MY UNKNOWN CHUM

"AGUECHEEK"

AGUECHEEK.

I am old,
And my infirmities have chained me here
To suffer and to vex my weary soul
With the vain hope of cure. * * *
Yet my captivity is not so joyless
As you would think, my masters. Here I sit
And look upon this eager, anxious world, —
Not with the eyes of sour misanthropy,
Nor envious of its pleasures, — but content, —
Yea, blessedly content, 'mid all my pains,
That I no more may mingle with its brawlings.
                                        ROWLEY.

MY UNKNOWN CHUM

"AGUECHEEK"

with a foreword by
HENRY GARRITY

WILDSIDE PRESS

THE AUTHOR'S PREFACE

The principal part of the sketches and essays of which this volume is composed, was first given to the public in the columns of the Boston *Saturday Evening Gazette,* under the signature of Aguecheek. The sketches of foreign travel have been mostly rewritten, and several of them are entirely new. In them the author has endeavoured to avoid the details which he always found tiresome in the works of many foreign tourists, and to confine himself to his individual experience. For, if any one wishes to read the history and description of a European city, or the public edifices thereof, are not all these things written in the guide-books of the infallible Murray? And who would wish to steal the well-earned laurels of that inseparable companion of the European traveller, when his theft could not possibly be concealed from any discerning eye?

There are, in several of the essays, certain local allusions, which the author thinks will be understood by a sufficiently large proportion of his readers to justify their retention.

Boston, June 1, 1859

FOREWORD

Life is too short for reading inferior books.

BRYCE.

IN 1878 a letter of introduction to Mr. S—— of
Detroit was instrumental in securing for me the
close friendship of a man some twenty years my
senior—a man of unusual poise of mind and of such
superb character that I have ever looked upon him
as a perfect type of Newman's ideal gentleman.

My new friend was fond of all that is best in art
and literature. His pet possession, however, was an
old book long out of print—"Aguecheek." He spoke
to me of its classic charm and of the recurring pleasure he found in reading and rereading the delightful
pages of its unknown author, who saw in travel, in
art, in literature, in life and humanity, much that
other travellers and other writers and scholars had
failed to observe—seeing all with a purity of vision,
a clearness of intellect, and recording it with a grace
and ease of phrase that suggest that he himself had
perhaps been taught by the Angelic Doctor referred
to in the closing lines of his last essay.

A proffered loan of the book was eagerly accepted.
Though still in my teens, I soon became a convert to
all that my cultured friend had said in its praise.

With the aid of a Murray Street dealer in old

books, I was fortunate enough to get a copy for myself. I read it again and again. Obliged to travel
much, I was rarely without its companionship; for I
knew that if other reading-matter proved uninteresting, I could always find some new conversational
charm in the views and words of the World-Con-
versant Author.

Fearing that I weighed the merits of the work
with a mental scale wanting in balance, I asked
others what they thought of it. Much to my surprise, they had never even heard of it. In fact, in
these thirty-four years I have found but three persons who knew the book at all. Recently at The
Players I asked Mr. Evert Jansen Wendell if he
knew "Aguecheek." "Why," said he, "it was in my
hands only yesterday. It is in my library—my dramatic library." The late John E. Grote Higgens,
President of the St. George Society, knew its interesting pages well; and it is, I am assured, a "prized
unit" in the library of His Eminence Cardinal
Farley.

I lent my copy to young and old, to men and
women of various professions and to friends in the
world of commerce. The opinion of all might be
summed up in the appreciation of a well-known Mon-
signor—himself an observant traveller and an ardent
lover of "real" literature. Returning the book, he
said, "I have read it with the greatest of pleasure,

and have turned to it often. I could read it a hundred times. It is a great book. Its fine humor, its depth, its simplicity and high ideals, commend it to all, especially the highly educated—the scholar."

Charles B. Fairbanks is the reputed author, but the records show that he died in 1859, when but thirty-two years old—an age that the text repeatedly discredits. Whether written by Mr. Fairbanks or not, the modest author hid his identity in an obscure pen-name that he might thus be free to make his book "his heart in other men's hands."

Some necessary changes have been made in the text. In offering the book to the public and in reluctantly changing the title, I am but following the insistent advice of friends—critics and scholars— whose judgment is superior to my own. No one seemed to know the meaning of "Aguecheek" (taken, no doubt, from a character in "Twelfth Night"), and few could even spell or pronounce the word; moreover, there is not the remotest connection between title and text. The old book has been the best of comrades, "the joy of my youth, the consolation of my riper years." If the new name lacks dignity as well as euphony, the reader will, I am sure, understand and appreciate the spirit of affection that inspired "My Unknown Chum."

HENRY GARRITY.

CONTENTS

SKETCHES OF FOREIGN TRAVEL

ESSAYS

SKETCHES
OF FOREIGN TRAVEL

Sketches of Foreign Travel

A PASSAGE ACROSS
THE ATLANTIC

'TO an American visiting Europe for the first
time," saith Geoffrey Crayon, "the long voyage which he has to make is an excellent prepara-
tive." To the greater proportion of those who
revisit the old world, the voyage is only an interval
of ennui and impatience. Not such is it to the writer
of this sentence. For him the sea has charms which
age cannot wither, nor head winds abate. For him
the voyage is a retreat from the cares of business, a
rest from the pursuit of wealth, and a prolonged re-
miniscence of his youthful days, when he first trod
the same restless pathway, and the glories of England and the Continent rose up resplendent before
him, very much as the gorgeous city in the clouds
looms up before the young gentleman in one of the
late lamented Mr. Cole's pictures. For it is a satisfaction to him to remember that such things were,—
even though the performances of life have not by
any means equalled the promises of the programme
of youth,—though age and the cares of an increasing
family have stifled poetry, and the genius of Romance has long since taken his hat.

The recollections of youthful Mediterranean voy-
ages are a mine of wealth to an old man. They have
transformed ancient history into a majestic reality
for him, and the pages of his dog's-eared Lemprière

become instinct with life as he recalls those halcyon days when he reclined on deck beneath an awning, and gazed on Crete and Lesbos, and the mountains that look on Marathon. Neither age nor misfortune can ever rob him of the joy he feels when he looks back to the cloudless afternoon when he passed from the stormy Atlantic to that blue inland sea,— when he saw where Africa has so long striven to shake hands with Europe,—and thrilled at the thought that the sea then glowing with the hues of sunset was once ploughed by the invincible galleys of the Cæsars, and dashed its angry surges over the shipwrecked Apostle of the Gentiles.

It is rather a pleasant thing to report one's self on board a fine packet ship on a bright morning in May —the old portmanteau packed again, and thoughts turned seaward. There is a kind of inspiration in the song of the sailors at the windlass, (that is, as many of them as are able to maintain a perpendicular position at that early period of the voyage;) the very clanking of the anchor chains seems to speak of speedy liberation, and the ship sways about as if yearning for the freedom of the open sea. At last the anchor is up, and the ship swings around, and soon is gliding down the channel; and slowly the new gas-ometer, and Bunker Hill Monument, and the old gasometer (with the dome) on Beacon Hill, begin to diminish in size. (I might introduce a fine mis-quotation here about growing "small by degrees, and beautifully less," but that I don't like novelties in a correspondence like this.) The embankments of Fort Warren seem brighter and more verdurous than ever, and the dew-drops glitter in the sunbeams, as dear Nellie's tears did, when she said good-by, that very morning. Then, as we get into the bay, the tocsin calls to lunch—and the appetite for lobsters, sardines, ale, and olives makes us all forget how much we fear lest business of immediate importance may prevent an early return to the festive mahogany. And shortly after, the pilot takes his leave, and with him the small knot of friends, who have gone as far as friendship, circumstances, and the tide will allow. And so the voyage commences—the captain takes command—and all feel that the jib-boom points towards Motherland, and begin to calculate the distance, and anticipate the time when the ship shall be boarded by a blue-coated beef-eater, who will take her safely "round 'Oly'ead, and dock 'er." The day wears away, and the sunset finds the passengers well acquainted, and a healthy family feeling growing up among them. The next morning we greet the sea and skies, but not our mother earth. The breeze is light—the weather is fine—so that the breakfast is discussed before a full bench. Every body feels well, but sleepy, and the day is spent in conversation and enjoyment of the novelty of life at sea. The gentle heaving of the ocean is rather agreeable than otherwise, and the young ladies promenade the deck, and flatter themselves that they have (if I might use such an expression) their sea legs on. But the next day the gentle heaving has become a heavy swell,—locomotion is attended with great difficulties,—the process of dressing is a severe practical joke,—and the timorous approach to the breakfast table and precipitous retreat from it, are very interesting studies to a disinterested spectator. The dining-saloon is

thinly populated when the bell rings—the gentlemen
preferring to lounge about on deck—they have slight
headaches—not seasick—of course not—the gentleman who had taken eight sherry cobblers was not
intoxicated at all—it was a glass of lemonade, that
he took afterwards, that disagreed with him and
made his footing rather unsteady. But Neptune is
inexorable, and exacts his tribute, and the payers
show their receipts in pale faces and dull eyes,
whether they acknowledge it or no; and many a poor
victim curses the pernicious hour that ever saw him
shipped, and comes to the Irishman's conclusion that
the pleasantest part of going away from home is the
getting back again.

But a few days suffice to set all minds and stom-
achs at rest, and we settle down into the ordinary
routine of life at sea. The days glide by rapidly, as
Shakspeare says, "with books, and work, and healthful play," and as we take a retrospective view of the
passage, it seems to be a maze of books, backgammon, bad jokes, cigars, *crochet*, cribbage, and conversation. Contentment obtains absolute sway,
which even ten days of head winds and calms cannot
shake off. Perhaps this is owing in a great measure
to the good temper and gentlemanly bearing of the
captain, who never yielded to the temptation, before
which so many intrepid mariners have fallen, to
speak in disrespectful and condemnatory terms of
the weather. How varied must be the qualities
which make a good commander of a packet ship;
what a model of patience he must be—patience not
only with the winds, but also with variable elements
of humanity which surround him. He must have a

good word for every body and a smiling face, although he knows that the ship will not head her course by four points of the compass on either tack; and must put aside with a jest the unconscious professional gentleman whose hat intervenes between his sextant and the horizon. In short, he must possess in an eminent degree what Virgil calls the *suaviter in* what's-his-name with the *fortiter in* whatd'ye-call-it. I am much disposed to think that had Job been a sea captain with a protracted head wind, the land of Uz would not have attained celebrity as the abode of the most patient of men.

An eminent Boston divine, not long since deceased, who was noted alike for his Johnsonian style and his very un-Johnsonian meekness of manner, once said to a sea captain, "I have, sir, in the course of my professional career, encountered many gentlemen of your calling; but I really must say that I have never been powerfully impressed in a moral way by them, for their conversation abounded in expressions savouring more of strength than of righteousness; indeed, but few of them seemed capable of enunciating the simplest sentence without prefacing it with a profane allusion to the possible ultimate fate of their visual organs, which I will not shock your fastidiousness by repeating." The profanity of seafaring men has always been remarked; it has been a staple article for the lamentations of the moralist and the jests of the immoralist; but I must say that I am not greatly surprised at its prevalence, for when I have seen a thunder squall strike a ship at sea, and every effort was making to save the rent canvas, it has seemed to me as if those whose dealings were with the elements actually needed a stronger vocabulary than is required for less sublime transactions. To speak in ordinary terms on such occasions would be as absurd as the Cockney's application of the epithets "clever" and "neat" to Niagara. I am not attempting to palliate every-day profanity, for I was brought up in the abhorrence of it, having been taken at an early age from the care of the lady "who ran to catch me when I fell, and kissed the place to make it well," and placed in the country under the superintendence of a maiden aunt, who was very moral indeed, and who instilled her principles into my young heart with wonderful eloquence and power. "Andrew," she used to say to me, "you must n't laugh in meetin'; I 've no doubt that the man who was hung last week (for this was in those unenlightened days when the punishment of crime was deemed a duty, and not a sin) began his wicked course by laughing in meetin'; and just think, if you were to commit a murder—for those who murder will steal—and those who steal will swear and lie—and those who swear and lie will drink rum—and then if they don't stop in their sinful ways, they get so bad that they will smoke cigars and break the Sabbath; and you know what becomes of 'em then."

The ordinary routine of life at sea, which is so irksome to most people, has a wonderful charm for me. There is something about a well-manned ship that commands my deepest enthusiasm. Each day is filled with a quiet and satisfactory kind of enjoyment. From that early hour of the morning when the captain turns out to see what is the prospect of the day, and to drink a mug of boiling coffee as strong as aquafortis, and as black as the newly-opened fluid Day & Martin, from No. 97, High Holborn, to that quiet time in the evening when that responsible functionary goes below and turns in, with a sententious instruction to the officer of the watch to "wake him at twelve, if there 's any change in the weather," there is no moment that hangs heavy on my hands. I love the regular striking of the bells, reminding me every half hour how rapidly time and I are getting on. The regularity with which every thing goes on, from the early washing of the decks to the sweeping of the same at four bells in the evening, makes me think of those ancient monasteries in the south of Europe, where the unvarying round of duties creates a paradise which those who are subject to the unexpected fluctuations of common life might be pardoned for coveting. If the rude voices that swell the boisterous chorus which hoists the tugging studding-sail up by three-feet pulls, only imperfectly remind one of the sounds he hears when the full choir of the monastery makes the grim arches of the chapel vibrate with the solemn tones of the Gregorian chant, certainly the unbroken calmness of the morning watch may well be allowed to symbolize the rapt meditation and unspoken devotion which finds its home within the "studious cloister's pale"; and I may be pardoned for comparing the close attention of the captain and his mates in getting the sun's altitude and working out the ship's position to the "examination of conscience" among the devout dwellers in the convent, and the working out of the spiritual reckoning which shows them how much they have varied from the course laid down on the divine chart, and how far they are from the wished-for port of perfection.

I have a profound respect for the sea as a moral teacher. No man can be tossed about upon it without feeling his impotence and insignificance, and having his heart opened to the companions of his danger as it has never been opened before. The sea brings out the real character of every man; and those who journey over its "deep invisible paths" find themselves intrusting their most sacred confidences to the keeping of comparative strangers. The conventionalities of society cannot thrive in a salt atmosphere; and you shall be delighted to see how frank and agreeable the "world's people" can be when they are caught where the laws of fashion are silent, and what a wholesome neglect of personal appearances prevails among them when that sternest of democrats, Neptune, has placed them where they feel that it would be folly to try to produce an impression. The gentleman of the prize ring, whom Dickens introduces looking with admiration at the stately Mr. Dombey, gave it as his opinion that there was a way within the resources of science of "doubling-up" that incarnation of dignity; but, for the accomplishment of such an end, one good, pitching, head-sea would be far more effectual than all the resources of the "manly art." The most unbending assumption could not survive that dreadful sinking of the stomach, that convulsive clutch at the nearest object for support, and the faint, gurgling cry of *"stew'rd,"* which announces that the victim has found his natural level. A thorough novitiate of seasickness is as indispensable, in my opinion, to the formation of true manly character, as the measles to a well-regulated childhood. Mentally as well as corporeally, seasickness is a wonderful renovator. We are such victims of habit, so prone to run in a groove, (most of us in a groove that may well be called a "vicious circle,") that we need to be thoroughly shaken up, and made to take a new view of the *rationale* of our way of life. I do not believe that any man ever celebrated his recovery from that marine malady by eating the pickles and biscuit which always taste so good on such an occasion, without having acquired a new set of ideas, and being made generally wiser and better by his severe experience. I meet many unamiable persons "whene'er I take my walks abroad," who only need two days of seasickness to convert them into positive ornaments to society.

But, pardon me; all this has little to do with the voyage to Liverpool. The days follow each other rapidly, and it begins to seem as if the voyage would stretch out to the crack of doom, for the head wind stands by us with the constancy of a sheriff, and when that lacks power to retard us we have a calm. But the weather is beautiful, and all the time is spent in the open air. Nut brown maids work worsted and crochet on the cooler side of the deck, and gentlemen in rusty suits, with untrimmed beards, wearing the "shadowy livery of the burning sun," talk of the prospects of a fair wind or read innumerous novels. The evenings are spent in gazing at a cloudless sky, and promenading in the moonshine. Music lends its aid and banishes impatience; my young co-voyagers seem not to have forgotten "Sweet Home," and the "Old Folks at Home" would be very much gratified to know how green their memory is kept.

At length we all begin to grow tired of fair weather. The cloudless sky, the gorgeous sunrises and sunsets, and the bright blue sea, with its lazily spouting whales and its lively porpoises playing around our bows,—grow positively distasteful to us; and we begin to think that any change would be an agreeable one. We do not have to wait many days before we are awaked very early in the morning, by the throwing down of heavy cordage on deck, and the shouts of the sailors, and are soon aware that we are subject to an unusual motion—as if the ship were being propelled by a strong force over a corduroy road constructed on an enormous scale. Garments, which yesterday were content to hang in an orderly manner against the partitions of one's state-room, now obstinately persist in hanging at all sorts of peculiar and disgraceful angles. Hat boxes, trunks, and the other movables of the voyager manifest great hilarity at the change in the weather, and dance about the floor in a manner that must satisfy the most fastidious beholder. Every timber in the ship groans as if in pain. The omnipresent steward rushes about, closing up sky-lights and dead lights, and "chocking" his rattling crockery and glassware. On deck the change from the even keel and the clear sunlight of the day before is still more wonderful. The colour of the sky reminds you of the leaden lining of a tea-chest; that of the sea, of the dingy green paper which covers the same. The sails, which so many days of sunshine have bleached to a dazzling whiteness, are now all furled, except those which are necessary to keep some little headway on the ship. The captain has adorned his manly frame with a suit of India rubber, which certainly could not have been selected for its gracefulness, and has overshadowed his honest face with a sou'wester of stupendous proportions. With the exception of occasional visits to the sinking barometer, he spends his weary day on the wet deck, and tries to read the future in the blackening waves and stormy sky. The wheel, which heretofore has required but one man, now taxes the strength of two of the stoutest of our crew;—so hard is it to keep our bashful ship heading up to that rude sea, and to "ease her when she pitches." The breakfast suffers sadly from neglect, for every one is engrossed with the care of the weather. At noon there is a lull for half an hour or so, and, in spite of the threats of the remorseless barometer, some of our company try to look for an amelioration in the meteorological line. But their hopes are crushed when they find that the wind has shifted one or two points, and has set in to blow more violently than before. The sea, too, begins to behave in a most capricious and disagreeable style. When the ship has, with a great deal of straining and cracking, ridden safely over two mighty ridges of water, and seems to be easily settling down into a black valley between two foam-capped hills, there comes a sudden shock, as if she had met the Palisades of the Hudson in her path, -a crackling, grating sound, like that of a huge nutmeg-grater operating on a coral reef, a crash like the combined force of all the battering-rams of Titus Flavius Vespasianus on one of the gates of Jerusalem,—and a hundred tons of angry water roll aft against the cabin doors, in a manner not at all agreeable to weak nerves. For a moment the ship seems to stand perfectly still, as if deliberating whether to go on or turn back; then, realizing that the ship that deliberates in such a time is lost, she rises gracefully over a huge pile of water which was threatening to submerge her.

The afternoon wears away slowly with the passengers. They say but little to one another, but look about them from the security of the wheel-house as if they were oppressed with a sense of the inestimable value of strong cordage. As twilight approaches, and all hands are just engaged in taking supper, after having "mended the reefs," the ship meets a staggering sea, which seems to start every timber in her firm-set frame, and our main-top-gallant-mast breaks off like a stick of candy. Such things generally happen just at night, the sailors say, when the difficulties of clearing away the broken rigging are increased by the darkness. Straightway the captain's big, manly voice is heard above the war-whoop of the gale, ringing out as Signor Badiali's was wont to in the third act of Ernani. The wind seems to pin the men to the ratlines as they clamber up; but all the difficulties are overcome at length; the broken mast is lowered down, and snugly stowed away; and before nine o'clock all is quiet, except the howling wind, which seems to have determined to make a night of it. And such a night! It is one of those times that make one want one's mother. There is little sleeping done except among the "watch below" in the forecastle, who snore away their four hours as if they appreciated the reasoning of Mr. Dibdin when he extols the safety of the open sea as compared with the town with its falling chimneys and flying tiles, and commiserates the condition of the unhappy shore-folks in such a tempestuous time. The thumping of the sea against our wooden walls, the swash of water on deck as the ship rolls and pitches as you would think it impossible for any thing addicted to the cold water movement to roll or pitch, and over all the wild, changeless, shrieking of the gale, will not suffer sleep to visit those who are not inured to such things. Tired of bracing up with knee, and hand, and heel, to keep in their berths, they lie and wonder how many such blows as that our good ship could endure, and think that if June gets up such gales on the North Atlantic, they have no wish to try the quality of those of January.

Morning comes at last, and every heart is cheered by the captain's announcement, as he passes through the cabin, that the barometer is rising, and the weather has begun to improve. Some of the more hopeful and energetic of our company turn out and repair to the deck. The leaden clouds are broken up, and the sun trying to struggle through them; but to the inexperienced the gale appears to be as severe as it was yesterday. All the discomfort and danger of the time are forgotten, however, in the fearful magnificence of the spectacle that surrounds us. As far as the eye can reach it seems like a confused field of battle, where snowy plumes and white flowing manes show where the shock of war is felt most severely. To watch the gathering of one of those mighty seas that so often work destruction with the noblest ships,—to see it gradually piling up until it seems to be impelled by a fury almost intelligent,—to be dazzled by its emerald flash when it erects its stormy head the highest, and breaks into a field of boiling foam, as if enraged at being unable to reach us;—these are things which are worth all the anxiety and peril that they cost.

The captain's prognostications prove correct. Our appetites at dinner bear witness to them; and before sunset we find our ship (curtailed of its fair proportion, it is true, by the loss of its main-top-gallant-mast) is under full sail once more. The next day we have a few hours' calm, and when a light breeze does spring up, it comes from the old easterly quarter. It begins to seem as if we were fated to sail forever, and never get any where. But patience wears out even a head wind, and at last the long-looked-for change takes place. The wind slowly hauls to the south, and many are the looks taken at the compass to see how nearly the ship can come up to her course. Then our impatience is somewhat allayed by speaking a ship which has been out twelve days longer than our own—for, if it be true, as Rochefoucauld says, that "there is something not unpleasing to us in the misfortunes of our best friends,"—how keen must be the satisfaction of finding a stranger-companion in adversity. The wind, though steady, is not very strong, and many fears are expressed lest it should die away and give Eurus another three weeks' chance. But our forebodings are not realized, and a sunshiny day comes when we are all called up from dinner to see a long cloud-like affair, (very like a whale,) which, we are told, is the

A PASSAGE ACROSS THE ATLANTIC

Old Head of Kinsale. Straightway all begin to talk of getting on shore the next day; but when that comes, we find that we are drawing towards Holyhead very rapidly, as our favourable wind has increased to a gale—so that when we have got round Holyhead, and have taken our pilot, (that burly visitor whose coming every one welcomes, and whose departure every one would speed,) the aforesaid pilot heaves the ship to, and, having a bed made up on the cabin floor, composes himself to sleep. The next morning finds the gale abated, and early in the forenoon we are running up to the mouth of the river. The smoke (that first premonitory symptom of an English town) hangs over Liverpool, and forms a strong contrast with the bright green fields and verdant hedges which deck the banks of the Mersey. The ship, after an immense amount of vocal power has been expended in that forcible diction which may be termed the marine vernacular, is got into dock, and in the afternoon a passage of thirty-three days is concluded by our stepping once more upon the "inviolate island of the sage and free," and following our luggage up the pier, with a swing in our gait which any stage sailor would have viewed with envy. The examination at the Custom House is conducted with a politeness and despatch worthy of imitation among the officials of our Uncle Samuel. The party of passengers disperses itself about in various hotels, without any circumstance to hinder their progress except falling in with an exhibition of Punch and Judy, which makes the company prolific in quotations from the sayings of Messrs. Codlin and Short, and at last the family which never had its harmonious unity disturbed by any thing, is broken up forever.

Liverpool wears its old thriving commercial look —perhaps it is a few shades darker with smoke. The posters are on a more magnificent scale, both as regards size and colour, than ever before, and tell not only of the night's amusements, but promise the acquisition of wealth outrunning the dreams of avarice in lands beyond the farthest Thule. Melbourne and Port Philip vie in the most gorgeous colours with San Francisco; and the United States seem to have spread wide their capacious arms to welcome the down-trodden Irishman. Liverpool seems to be the gate to all the rest of the world. I almost fear to walk about lest I should find myself starting off, in a moment of temporary insanity, for Greenland's icy mountains, or India's coral strand.

LONDON

DULL must he be of soul who could make the journey from Liverpool to the metropolis in the month of June, and not be lifted above himself by the surpassing loveliness of dear mother Nature. Even if he were chained to a ledger and cash book—if he never had a thought or wish beyond the broker's board, and his entire reading were the prices current—he must forget them all, and feel for the time what a miserable sham his life is—or he does not deserve the gift of sight. It is Thackeray, I think, who speaks somewhere of the "charming friendly English landscape that seems to shake hands with you as you pass along"—and any body who has seen it in June will say that this is hardly a figurative expression. I used to think that it was my enthusiastic love for the land of the great Alfred which made it seem so beautiful to me when I was younger; but I find that it wears too well to be a mere fancy of my own brain. People may complain of the humid climate of England, and curse the umbrella which must accompany them whenever they walk out; but when the sun does shine, it shines upon a scene of beautiful fertility unequalled elsewhere in the world, and which the moist climate produces and preserves. And then, too, it seems doubly grateful to the eyes of one just come from sea. The bright freshness of the whole landscape, the varied tints of green, the trim hedges, the luxuriant foliage which springs from the very trunks of the trees, and the high state of cultivation which makes the whole country look as if it had been swept and dusted that morning,—all these things strike an American, for he cannot help contrasting them with the parched fields of his own land in summer, surrounded by their rough fences and hastily piled-up stone walls. The solidity of the houses and cottages, which look as if they were built, not for an age, but for all time, makes him think of the country houses of America, which seem to have grown up in a night, like our friend Aladdin's, and whose frailty is so apparent that you cannot sneeze in one of them without apprehending a serious calamity. Then the embankments of the railways present not only a pleasant sight to the eye of the traveller, but a pretty little hay crop to the corporation; and at every station, and bridge, and crossing, wherever there is a switch to be tended, you see the neat cottages of the keepers, and the gardens thereof —the railway companies having learned that the expenditure of a few hundred pounds in this way saves an expenditure of many thousands in surgeons' bills and damages, and is far more satisfactory to all concerned.

What a charming sight is a cow—what a look of contentment she has—ambitious of nothing beyond the field of daily duty, and never looking happier than when she comes at night to yield a plenteousness of that fluid without which custards were an impossibility! Wordsworth says that "heaven lies about us in our infancy"—surely he must mean that portion of the heavens called by astronomers the Milky Way.

LONDON

It is pleasant to see a cow by the side of a railway—
provided she is fenced from danger—to see her lift
her head slowly as the train goes whizzing by, and
gaze with those mild, tranquil eyes upon the noisy,
smoke-puffing monster,—just as the saintly hermits
of olden times might have looked from their serene
heights of contemplation upon the dusty, bustling
world. The taste of the English farmers for fine
cattle is attested by a glance at any of their pastures.
On every side you see the representatives of Alder-
ney's bovine aristocracy; and scores of cattle crop
the juicy grass, rivalling in their snowy whiteness any
that ever reclined upon Clitumno's "mild declivity of
hill," or admired their graceful horns in its clear
waters. Until I saw them, I never comprehended
what farmers meant when they spoke of "neat
cattle."

What an eloquent preacher is an old church-tower!
Moss-crowned and ivy-robed, it lifts its head, unshaken by the tempests of centuries, as it did in the
days when King John granted the Great Charter or
the holy Edward ruled the realm, and tells of the
ages when England was one in faith, and not a poor-
house existed throughout the land. Like a faithful
sentinel, it stands guard over the humbler edifices
around it, and warns their inhabitants alike of their
dangers and their duties by the music of its bells.
Erect in silent dignity, it receives the first beams of
the morning, and when twilight has begun to shroud
every thing in its neighbourhood, the flash of sunset
lingers on its gray summit. It looks down with sublime indifference upon the changing scene below, as if
it would reproach the actors there with their forget-

fulness of the transitoriness of human pursuits, and remind them, by its unchangeableness, of the eternal years.

At last we draw near London. A gentleman, whose age I would not attempt to guess,—for he was very carefully made up, and boasted a deportment which would have excited the envy of Mr. Turvey-drop, senior,—so far forgot his dignity as to lean forward and inform me that the place we were pass-ing was " 'Arrow on the 'Ill," which made me forget for the moment both his appearance and his un-called-for "exasperation of the haitches." Not long after, I found myself issuing from the magnificent terminus of the North Western Railway, in Euston Square, in a cab marked V. R. 10,276. The cab and omnibus drivers of London are a distinct race of beings. Who can write their natural history? Who is competent to such a task? The researches of a Pritchard, a Pickering, a Smyth, would seem to cover the whole subject of the history of the human species from the anthropophagi and bosjesmen to the drinkers of train oil in the polar regions; but the cab-men are not included. They would require a master mind. The subject would demand the patient in-vestigation of a Humboldt, the eloquence of a Macaulay, and the humour of a Dickens—and even then would fall short, I fear, of giving an adequate idea of them. Your London cab driver has no idea of distance; as, for instance, I ask one the simple question,—

"How far is it to the Angel in Islington?"

"Wot, sir?"

I repeat my interrogatory.

"Oh, the Hangel, sir! Four shillings."

"No, no. I mean what distance."

"Well, say three, then, sir."

"But I mean—what distance? How many miles?"

"O, come, sir, jump in—don't be 'ard on a fellow —I 'aven't 'ad a fare to-day. Call it 'arf a crown, sir."

Leigh Hunt says somewhere that if there were such a thing as metamorphosis, Dr. Johnson would desire to be transformed into an omnibus, that he might go rolling along the streets whose very pavements were the objects of his ardent affection. And he was about right. What better place is there in this world to study human nature than an omnibus? All classes meet there; in the same coach you may see them all—from the poor workwoman to the genteelly dressed lady, who looks as if she disapproved of such conveyances, but must ride nevertheless— from the young sprig, who is constantly anxious lest some profane foot should dim the polish of his boots, to the urbane old gentleman, who regrets his corpulence, and would take less room if he could. And then the top of the omnibus, which usually carries four or more passengers, what a place is that to see the tide of life which flows unceasingly through the streets of London! I know of nothing which can furnish more food for thought than a ride on an omnibus from Brompton to the Bank on a fine day. It is a pageant, in which all the wealth, pomp, power, and prosperity of this world pass before you; and for a moral to the whirling scene, you must go to the nearest churchyard.

London is ever the same. The omnibuses follow

each other as rapidly as ever up and down the Strand, the white-gloved, respectable-looking policemen walk about as deliberately, and the tail of the lion over the gate of Northumberland House sticks out as straight as ever. The only great change visible here is in the newspapers. The tone of society is so different from what it was formerly, in all that concerns France, that the editors must experience considerable trouble in accustoming themselves to the new state of things. Once, France and Louis Napoleon furnished Punch with his chief materials for satire and amusement, and if any of the larger and more dignified journals wished to let off a little ill humour, or to say any thing particularly bitter, they only had to dip their pens in *Gaul;* but times are changed, and now nothing can be said too strong in favour of "our chivalric allies, the French." The memory of St. Helena seems to have given place to what they call here the *entente cordiale,* which those who are acquainted with the French language assure me means an agreement by which one party contracts to "play second fiddle" to another, through fear that if he does not he will not be permitted to play at all.

To the man who thoroughly appreciates the Essays of Elia, and Boswell's Life of Johnson, London can never grow tiresome. He can never turn a corner without finding "something new, something to please, and something to instruct." Its very pavements are classical. And there is nothing to abate, nor detract from, such a man's enthusiasm. The traveller who visits the Roman Forum, or the Palace of the Cæsars, experiences a sad check when he finds his progress impeded by unpoetical obstacles. But in London, all is harmonious; he sees on every side, not only that which tells of present life and prosperity, but the perennial glories of England's former days. Would he study history, he goes to the Tower, "rich with the spoils of time"; or to Whitehall, where mad fanaticism consummated its treasonable work with the murder of a sovereign; or to the towering minster, to gaze upon the chair in which the monarchs of a thousand years have sat; or to view the monuments, and read the epitaphs, of that host of

"Bards, heroes, sages, side by side,
Who darkened nations when they died."

Is he a lover of English literature? Here are scenes eloquent of that goodly company of wits and worthies, whose glowing pages have been the delight of his youth and the consolation of his riper years; here are the streets in which they walked, the taverns in which they feasted, the churches where they prayed, the tombs where they repose.

And London wears well. To revisit it when age has sobered down the enthusiasm of youth, is not like seeing a theatre by daylight; but you think almost that you have under-estimated your privileges. How well I remember the night when I first arrived in the metropolis! It was after ten o'clock, and I was much fatigued; but before I booked myself in my hotel, or looked at my room, I rushed out into the Strand, "with breathless speed, like a soul in chase." I pushed along, now turning to look at Temple Bar, now pausing to take breath as I went up Ludgate Hill. I saw St. Paul's and its dome before me, and I was satisfied. No, I was not satis-

fied; for when I returned up Fleet Street, I looked
out dear old Bolt Court, and entered its Johnsonian
precincts with an awe and veneration which a devout
Mussulman, taking the early train for Mecca, would
gladly imitate. And then I posted down Inner Temple Lane, and looked at the house in which Charles
Lamb and his companions held their "Wednesday
nights"; and, going still farther, I saw the river—I
stood on the bank of the Thames, and I was satisfied. I looked, and all the associations of English
history and literature which are connected with it
filled my mind—but just as I was getting into a fine
frenzy about it, a watchman hove in sight, and the
old clock chimed out eleven. So I started on, and
soon reached my hotel. I was accosted on my way
thither by a young and gayly dressed lady, whom I
did not remember ever to have seen before, but who
expressed her satisfaction at meeting me, in the most
cordial terms. I told her that I thought that it must
be a mistake, and she responded with a laugh which
very much shocked an elderly gentleman who was
passing, who looked as if he might have been got up
for the part of the uncle of the unhappy G. Barnwell.
I have since learned that such mistakes and personal
misapprehensions very frequently occur in London in
the evening.

Speaking of Temple Bar, it gratifies me to see that
this venerable gateway still stands, "unshaken, un-
seduced, unterrified," by any of the recent attempts
to effect its removal. The old battered and splashed
doors are perhaps more unsightly than before; but
the statues look down with the same benignity upon
the crowd of cabs and omnibuses, and the never-

ending tide of humanity which flows beneath them, as they did upon the Rake's Progress, so many years ago. The sacrilegious commissioners of streets long to get at it with their crows and picks, but the shade of Dr. Johnson watches over the barrier of his earthly home. It is not an ornamental affair, to be sure, and it would be difficult for Mr. Choate, even, to defend it against the charge of being an obstruction; but its associations with the literature and history of the last two or three centuries ought to entitle its dingy arches to a certain degree of reverence, even in our progressive and irreverent age. The world would be a loser by the demolition of this ancient landmark, and London, if it should lose this, though it might still be the metropolis of the British empire, would cease to be the London of Johnson and Goldsmith, of Addison and Pope, of Swift and Hogarth.

Perhaps some may think, from what I have said in the commencement of this letter, that my enthusiasm has blinded me to those great moral and social evils which are apparent in English civilization: but it is not so. I love England rather for what she has been than for what she is; I love the England of Alfred and St. Edward; and when I contrast the present state with what it might have been under a succession of such rulers, I cannot but grieve. Truly the court of St. James under Victoria is not what it was under Charles II., nor even under Mr. Thackeray's favourite hero, "the great George IV.,"—but are not St. James and St. Giles farther apart than ever before? Is not Lazarus looked upon as a nuisance, which legislation ought, for decency's sake, to put out of the way? What does England do for the poor? Nothing; absolutely nothing, if you except a system of workhouses, compared with which prisons are delightful residences, and which seems to have been intended more for the punishment of poverty than as a work of charity. No; on the contrary, she discountenances works of charity; when a few earnest men among the clergy of her divided church make an effort in that direction, there is an outcry, and they must be put down; and their bishops, whose annual incomes are larger than the whole treasury of Alfred, admonish them to beware how they thus imitate the superstitions of the middle ages. No; your Englishman of the present day has something better to do than to look after the beggar at his doorstep; he is too respectable a man for that; he pays his "poor rates," and the police must order the thing of shreds and patches to "move on"; his progress must not be impeded, for his presence is required at a meeting of the friends of Poland, or of Italy, or of a society for the abolition of American slavery, and he has no time to waste on such common, everyday matters as the improvement of the miserable wretches who work his coal mines, or of those quarters of the town where vice parades its deformity with exulting pride, and the air is heavy with pestilence. There is proportionably more beggary in London at this hour than in any continental city. And such beggary! Not the comfortable, jolly-looking beggars you may see in Rome or Naples, who know that charity is enjoined upon the people as a religious duty, but the thin, pallid, high-cheeked supplicants, whose look is a petition which tells a more effective story than words can frame of destitution and starvation.

But there is another phase of this part of London life, sadder by far than that of mere poverty. It is an evil which no attempt is made to prevent, and so great an evil that its very mention is forbidden by the spirit of this age of "superficial morality and skin-deep propriety." I pity the man who can walk through Regent Street or the Strand in the evening, unsaddened by what he shall see on every side. How ridiculous do our boasts of this Christian nineteenth century seem there! Here is this mighty Anglo-Saxon race, which can build steam engines, and telegraphs, and clipper ships, which tunnels mountains, and exerts an almost incredible mastery over the forces of nature,—and yet, when Magdalene looks up to it for a merciful hand to lift her from degradation and sin, she finds it either deaf or powerless. There is a work yet to be done in London which would stagger a philanthropist, if he were gifted with thrice the heroism, and patience, and self-forgetfulness of a St. Vincent of Paul.

I cannot resist the inclination to give in this connection a passage from the personal experience of a friend in London, which, had I read it in any book or newspaper, I should have hesitated to believe. One evening, as he was passing along Pall Mall, he was addressed by a young woman, who, when she saw that he was going to pass on and take no notice of her, ran before him, and said in a tone of the most pathetic earnestness,—

"Well, if you'll not go with me, for God's sake, sir, give me a trifle to buy bread!"

Thus appealed to, and somewhat shaken by the voice and manner, he stopped under a gaslight, and looked at the speaker. Vice had not impressed its distinctive seal so strongly upon her as upon most of the unfortunate creatures one meets in London's streets; indeed, there was a shade of melancholy on her face which harmonized well with her voice and manner. So my friend resolved to have a few words more with her, and buttoning up his coat, to protect his watch and purse, he told her that he feared she wanted money to buy gin rather than bread. She assured him that it was not so, but that she wished to buy food for her little child, a girl of two or three years. Then he asked how she could lead such a life, if she had a child growing up, upon whom her example would have such an influence; and she said that she would gladly take up with an honest occupation, if she could find one,—indeed, she did try to earn enough for the daily wants of herself and child with her needle, but it was impossible,—and her only choice was between starvation and the street. At that time she said that she was learning the trade of a dressmaker, and she hoped that before long she should be able to keep herself above absolute necessity. Encouraged by a kind word from my friend, she went on in a simple, womanly manner, and told him of her whole career. It was the old story of plighted troth, betrayed affection, and flight from her village home, to escape the shame and reproach she would there be visited with. She arrived in London without money, without friends, without employment,—without any thing save that natural womanly self-respect which had received such a severe blow:

—necessity stared her in the face, and she sank before it. My friend was impressed by the recital of her misfortunes, and thinking that she must be sincere, he took a sovereign from his purse and gave it to her. She looked from the gift to the giver, and thanked him again and again. He continued his walk, but had not gone more than three or four rods, when she came running after him, and reiterated her expressions of thankfulness with a trembling voice. He then walked on, and crossed over to the front of the Church of St. Martin, (that glorious soldier who with his sword divided his cloak with the beggar,) when she came after him yet again, and seizing hold of his hand, she looked up at him with streaming eyes, and said, holding the sovereign in her hand,—

"God bless you, sir, again and again for your kindness to me! Pray pardon me, sir, for troubling you so much—but—but—perhaps you meant to give me a shilling, sir,—perhaps you don't know that you gave me a sovereign."

How many models of propriety and respectability in every rank of life,—how many persons who have the technical language of religion constantly on their lips,—how many of those who, nurtured amid the influences of a good home, have never really known what temptation is,—how many such persons are there who might learn a startling lesson from this fallen woman, whom they seem to consider themselves religiously bound to despise and neglect! I have a great dread of these severely virtuous people, who are so superior to all human frailty that they cannot afford a kind word to those who have not the good fortune to be impeccable. But we all of us, I fear, need to be reminded of Burns's lines—

> "What's done we partly may compute,
> But know not what's resisted."

If we thought of this, keeping our own weaknesses in view, which of us would not shrink from judging uncharitably, or casting the first stone at an erring fellow-creature? Which of us would dare to condemn the poor girl who preserved so much of the spirit of honesty in her degradation, and to commend the negative virtues which make up so many of what the world calls good lives?

ANTWERP AND BRUSSELS

IT is a very pleasant thing to get one's passport *viséd* (even though a pretty good fee is demanded for it,) and to make preparations for leaving London, at almost any time; but it is particularly so when the weather has been doing its worst for a fortnight, and the atmosphere is so "thick and slab" that to compare it to pea-soup would be doing that excellent compound a great injustice. It is very pleasant to think of getting out from under that blanket of smoke and fog, and escaping to a land where the sun shines occasionally, and where the manners of the people make a perpetual sunshine which renders you independent of the weather. If there ever was a day to which that expressive old Saxon epithet *nasty* might be justly applied, it was the one on which I left the greasy pavements of London, and (after a contest with a cabman, which ended, as such things generally do, in a compromise) found myself on board one of the fast-sailing packets of the General Steam Navigation Company, at St. Catharine's Wharf, just below the esplanade of the Tower. The beautiful banks of the river below the city, the fine pile of buildings, and the rich foliage of the park at Greenwich, seemed to have laid aside their charms, and shrouded themselves in mourning for the death of sunshine. The steamer was larger than most of those which ply in the Channel; but the crowded cabins and diminutive state-rooms made me think with envy of the passengers from New York to Fall River that afternoon. And there was a want of attention to those details which would have improved the appearance of the boat greatly—which made me wish that her commander might have served his apprenticeship on Long Island Sound or on the Hudson.

The company was composed of about the usual admixture of English and foreign beauty and manliness; and the English, French, Dutch, and German languages were confounded in such a manner as to bring to mind the doings of the committee on the construction of public works recorded in Genesis. Among the crowd of young Cockneys in jockeyish-looking caps, with travelling pouches strapped to their sides, there was a rather tall gentleman in a clerical suit, with his throat covered with the usual white bandages. His highly respectable look, and the eminently "evangelical" expression of the corners of his mouth, made me feel quite sure that I had found a character. He had three little boys with him; and as far as appearance went, he might have been Dickens's model for Dr. Blimber, (the principal of that celebrated academy where they had mental green peas and intellectual asparagus all the year round,) for he had the eye of a pedagogue "to threaten and command," and his fixed look was the one which my old schoolmaster's face wore when he turned up his wristbands, and, taking his ruler, said, "I am very sorry, Andrew; but you know that it is for your good." His conversation savoured so strongly of the dictionary, that, even if I had been blind, I should have said that the speaker had spent years in correcting the compositions of ingenuous youth. I shall not forget his look of wonder when he asked one of the engineers what was the matter with a dog that was yelping about the deck, and received for a reply that he tumbled off the quarter deck, and was *strained in the garret.* However, I enjoyed two or three hours' conversation with him very much—if it could be called conversation when he did all the talking.

Towards evening, when we found ourselves in the open sea, the south-westerly swell rolled up finely from the Goodwin Sands, and produced a scene to remind a disinterested spectator of Punch's touching pictorial representation of the commencement of the continental tour of Messrs. Brown, Jones, and Robinson. I soon perceived that a conspicuous collection of white bowls, which adorned the main saloon, was not a mere matter of ornament. The amount of medicine for the prevention or cure of seasickness, which was taken by my fellow-voyagers from flat bottles covered with wicker-work, would have astonished the most ardent upholder of the old allopathic practice. But all the pitching and rolling of the steamer, and the varied occupations of the passengers, did not interfere with my repose. I slept as soundly in my narrow accommodations as if I had been within hearing of the rattling of the omnibuses of my native city.

The next morning I was out in good season; and though I do not consider myself either "remote," "unfriended," "melancholy," or "slow," I found myself upon the "lazy Scheldt," with Antwerp's heaven-kissing spire climbing up the hazy perspective. The banks of the Scheldt are not very picturesque; indeed, a person of the strongest poetical susceptibilities might approach Flanders without the slightest apprehension of an attack of his weakness. I could not help congratulating myself, though, on having been spared to see the country which was immortalized by the profanity of a great military force.

We Americans usually consider ourselves up to the times, and are prone to sneer at Russia for being eleven days behind the age; but we do not yet "beat the Dutch" in progress, for they are half an hour in advance, as I found, very soon after landing, that all the church clocks, with a great deal of formality and precision, struck nine, when the hands only pointed to half past eight; and I noted a similar phenomenon while I was taking breakfast an hour after. Antwerp is a beautiful old city, and its quiet streets are very pleasant, after the tumult and roar of London; but—there is one drawback—it is too scrupulously clean. I almost feared to walk about, lest I should unknowingly do some damage; and every door-handle and bell-pull had a most unhospitable polish, which seemed to say with the placards in the Crystal Palace, "Please not to handle." Cleanliness is a great virtue; but when it is carried to such an extent that you cannot find your books and papers which you left carefully arranged yesterday on your table, —when it gets to be a monomania with man or woman,—it becomes a bore. How strangely the first two or three hours in a Dutch town strike a stranger!—the odd, high-gabled houses, the queer head-dresses, (graceful because of their very ungracefulness,) the wooden shoes, and the language, which sounds like English spoken by a toothless person. But one very soon gets accustomed to it. It is like being in an Oriental city, where the great variety of costumes and languages, and the different manners of the people, make up an *ensemble* which a stranger thinks will be a lasting novelty; but on his second day he finds himself taking about as much notice of a Persian caravan as he would of a Canton Street or Sixth Avenue omnibus.

I might here indulge in a little harmless enthusiasm about this grand old cathedral of Antwerp. I might talk about the "long-drawn aisle and fretted vault," and give an elaborate description of it,—its enormous dimensions and artistic glories,—if I did not know that any reader who desires such things can find them set down with greater exactness than becomes me, in any of the guide books for Belgium. I spent the greater proportion of my waking hours in Antwerp under the solemn arches of that majestic old church. I wonder, shall we ever see any thing in America to remind us even faintly of the glories of Antwerp, Cologne, Rouen, Amiens, York, or Milan? I fear not. The ages that built those glorious piles thought less of fat dividends than this boastful nineteenth century of ours, and their religion was not the mere one-day-out-of-seven affair that the improved Christianity of to-day is. The architects who conceived and executed those marvels of sublimity never troubled themselves with our popular query, "Will it pay?" any more than Dante interrupted the inspiration of his *Paradiso*, or Beethoven the linked harmony of his matchless symphonies, with their solicitude about the amount of their copyright. No; their work inspired them, and while it reflected their genius, it imparted to them something of its own divine dignity. Their art became religion, and its laborious processes acts of the most fervent devotion. But we have reformed all that, and now inspiration has to give way to considerations of the greatest number of "sittings," that can possibly be provided, and if the expenses of the sacred enterprise can be lessened by contriving accommodation for shops or storage in the basement, who does not rejoice? There are too many churches nowadays built upon the foundation of the *profits*, leaving the apostles entirely out of the question.

But while I lament our want of those wonderful constructions whose very stones seem to have grown consciously into forms of beauty, I must record my satisfaction at the improvement in architectural taste which is visible in most of our cities at home. If we must have banks, and railway stations, and shops, it is some compensation to have them made pleasant to our sight. Buildings are the books that every body unconsciously reads; and if they are a libel on the laws of architecture, they will surely vitiate in time the taste of those who become familiarized to their deformity. Dr. Johnson said, that "if a man's hands were dirty, his thoughts would be dirty"; and it may be declared, with much more reason, that those who are obliged to look, day after day, at ungraceful, mean, and unsubstantial objects, lose, by degrees, their sense of the beautiful and the harmonious, and set forth, in the poverty of their minds, the meanness of their surroundings.

ANTWERP AND BRUSSELS

On one account I have again and again blessed the star that guided me to Antwerp,—that is, for the pleasure afforded me by its treasures of art. I have, in times past, fed fat my appetite for the beautiful in the galleries of Italy, and therefore counted but little on the contents of the museum and churches of this ancient city. Do not be frightened, beloved reader; I am not going to launch out into the muddy stream of artistic criticism. I despise most of that which passes current under that dignified name, as heartily as you do. Even the laurels of Mr. Ruskin cannot rob me of a moment's repose. I cannot if I would, nor would I if I could, talk learnedly about pictures. So I can safely promise not to bore you with any "breadth of colouring," and to keep very "shady" about *chiaro 'scuro*. I only wish to say that he who has never been in Antwerp does not know who Rubens was. He may know that an industrious painter of that name once lived, and painted (as I used to think, judging from most of his works that I had seen elsewhere) a variety of fat, flaxen-haired women; but of Rubens, the great master, the painter of the Crucifixion, and the Descent from the Cross, he is as ignorant as a fourth-form boy in the public schools of Patagonia. It is worth a month of sea-sick voyaging to see the works of Rubens and Vandyck which Antwerp possesses; and the only regret connected with my visit there has been, that I could not give more days to the study of them than I could hours.

It is but fifteen miles from Antwerp to Mechlin, or Malines, (as the people here, in the depths of their ignorance, insist upon calling it,) and as a rep-

resentative of a nation whose sole criterion is success, and whose list of the cardinal virtues is headed
by Prosperity, I felt that it would be a grievous sin
of omission for me not to stop and visit that thriving
old town. It did not require much time to walk
through its nice, quiet streets, and look at the pictures and wood carvings in its venerable churches.
The white-capped and bright-eyed lace-makers sat in
windows and doorways, their busy fingers forming
fabrics, the sight of which would kindle the fire of
covetousness in any female heart. Three hours in
Mechlin sufficed to make me about as well acquainted
with it as if I had daily waked up its echoes with the
creaking of my shoes, until their thick soles were
worn out past all hope of tapping. Selecting one of
the numerous railways that branch out from Mechlin, like the reins from the hand of a popular circus
rider in his favourite "six-horse-act," the "Courier
of St. Petersburg," I took a ticket for Brussels, and
soon found myself spinning along over these fertile
plains, whose joyous verdure I had not sufficient time
to appreciate before I found myself in the capital of
Belgium.

And what a charming place this city of lace and
carpets is! Clean as a parlour, not a speck nor a stain
to be seen any where, with less of Dutch stiffness
and more of French ease, so that you do not feel so
much like an intruder as in most other strange cities.
Brussels is a kind of vestibule to Paris; its streets, its
shops, its public edifices are all reflections in miniature of those of the French metropolis. It has long
seemed to me so natural a preparation for the
meridian splendours of Paris, that to go thither in

any other way than through Brussels, is as if you should enter a saloon by a back window, rather than through the legitimate front door. In one respect I prefer Brussels to Paris; it is smaller, and your mind takes it all in at once. In the French capital, its very vastness bewilders you. You are in the condition of the gentleman whose wife was so fat that when he wished to embrace her, he was obliged to make two actions of the feat, and use a bit of chalk to insure the proper distribution of his caress. But in Brussels every thing is so harmoniously and compactly combined, that you can enjoy it all at once. How does one's mind treasure up his rambles through these fair streets and gay arcades, his leisurely walks on these spacious boulevards, or under the dense shade of this lovely park, his musings in this fine old church of Ste. Gudule, whose gorgeous windows symbolize the heavenly bow, and whose air of devotion is eloquent of the undying hope which abides within its consecrated precincts! How one looks back years after leaving Brussels, and conjures up, in his memory, its public monuments, from that exceedingly diminutive and peculiar statue near the Hôtel de Ville, which has pursued its useful and ornamental career for so many centuries, to the heroic equestrian figure of Godfrey of Bouillon, in the Place Royale! How vividly does one remember the old Gothic hall, which has remained unchanged during the many years that have passed since the Emperor Charles V. there laid down the burden of his power, and exchanged the throne for the cloister.

One of the most delightful recollections of my term of residence in Brussels, is of a bright summer

day, when I made an excursion to the field of Waterloo. Some Englishmen have established a line of
coaches for the purpose—real old fashioned coaches,
with a driver and a guard, which latter functionary
performed Yankee Doodle most admirably on his
melodious horn as we rattled out of town. The
roadside views cannot have changed much since the
night when the pavement shook beneath the heavy
artillery and thundering tramp of Wellington's
army. The forest of Soignies (or, to use its poetical
name, Arden) looked as it might have looked before
it was immortalized by a Tacitus and a Shakspeare;
and its fresh foliage was "dewy with Nature's tear-
drops," over our two coach loads of pleasure-seek-
ers, just as Byron describes it to have been over the
"unreturning brave," who passed beneath it forty
years ago. Our party was shown over the memorable field by an old English sergeant who was in the
battle; a fine bluff old fellow, and a gentleman withal,
who, though his head was white, had all the enthusiasm of a young soldier. It was the most interesting trip of the kind that I ever made, far surpassing
my expectations, for the ground remains literally *in
statu quo ante bellum*. No commissioners of high-
ways have interfered with its historical boundaries.
It remains, for the most part, under cultivation, as it
was before it became famous, and the grain grows,
perhaps, more luxuriantly for the chivalric blood
once shed there. There they are, unchanged, those
localities which seem to so many mere inventions of
the historian, Mont St. Jean, the farm of La Haye
Sainte, the château of Hougoumont, the orchard
with its low brick wall, over which the chosen troops

of France and England fought hand to hand, and the spot where the last great charge was made, and the spell which held Europe in awe of the name of Napoleon, and made that name his country's watchword, and the synonyme of victory, was broken forever. Perhaps I err in saying forever, for France is certainly not unmindful of that name even now. That showery afternoon, when the great conqueror saw his veterans, against whom scores of battle fields, and all the terrors of a Russian campaign, proved powerless, cut to pieces and dispersed by a superior force, to which the news of coming reënforcements gave new strength and courage,—that very afternoon a boy, without a thought of battles or their consequences, was playing in the quiet grounds of the château of Malmaison. If Napoleon could have looked forward forty years, if he could have foreseen the romantic career of that child, and followed him through thirty years of exile, imprisonment, and discouragement, until he saw him reëstablish the empire which was then overthrown, and place France on a higher pinnacle of power than she ever knew before, how comparatively insignificant would have seemed to him the consequences of that last desperate charge! If he could have seen that it was reserved to his nephew, the grandchild of his divorced but faithful Josephine, to avenge Waterloo by an alliance more fatal to England's prestige than any invasion could be, and that the armies which had that day borne such bloody witness to their unconquerable daring, would forty years later be united to resist the encroachments of the power which first checked him in his career of victory, he would have had something to think of during that gloomy night besides the sad events that had wrought such a fearful change in his condition.

I returned to Brussels in the afternoon, meditating on the scenes I had visited, and repeating the five stanzas of Childe Harold in which Byron has commemorated the battle of Waterloo. In the evening I read, with new pleasure, Thackeray's graphic Waterloo chapter in Vanity Fair, and dreamed all night of falling empires and "garments rolled in blood." And now I turn my face towards Italy.

GENOA AND FLORENCE

IT is a happy day in every one's life when he com‧ mences his journey into Italy. That glorious land, "rich with the spoils of time" above all others, endeared to every heart possessing any sense of the beautiful in poetry and art, or of the heroic in his‧ tory, rises up before him as it was wont to do in the days of his youth, when Childe Harold's glowing numbers gave a tone of enthusiasm to his every thought, and filled him with longings, for the realization of which he hardly dared to hope. For the time, the commonest actions of the traveller seem to catch something of the indescribable charm of the land to which he is journeying. The ticketing of luggage and the securing of a berth on board a steamer—occupations which are not ordinarily considered particularly agreeable—become invested with an attractiveness that makes him wonder how he could ever have found them irksome. If he approaches Italy by land from France or Switzerland, with what curiosity does he study the varied features of the Piedmontese landscape! He recognizes the fertile fields which he read about in Tacitus years ago, and endeavours to find in the strange dialect which he hears spoken in the brief stops of the diligence to change horses, something to remind him even faintly of the melodious tongue with whose accents Grisi and Bosio had long since made him familiar. Meanwhile his imagination is not idle, and his mind is filled with historical pictures drawn from the classical pages which he once found any thing but entertaining. Though he may be fresh from the cloudless atmosphere of fair Provence, he fancies that the sky is bluer and the air more pure than he ever saw before.

It is a great advantage to enter Italy from the sea. In this way you perceive more clearly the national characteristics, and enter at once into the Italian way of life. You avoid in this way that gradual change from one pure nationality to another, which is eminently unsatisfactory. You do not weary yourself with the mixed population and customs of those border towns which bear about the same relation to Italy that Boulogne, with its multitude of English residents, bears to France. It was my good fortune when I first visited Italy, years ago, to make the voyage from America direct to the proud city of Genoa. Fifty-five weary days passed away before the end of the voyage was reached. Twenty-six of those days were spent in battling with a terrible north-easter, before whose might many a better craft than the one I was in went down into the insatiable depths. My Italian anticipations kept me up through all the cheerlessness of that time. The stormy sky, the wet, the cold, and all the discomfort could not keep from my mind's eye the vineyards, palaces, churches, and majestic ruins which made up the Italy I had looked forward to from childhood. My first sight of that romantic land did somewhat shock, I must acknowledge, my preconceived notions. I was called on deck early one December morning to see the land which is associated in most minds with perpetual sunshine. Facing a biting, northerly blast, I saw the maritime range of the Alps covered with snow and looking as relentless as arctic icebergs. My disappointment was forgotten, however, two mornings after, when Genoa, wearing "the beauty of the morning," lay before our weather-beaten bark. It was something to remember to my dying day—that approach to the city of palaces. Surrounded by its amphitheatre of hills crested on every side with heavy fortifications, its palaces, and towers, and domes, and terraced gardens rising apparently from the very edge of that tideless sea, there sat Genoa, surpassing in its splendour the wildest imaginings of my youth. I shall never forget the thrill that ran through every fibre of my frame, when the sun rose above those embattled ridges, and poured his flood of saffron glory over the whole wonderful scene, and the bells from a hundred churches and convents rang out as cheerily as if the sunbeams made them musical, like the statue in the ancient fable, and there was no further need of bell ropes. The astonishment of Aladdin when he rubbed the lamp and saw the effects of that operation could not have equalled mine, when I saw Genoa put on the light and life of day like a garment. It was like a scene in a theatrical pageant, or one of the brilliant changes in a great firework, so instantaneous was the transition from the subdued light and calmness of early morning to the activity and golden light of day. All the discomfort of the eight preceding weeks was forgotten in the exultation of that moment. I had found the Italy of my young dreams, and my happiness was complete.

This time, however, I entered Italy from the north. I pass by clean, prosperous-looking Milan, with its elegant churches, and its white-coated Austrian soldiers standing guard in every public place. I have not a word of lament to utter at seeing a stranger force sustaining social order there. It is better that it should be sustained by a despotism far more cruel than that of Austria, than to become the prey of that sanguinary anarchy which is dignified in Europe with the name of republicanism. The most absolute of all absolute monarchies is to be preferred to the best government that could possibly be built upon such a foundation as Mazzini's stiletto. Far better is the severest military despotism than the irresponsible tyranny of those who deny the first principles of government and common morality, and who seem to consider assassination the chief of virtues and the most heroic of actions. I pass by that magnificent cathedral, with its thousands of pinnacles and shining statues piercing the clear atmosphere like the peaks of a stupendous iceberg, and its subterranean chapel, glittering with precious metals and jewels, where, in a crystal shrine, repose the relics of the great St. Charles, and the lamps of gold and silver burn unceasingly, and symbolize the shining virtues of the self-forgetful successor of St. Ambrose, and the glowing gratitude of the faithful Milanese for his devotion to the welfare of their forefathers.

I lingered among the attractions of Genoa for a few days. I enjoy not only those magnificent palaces with their spacious quadrangles, broad staircases, and sculptured façades, but those narrow, winding streets of which three quarters of the city are composed—so narrow indeed that a carriage never is seen in them, and a donkey, pannier-laden, after the manner of Ali Baba's faithful animal, compels you to keep very close to the buildings. Genoa is the very reverse of Philadelphia. Its streets are as narrow and crooked as those of Philadelphia are broad and straight. The Quaker City was always a wearisome place to me. Its rectangular avenues—so wide that they afford no protection from the wintry blast nor shelter from the canicular sunshine, and as interminable as a tale in a weekly newspaper—tire me out. They make me long for something more social and natural than their straight lines. Man is a gregarious animal. It is his nature to snuggify himself. But the Quaker affects a contempt for snugness, and includes Hogarth's line of beauty among the worldly vanities which his religion obliges him to shun. Every time I think of Philadelphia my disrespect for the science of geometry is increased, and I find myself more and more inclined to believe the most unkind things that Lord Macaulay can say about Mr. Penn, its founder. Cherishing such sentiments as these, is it wonderful that I find Genoa a pleasant city? I enjoy its gay port, its thronged market place, its sumptuous churches, with gilded vaults and panels, and checkered exteriors, its well-dressed people, from the bluff coachman, who laughed at my attempts to understand the Genoese dialect, to the devout feminines in their graceful white veils, which give the whole city a peculiarly festive and nuptial appearance: but it must be acknowledged, that the

up-and-down-stairsy feature of the town is not grate‹
ful to my gouty feet.

I must not weary you, dear reader, with any
attempts to describe the delightful four days' journey from Genoa to Florence, in a *vettura*. The
Cornice road, with its steep cliffs or trim villas on one
side, and the clear blue Mediterranean on the other,
—those pleasant old towns, pervaded with an air of
respectable antiquity, Chiavari, Sestri, Sarzana,
Spezzia, with its beautiful gulf, whose waters looked
so pure and calm that it was difficult to think that
they could ever have swallowed poor Percy Shelley,
and robbed English literature of one of its brightest
ornaments,—Pietra Santa, Carrara, with its queer
old church, its quarries, its door-steps and window-
sills of milk-white marble, and its throng of artists,
—the little marble city of Massa Ducale, nestling
among the mountains,—the vast groves of olives,
whose ash-coloured leaves made noontide seem like
twilight,—all these things would require a great expenditure of time and rhetoric, and therefore I will
not even allude to them.

Neither will I tire you with any reference to my
brief sojourn in Pisa. I will not tell how delightful
it was to perambulate the clean streets of that peaceful city,—how I enjoyed the view from the bridges,
the ancient towers and domes, and the lofty palaces,
whose fair fronts are mirrored in the soft-flowing
Arno. I will not attempt to describe the enchantment produced by that noble architectural group,—
the Cathedral, the Baptistery, the Campanile, and
the Campo Santo,—nor the joy I felt on making a
closer acquaintance with that graceful tower, whose

inexplicable dereliction from the perfect uprightness which is inculcated as a primary duty in all similar structures, was made familiar to me at an early age, through the medium of a remarkable wood-cut in my school Geography. I will not tell how I fatigued my sense with the forms of beauty with which that glorious church is filled,—how refreshing its holy quiet and subdued light were to my travel-worn spirit,—nor how the majestic cloisters of the Campo Santo, with their delicate traceries, antique frescoes, and constantly varying light and shade, elevated and purified my heart of the sordid spirit of this mean, practical age, until I felt that to live amid such scenes, and to be buried at last in the earth of Palestine, under the shade of those solemn arches, was the only worthy object of human ambition.

I entered Florence late in the afternoon, under cover of a fog that would have done credit to London in the depths of its November nebulosity. It was rather an unbecoming dress for the style of beauty of the Tuscan capital,—that mantle of chill vapour,—but it was worn but a few hours, and the sun rose the next morning in all his legitimate splendour, and darted his rays through as clear and frosty an atmosphere as ever fell to the lot of even that favoured country. I have once or twice heard the epithet "beautiful" applied to this city; indeed, I will not be sure that I have not met with it in some book or other. It is, in fact, the only word that can be used with any propriety concerning this charming place. It is not vast like Rome, nor is the soul of its beholder saddened by the sight of mighty ruins, or burdened with the weight of thousands of years of heroic history. It does not possess the broad Bay of Naples, nor is it watched over by a stupendous volcano, smoking leisurely for want of some better occupation. But it lies in the valley of the Arno, one of the most harmonious and impressive works of art that the world has ever seen, surrounded by natural beauties that realize the most ecstatic dreams of poesy.

Firenze la bella! Who can look at her from any of the terraced hills that enclose her from the rude world, and deny her that title? That fertile plain which stretches from her very walls to the edge of the horizon—those picturesque hills, dotted with lovely villas—those orchards and vineyards, in their glory of gold and purple—that river, stealing noiselessly to the sea—and far away the hoary peaks of the Apennines, changing their hue with every hour of sun-light, and displaying their most gorgeous robes, in honour of the departing day,—I pity the man who can look upon them without a momentary feeling of inspiration. The view from Fiesole is consolation enough for a life of disappointment, and ought to make all future earthly trials seem as nothing to him who is permitted to enjoy it.

And then, those domes and towers, so eloquent of the genius of Giotto and Brunelleschi and of the public spirit and earnest devotion of ages which modern ignorance stigmatizes as "dark,"—who can behold them without a thrill? The battlemented tower of the Palazzo Vecchio—which seems as if it had been hewn out of solid rock, rather than built up by the patient labour of the mason—looks down upon the peaceful city with a composure that seems almost intelligent, and makes you wonder whether it appeared the same when the signiory of Florence held their councils under its massive walls, and in those dark days when the tyrannous factions of Guelph and Ghibelline celebrated their bloody carnival. The graceful Campanile of the cathedral, with its coloured marbles, seems too much like a mantel ornament to be exposed to the changes of the weather. Amid the other domes and towers of the city rises the vast dome of the cathedral, the forerunner of that of St. Peter's, and almost its equal. It appears to be conscious of its superiority to the neighbouring architectural monuments, and merits Hallam's description—"an emblem of the Catholic hierarchy under its supreme head; like Rome itself, imposing, unbroken, unchangeable, radiating in equal expansion to every part of the earth, and directing its convergent curves to heaven."

There is no city in the world so full of memories of the middle ages as Florence. Its very palaces, with their heavily barred basement windows, look as if they were built to stand a siege. Their sombre walls are in strong contrast with the bloom and sunshine which we naturally associate with the valley of the Arno. Their magnificent proportions and the massiveness of their construction oppress you with recollections of the warlike days in which they were erected. You wonder, as you stand in their courtyards, or perambulate the streets darkened by their overhanging cornices, what has become of all the cavaliers; and if a gentleman in "complete steel" should lift his visor to accost you, it would not startle you so much as to hear two English tourists with the

inevitable red guide-books under their arms, conversing about the "Grand Juke." Wherever one
may turn his steps in Florence, he meets with some
object of beauty or historical interest; yet among all
these charms and wonders there is one building upon
which my eyes and mind are never tired of feeding.
The Palazzo Riccardi, the cradle of the great Medici family, is not less impressive in its architecture
than in its historic associations. Its black walls have
a greater charm for me than the variegated marbles
of the Duomo. It was built by the great Cosmo de'
Medici, and was the home of that family of merchant
princes in the most glorious period of its history,
when a grateful people delighted to render to its
members that homage which is equally honourable to
"him that gives and him that takes." The genius of
Michel Angelo and Donatello is impressed upon it.
It was within those lofty halls that Cosmo and his
grandson, Lorenzo the Magnificent, welcomed pontiffs and princes, and the illustrious but untitled
nobility of literature and art, which was the boast of
their age. The ancient glories of the majestic pile
are kept in mind by an inscription which greets him
who enters it with an exhortation to "reverence with
gratitude the ancient mansion of the Medici, in
which not merely so many illustrious men, but Wisdom herself abode—a house which was the nurse of
revived learning."

I wonder whether any one ever was tired of stroll-
ing about these old streets and squares. At my time
of life, walking is not particularly agreeable, even if
it be not interfered with by either of those foes to
active exercise and grace of movement—rheumatism

or gout; but I must acknowledge that I have found such pleasure in rambling through the familiar streets of this delightful city, that I have taken no note of bodily fatigue, and have forgotten the crutch or cane which is my inseparable companion. It is all the same to me whether I walk about the streets, or loiter in the Boboli Gardens, or listen to the delicious music of the full military band that plays daily for an hour before sunset under the shade of the Cascine. They all afford me a kind of vague pleasure—very much that sort of satisfaction which springs from hearing a cat purr, or from watching the fitful blaze of a wood fire. I have no fondness for jewelry, and the great Kohinoor diamond and all the crown jewels of Russia could not invest respectable useless-ness or aristocratic vice with any beauty for me, nor add any charm to a bright, intelligent face, such as lights up many a home in this selfish world; yet I have spent hours in looking at the stalls on the Jeweller's Bridge, and enjoying the covetous looks bestowed by so many passers-by upon their glittering contents.

There are some excellent bookstalls here, and I have renewed the joys of past years and the memory of Paternoster Row, Fleet Street, Holborn, the Strand, and of the quays of Paris, in the inspection of their stock. I have a strong affection for book-stalls, and had much rather buy a book at one than in a shop. In the first place it would be cheaper; in the second place it would be a little worn, and I should become the possessor, not only of the volume, but of its associations with other lovers of books who turned over its leaves, reading here and there, envying the future purchaser. For books, so long as they are well used, increase in value as they grow in age. Sir William Jones's assertion, that "the best monument that can be erected to a man of literary talents is a good edition of his works," is not to be denied; but who would think of reading, for the enjoyment of the thing, a modern edition of Sir Thomas Browne, or Izaak Walton? Who would wish to read Hamlet in a volume redolent of printers' ink and binders' glue? Who would read a clean new copy of Robinson Crusoe when he might have one that had seen service in a circulating library, or had been well thumbed by several generations of adventure-loving boys? A book is to me like a hat or coat —a very uncomfortable thing until the newness has been worn off.

It is in the churches of Florence that my enthusiasm reaches its meridian. This solemn cathedral, with its richly dight windows,—whose warm hues must have been stolen from the palette of Titian or Tintoretto,—makes me forget all earthly hopes and sorrows; and the majestic Santa Maria Novella and San Lorenzo, with their peaceful cloisters and treasures of literature and art, appeal strongly to my religious sensibilities, while they completely satisfy my taste. And then Santa Croce, solemn, not merely as a place of worship, but as the repository of the dust of many of those illustrious men whose genius illumined the world during the fourteenth and fifteenth centuries! I have enjoyed Santa Croce particularly, because I have seen more of the religious life of the Florentine people there. For more than a week I have been there every evening, just after sunset, when the only light that illuminated those ancient arches came from the high altar, which appeared like a vision of heaven in the midst of the thickest darkness of earth. The nave and aisles of that vast edifice were thronged: men, women, and children were kneeling upon that pavement which contains the records of so much goodness and greatness. I have heard great choirs; I have been thrilled by the wondrous power of voices that seemed too much like those of angels for poor humanity to listen to; but I have never before been so overwhelmed as by the hearty music of that vast multitude.

The galleries of art need another volume and an abler pen than mine. Free to the people as the sunlight and the shade of the public gardens, they make an American blush to think of the niggardly spirit that prevails in the country which he would fain persuade himself is the most favoured of all earthly abodes. The Academy, the Pitti, the Uffizi, make you think that life is too short, and that art is indeed long. You wish that you had more months to devote to them than you have days. Great as is the pleasure that I have found in them, I have found myself lingering more fondly in the cloisters and corridors of San Marco than amid the wonderful works that deck the walls of the palaces. The pencil of Beato Angelico has consecrated that dead plastering, and given to it a divine life. The rapt devotion and holy tranquillity of those faces reflect the glory of the eternal world. I ask no more convincing proof of the immortality of the soul, than the fact that those forms of beauty and holiness were conceived and executed by a mortal.

MY UNKNOWN CHUM

It is enough to excite the indignation of any re-
flective Englishman or American to visit Florence,
and compare—or perhaps I ought rather to say contrast—the facts which force themselves upon his attention, with the prejudices implanted in his mind by
early education. Surely, he has a right to be astonished, and may be excused if he indulges in a little
honest anger, when he looks for the first time at the
masterpieces of art which had their origin in those
ages which he has been taught to consider a period of
ignorance and barbarism. He certainly obtains a new
idea of the "barbarism" of the middle ages, when he
visits the benevolent institutions which they have
bequeathed to our times, and when he sees the admirable working of the *Compagnia della Misericor-
dia,* which unites all classes of society, from the
grand duke to his humblest subject, in the bonds of
religion and philanthropy. He may be pardoned,
too, if he comes to the conclusion that the liberal arts
were not entirely neglected in the age that produced
a Dante and a Petrarch, a Cimabue and a Giotto,—
not to mention a host of other names, which may not
shine so brightly as these, but are alike superior to
temporal accidents,—and he cannot be considered
unreasonable if he refuses to believe that the ages
which witnessed the establishment of universities like
those of Paris, Oxford, Cambridge, Prague, Bo-
logna, Salamanca, Vienna, Ferrara, Ingolstadt,
Louvain, Leipsic, &c., were quite so deeply sunk in
darkness, or were held in an intellectual bondage so
utterly hopeless, as the eulogists of the nineteenth
century would persuade him. The monuments of
learning, art, and benevolence, with which Florence

is filled, will convince any thinking man that those who speak of the times I have alluded to as the "dark ages," mean thereby the ages concerning which they are in the dark; and admirably exemplify in their own shallow self-sufficiency the ignorance they would impute to the ages when learning and all good arts were the handmaids of religion.

ANCIENT ROME

THE moment in which one takes his first look at Rome is an epoch in his life. Even if his education should have been a most illiberal one, and he himself should be as strenuous an opponent of pontifical prerogatives as John of Leyden or Dr. Dowling, he is sure to be, for the time, imbued in some measure with the feelings of a pilgrim. The sight of that city which has exercised such a mighty influence on the world, almost from its very foundation, fills his mind with "troublings of strange joy." His vague notions of ancient history assume a more distinct form. The twelve Cæsars pass before his mind's eye like the spectral kings before the Scotch usurper. The classics which he used to neglect so shamefully at school, the historical lessons which he thought so dull, have been endowed with life and interest by that one glance of his astonished eye. But if he loved the classics in his youth,—if the wanderings of Æneas and the woes of Dido charmed instead of tiring him,—if "Livy's pictured page," the polished periods of Sallust and Tacitus, and the mighty eloquence of Cicero, were to him a mine of delight rather than a task,—how does his eye glisten with renewed youth, and his heart swell as his old boyish enthusiasm is once more kindled within it! He feels that he has reached the goal to which his heart and mind were turned during his purest and most unselfish years; and if he were as unswayed by human respect as he was then, he would kneel down with the travel-worn pilgrims by the wayside to give utterance to his gratitude, and to greet the queen city of the world: *Salve, magna parens!*

I shall not easily forget the cloudless afternoon when I first took that long, wearisome ride from Civita Vecchia to Rome. There was no railway in those days, as there is now, and the diligence was of so rude and uncomfortable a make that I half suspected it to be the one upon the top of which Hannibal is said to have crossed the Alps, (*summâ diligentiâ.*) I shared the *coupé* with two other sufferers, and was, like them, so fatigued that it seemed as if a celestial vision would be powerless to make me forgetful of my aching joints, when (after a laborious pull up a hill which might be included among the "everlasting hills" spoken of in holy writ) our long-booted postilion turned his expressive face towards us, and banished all our weariness by exclaiming, as he pointed into the blue distance with his short whip-handle, *"Ecco! Roma! San Pietro!"*

A single glance of the eye served to overcome all our fatigue. There lay the world's capital, crowned by the mighty dome of the Vatican basilica, and we were every moment drawing nearer to it. It was evening before we found ourselves staring at those dark walls which have withstood so many sieges, and heard the welcome demand for passports, which informed us that we had reached the gate of the city.

I was really in Rome,—I was in that city hallowed by so many classical, historical, and sacred associations,—and it all seemed to me like a confused dream. Twice, before the diligence had gone a hundred yards inside the gate, I had pinched myself to ascertain whether I was really awake; and even after I passed through the lofty colonnade of St. Peter's, and had gazed at the front of the church and the vast square which art has made familiar to every one, and had seen the fountains with the moonbeams flashing in their silvery spray, I feared lest something should interrupt my dream, and I should wake to find myself in my snug bedroom at home, wondering at the weakness which allowed me to be seduced into the eating of a bit of cheese the evening before. It was not so, however; no disorganizing cheese had interfered with my digestion; it was no dream; and I was really in Rome. I slept soundly when I reached my hotel, for I felt sure that no hostile Brennus lay in wait to disturb the city's peace, and the grateful hardness of my bed convinced me that all the geese of the capital had not been killed, if the enemy should effect an entrance.

There are few people who love Rome at first sight. The ruins, that bear witness to her grandeur in the days of her worldly supremacy, oppress you at first with an inexpressible sadness. The absence of any thing like the business enterprise and energy of this commercial age makes English and American people long at first for a little of the bustle and roar of Broadway and the Strand. The small paving stones, which make the feet of those who are unaccustomed to them ache severely, the brick and stone floors of the houses, and the lack of the little comforts of modern civilization, render Rome a wearisome place, until one has caught its spirit. Little does he think who for the first time gazes on those gray, mouldering walls, on which "dull time feeds like slow fire upon a hoary brand," or walks those streets in which the past and present are so strangely commingled,— little does he realize how dear those scenes will one day be to him. He cannot foresee the regret with which he will leave those things that seem too common and familiar to deserve attention, nor the glowing enthusiasm which their mention will inspire in after years; and he would smile incredulously if any one were to predict to him that his heart, in after times, will swell with homesick longings as he recalls the memory of that ancient city, and that he will one day salute it from afar as his second home.

I make no claims to antiquarian knowledge; for I do not love antiquity for itself alone. It is only by force of association that antiquity has any charms for me. The pyramids of Egypt would awaken my respect, not so much by their age or size, as by the remembrance of the momentous scenes which have been enacted in their useless and ungraceful presence. Show me a scroll so ancient that human science can obtain no key to the mysteries locked up in the strange figures inscribed upon it, and you would move me but little. But place before me one of those manuscripts (filled with scholastic lore, instinct with classic eloquence, or luminous with the word of eternal life) which have come down to us from those nurseries of learning and piety, the monasteries of the middle ages, and you fill me with the intensest enthusiasm. There is food for the imagination hidden under those worm-eaten covers and brazen clasps. I see in those fair pages something more than the results of the patient toil which perpetuated those precious truths. From those carefully penned lines, and brilliant initial letters, the pale, thoughtful face of the transcriber looks upon me—his contempt of worldly ambition and sacrifice of human consolations are reflected there—and from the quiet of his austere cell, he seems to dart from his serene eyes a glance of patient reproach at the worldlier and more modern age which reaps the fruit of his labour, and repays him by slandering his character. Show me a building whose stupendous masonry seems the work of Titan hands, but whose history is lost in the twilight of the ages, so that no record remains of a time when it was any thing but an antique enigma, and its massive columns and Cyclopean proportions will not touch me so nearly as the stone in Florence where Dante used to stand and gaze upon that dome which Michel Angelo said he would not imitate, and could not excel.

Feeling thus about antiquities, I need not say that those of Rome, so crowned with the most thrilling historical and personal associations, are not wanting in charms for me. Yet I do not claim to be an antiquarian. It is all one to me whether the column of Phocas be forty feet high or sixty,—whether a ruin on the Palatine that fascinates me by its richness and grandeur, was once a Temple of Minerva or of Jupiter Stator; or whether its foundations are of travertine or tufa. I abhor details. My enjoyment of a landscape would be at an end if I were called upon to count the mild-eyed cattle that contribute so much to its picturesqueness; and I have no wish to disturb my appreciation of the spirit of a place consecrated by ages of heroic history, by entertaining any of the learned conjectures of professional antiquarians. It is enough for me to know that I am standing on the spot where Romulus built his straw-thatched palace, and his irreverent brother leaped over the walls of the future mistress of the nations. Standing in the midst of the relics of the grandeur of imperial Rome, the whole of her wonderful history is constantly acting over again in my mind. The stern simplicity of those who laid the foundations of her greatness, the patriotic daring of those who extended her power, the wisdom of those who terminated civil strife by compelling the divided citizens to unite against a foreign foe, are all present to me. In that august place where Cicero pleaded, gazing upon that mount where captive kings did homage to the masters of the world, your mere antiquarian, with his pestilent theories and measurements, seems to me little better than a profaner. When I see such a one scratching about the base of some majestic column in the Forum (although I cannot but be grateful to those whose researches have developed the greatness of the imperial city,) I do long to interrupt him, and remind him that his "tread is on an empire's dust." I wish to recall him from the petty details in which he delights, and have him enjoy with me the grandeur and dignity of the whole scene.

The triumphal arches,—the monuments of the cultivation of those remote ages, no less than of the power of the state which erected them,—the memorials of the luxury that paved the way to the decline of that power—all these things impress me with the thought of the long years that intervened between that splendour and the times when the seat of universal empire was inhabited only by shepherds and their flocks. It wearies me to think of the long centuries of human effort that were required to bring Rome to its culminating point of glory; and it affords me a melancholy kind of amusement to contrast the spirit of those who laid the deep and strong foundations of that prosperity and power, with that of some modern sages, to whom a hundred years are a respectable antiquity, and who seem to think that commercial enterprise and the will of a fickle populace form as secure a basis for a state as private virtue, and the principle of obedience to law. I know a country, yet in the first century of its national existence, full of hope and ambition, and possessing advantages such as never before fell to the lot of a young empire, but lacking in those powers which made Rome what she was. If that country, "the newest born of nations, the latest hope of mankind," which has so rapidly risen to a power surpassing in extent that of ancient Rome, and bears within itself the elements of the decay that ruined the old empire, —wealth, vice, corruption,—if she could overcome the vain notion that hers is an exceptional case, and that she is not subject to that great law of nature which makes personal virtue the corner-stone of national stability and the lack of that its bane, and could look calmly upon the remains of old Rome's grandeur, she might learn a great lesson. Contemplating the patient formation of that far-reaching dominion until it found its perfect consummation in the age of Augustus, (*Tantæ molis erat Romanam condere gentem,*) she would see that true national greatness is not "the hasty product of a day"; that demagogues and adventurers, who have made politics their trade, are not the architects of that greatness; and that the parchment on which the constitution and laws of a country are written, might as well be used for drum-heads when reverence and obedience have departed from the hearts of its people.

A gifted representative of a name which is classical in the history of the drama, some years ago gave to the world a journal, of her residence in Rome. She called her volume "A Year of Consolation"—a title as true as it is poetical. Indeed I know of nothing more soothing to the spirit than a walk through these ancient streets, or an hour of meditation amid these remains of fallen majesty. To stand in the arena of the Coliseum in the noonday glare, or when those ponderous arches cast their lengthened shadows on the spot where the first Roman Christians were sacrificed to make a holiday for a brutalized populace,—to muse in the Pantheon, that changeless temple of a living, and monument of a dead, worship, and reflect on the many generations that have passed beneath its majestic portico from the days of Agrippa to our own,—to listen to the birds that sing amid the shrubbery which decks the stupendous arches of the Baths of Caracalla,—to be overwhelmed by the stillness of the Campagna while the eye is filled with that rolling verdure which seems in the hazy distance like the waves of the unquiet sea— what are all these things but consolations in the truest sense of the word? What is the bitterest grief that ever pierced a human heart through a long life of sorrows, compared to the dumb woe of that mighty desolation? What are our brief sufferings, when they are brought into the august presence of a mourner who has seen her hopes one by one taken from her, through centuries of war and rapine, neglect and silent decay?

Among all of Rome's monuments of antiquity, there are few that impress me so strangely as those old Egyptian obelisks, the trophies of the victorious emperors, which the pontiffs have made to contribute so greatly to the adornment of their capital. It is almost impossible to turn a corner of one of the principal streets of the city without seeing one of these peculiar shafts that give a fine finish to the perspective. If their cold granite forms could speak, what a strange history they would reveal! They were witnesses of the achievements of a power which reached its noonday splendour centuries before the shepherd Faustulus took the foundling brothers into his cottage on the banks of the Tiber. The civilization of which they are the relics had declined before the Roman kings inaugurated that which afterwards reclaimed all Europe from the barbarians. Yet there they stand as grim and silent as if they had but yesterday been rescued from the captivity of the native quarry, and had never seen a nobler form than those of the dusty artisans who wrought them—as dull and unimpressible as some of the stupid tourists whom I see daily gazing upon these glorious monuments, and seeing only so much brick and stone.

MODERN ROME

ACKNOWLEDGING as I do the charms which the Rome of antiquity possesses for me, it must still be confessed that the Rome of the present time enchants me with attractions scarcely less potent. Religion has consecrated many of the spots which history had made venerable, and thus added a new lustre to their associations. I turn from the broken columns and gray mouldering walls of old Rome to those fanes, "so ancient, yet so new," in which the piety of centuries has found its enduring expression. Beneath their sounding arches, by the mild light of the lamps that burn unceasingly around their shrines, who would vex his brain with antiquarian lore? We may notice that the pavement is worn away by the multitudes which have been drawn thither by curiosity or devotion; but we feel that Heaven's chronology is not an affair of months and years, and that Peter and Paul, Gregory and Leo, are not mere personages in a drama upon the first acts of which the curtain long since descended. Who thinks of antiquity while he inhabits that world of art which Rome encloses within her walls? Those are not the triumphs of a past age alone; they are the triumphs of to-day. The Apollo's bearing is not less manly, its step not less elastic, than it was in that remote age when its unknown sculptor threw aside his chisel and gazed upon his finished work. To-day's sunshine is not more clear and golden than that which glows in the landscapes of Claude Lorraine, though he who thus made the sunbeams his servants has been sleeping for nearly two centuries in the dusty vaults of *Trinità de' Monti*. Were Raphael's deathless faces more real while he was living than they are now? Were Guido's and Domenichino's triumphs more worthy of admiration while the paint was wet upon them? or were the achievements of that giant of art, Michel Angelo, ever more wonderful than now? No; these great works take no note of time, and confer upon the city which contains them something of their own immortality.

I have heard people regret that so many of our artists should expatriate themselves, and spend their lives in Rome or Florence. To me, however, nothing seems more natural; and if I were a painter, or a sculptor, I feel certain that I should share the common weakness of the profession for a place of residence in harmony with my art. What sympathy can a true artist feel with a state of society in which he is regarded by nine people out of ten as a useless member, because he does not directly aid in the production of a given quantity of grain or of cloth? Every stroke of his brush, every movement of his hands in moulding the obedient clay, is a protest against the low, mean, materialistic views of life which prevail among us; and it is too much to ask of any man that he shall spend his days in trying to live peaceably in an enemy's camp. When figs and dates become common articles of food in Lapland, and the bleak sides of the hills of New Hampshire are adorned with the graceful palm tree and the luxuriant foliage of the tropics, you may expect art to flourish in a community whose god is commerce, and whose chief religious duty is money-getting.

Truly the life of an artist in Rome is about as near the perfection of earthly happiness as is commonly vouchsafed to mortal man. The tone of society, and all the surroundings of the artist, are so congenial that no poverty nor privation can seriously interfere with them. The streets, with their architectural marvels, the trim gardens and picturesque cloisters of the old religious establishments, the magnificent villas of the neighbourhood of the city, and the vast, mysterious Campagna, with its gigantic. aqueducts and its purple atmosphere, and those glorious galleries which at the same time gratify the taste of the artist and feed his ambition,—these are things which are as free to him as the blessed sunlight or the water that sparkles in the countless fountains of the Holy City. I do not wonder that artists who have lived any considerable time in Rome are discontented with the feverish restlessness of our American way of life, and that, after "stifling the mighty hunger of the heart" through two or three wearisome years in our western world, they turn to Rome as to a fond mother, upon whose breast they may find that peace which they had elsewhere sought in vain.

The churches of Rome impress me in a way which I have never heard described by any other person. I do not speak of St. Peter's, (that "noblest temple that human skill ever raised to the honour of the Creator,") nor do I refer to those other magnificent basilicas in which the Christian glories of eighteen centuries sit enthroned. These have a dignity and

majesty peculiarly their own, and the most thoughtless cannot tread their ancient pavement without
being for the time subdued into awe and veneration.
But the parish churches of Rome, the churches of the
various religious orders and congregations, and
those numerous little temples which are so thickly
scattered through the city, attract me in . manner
especially fascinating. There is an air of cosiness
and at-home-ativeness about them which cannot be
found in the grander fanes. Some of them seem by
their architectural finish to have been built in some
fine street or square, and to have wandered off in
search of .quiet to their present secluded positions.
It is beneath their arches that the Roman people may
be seen. Before those altars you may see men, women, and children kneeling, their lips scarcely moving with the petitions which are heard only in another
world. No intruding tourists, eye-glassed and Mur-
rayed, interfere with their devotions, and the silence
of the sacred place is unbroken, save by the rattling
of a rosary, or at stated times by the swell of voices
from the choir chapel. These are the places where
the real power of the Catholic religion makes itself
felt more unmistakably than in the grandest cathedrals, where every form and sound is eloquent of
worship. I remember with pleasure that once in
London, as I was passing through that miserable
quarter which lies between Westminster Abbey and
Buckingham Palace, I was attracted by the appearance of a number of people who were entering a narrow doorway. One or two stylish carriages, with
crests upon their panels, and drivers in livery, stood
before the dingy building which seemed to wear a

mysterious air of semi-cleanliness in the midst of the general squalour. I followed the strange collection of the representatives of opulence and the extremest poverty through a long passage-way, and found myself in a large room which was tastefully fitted up for a Catholic chapel. The simplicity of the place, joined with its strictly ecclesiastical look, the excellent music, the crowded and devout congregation, and the almost breathless attention which was paid to the simple and persuasive eloquence of the preacher, who was formerly one of the chief ornaments of the established church, whose highest honours he had cast aside that he might minister more effectually to the poor and despised,—all these things astonished and delighted me. To see that church preserving, even in its hiddenness and poverty, its regard for the comeliness of God's worship, and adorning that humble chapel in a manner which showed that the spirit which erected the shrines of Westminster, Salisbury and York, had not died out, carried me back in spirit to the catacombs of Rome, where the early Christians left the abiding evidences of their zeal for the beauty of the house of God. I was at that time fresh from the continent, and my mind was occupied with the remembrance of the gorgeous churches of Italy. Yet, despite my recollection of those "forests of porphyry and marble," those altars of *lapis lazuli,* those tabernacles glittering with gold, and silver, and precious stones, and those mosaics and frescoes whose beauty and variety almost fatigue the sense of the beholder,—I must say that it gave me a new sense of the dignity and grandeur of the ancient Church, to see her in the midst of the pov-

erty and obscurity to which she is now condemned in
the land which once professed her faith, and was
once thickly planted with those institutions of learning and charity which are the proudest monuments of
her progress. A large ship, under full sail, running
off before a pleasant breeze, is a beautiful sight; but
it is by no means so grandly impressive as that of the
same ship, under close canvas, gallantly riding out
the merciless gale that carried destruction to every
unseaworthy craft which came within its reach.

I am not one of those who lament over the millions which have been expended upon the churches of
Rome. I am *not* inclined to follow the sordid principle of that apostle who is generally held up rather
as a warning than an example, and say that it had
been better if the sums which have been devoted to
architectural ornament had been withheld and given
to the poor. Religion has no need, it is true, of
these visible splendours, any more than of set forms
and modes of speech. For it is the heart that be-
lieves, and loves, and prays. But we, poor mortals,
so enslaved by our senses, so susceptible to external
appearances, need every thing that can inspire in us
a respect for something higher than ourselves, or
remind us of the glories of the invisible, eternal
world. And can we doubt that He who praised the
action of that pious woman who poured the precious
ointment upon His sacred head, looks with compla-
cency upon the sacrifices which are made for the
adornment of the temples devoted to His worship?
Is it a right principle that people who are clad in expensive garments, who are not content unless they
are surrounded by carved or enamelled furniture,

and whose feet tread daily on costly tapestries, should find fault with the generous piety which has made the churches of Italy what they are, and should talk so impressively about the beauty of spiritual worship? I have no patience with these advocates for simplicity in every thing that does not relate to themselves and their own comforts.

"Shall we serve Heaven with less respect
Than we do minister to our gross selves?"

I care not how simple our private houses may be, but I advocate liberality and splendour in our public buildings of all kinds, for the sake of preserving a due respect for the institutions they enshrine. I remember, in reading one of the old classical writers, —Sallust, I think,—in my young days, being greatly impressed by his declaration that private luxury is a sure forerunner of a nation's downfall, and that it is a fatal sign for the dwellings of the citizens to be spacious and magnificent, while the public edifices are mean and unworthy. Purely intellectual as we may think ourselves, we are, nevertheless, somewhat deferential to the external proprieties of life, and I very much doubt whether the most reverential of us could long maintain his respect for the Supreme Court if its sessions were held in a tap-room, or for religion, if its ministers prayed and preached in pea-jackets and top-boots.

Displeasing as is the presence of most of the English-speaking tourists one meets in Rome, there are two places where they delight to congregate, which yet have charms for me that not even Cockney vulgarity or Yankee irreverence can destroy. The church of the convent of *Trinità de' Monti* wins me, in spite of the throng that fills its nave at the hour of evening every Sunday and festival day. Some years since, when I first visited Rome, the music which was heard there was of the highest order of merit. At present the nuns of the Sacred Heart have no such great artistes in their community as they had then, but the music of their choir is still one of those things which he who has once heard can never forget. It is the only church in Rome in which I have heard female voices; and, though I much prefer the great male choirs of the basilicas, there is a soothing simplicity in the music at *Trinità de' Monti* which goes home to almost every heart. I have seen giddy and unthinking girls, who laughed at the ceremonial they did not understand, subdued to reverence by those strains, and supercilious Englishmen reduced to the humiliating necessity of wiping their eyes. Indeed, the whole scene is so harmoniously impressive that its enchantment cannot be resisted. The solemn church, lighted only by the twilight rays, and the tapers upon the high altar,—the veiled forms of the pious sisterhood and their young pupils in the grated sanctuary,—the clouding of the fragrant incense,—the tinkling of that silvery bell and of the chains of the swinging censer,—those ancient and dignified rites,—and over all, those clear, angelic voices praying and praising, in litany and hymn—all combine to make up a worship, one moment of which would seem enough to wipe away the memory of a lifetime of folly, and disappointment, and sorrow.

The Sistine Chapel is another place to which I am bound by an almost supernatural fascination. My

imperfect eyesight will not permit me to enjoy fully
the frescoes that adorn its lofty walls; but I feel that
I am in the presence of the great master and some of
his mightiest conceptions. I do not know whether
the chapel is most impressive in its empty state, or
when thronged for some great religious function. In
the former condition, its fine proportions and its
simplicity satisfy me so completely, that I hardly
wish for the pomp and splendour which belong to it
on great occasions. I know of nothing more grand
than the sight of that simple throne of the Sovereign
Pontiff, when it is occupied by that benignant old
man, to whom more than two hundred millions of
people look with veneration as to a father and a
teacher,—and surrounded by those illustrious prelates and princes who compose a senate of moral and
intellectual worth, such as all the world beside cannot
parallel. Those venerable figures—those gray hairs
—those massive foreheads, and those resplendent
robes of office, seem to be a part of some great historical picture, rather than a reality before my eyes.
There is nothing more severe in actual experience,
or more satisfactory in the recollection, than Holy
Week in the Sistine Chapel. The crowd, the fatigue,
and the presence of so many sight-seers, who have
come with the same feeling that they would attend an
opera or a play, are not calculated to increase one's
bodily comfort, or to awaken the sentiments proper
to so sacred a season as that which is then commemorated. But after these have passed away, there remains the recollection, which time does not diminish,
but makes more precious, of that darkening chapel
and the bowed-down heads of the Pope and cardi-

nals, of the music, "yearning like a god in pain," of the melodious woe of the *Miserere,* the plaintive majesty of the Lamentations and the Reproaches, and the shrill dissonance of the shouts of the populace in the gospel narrative of the crucifixion. These are things which would outweigh a year of fatigue and pain. I know of no greater or more sincere tribute to the perfections of the Sistine choir, and the genius of Allegri and Palestrina, than the patience with which so many people submit to be packed, like herring in a box, into that small chapel. But old and gouty as I am, I would gladly undergo all the discomforts of that time to hear those sounds once more.

I hear some people complain of the beggars, and wonder why Rome, with her splendid system of charities for the relief of every form of suffering, permits mendicancy. For myself, I am not inclined to complain either of the beggars or of the merciful government, which refuses to look upon them as offenders against its laws. On the contrary, it appears to me rather creditable than otherwise to Rome, that she is so far behind the age, as not to class poverty with crime among social evils. I have a sincere respect for this feature of the Catholic Church; this regard for the poor as her most precious inheritance, and this unwillingness that her children should think that, because she has organized a vast system of benevolence, they are absolved of the duty of private charity. In this wisdom, which thus provides for the exercise of kindly feelings in alms-giving, may be found one of the most attractive characteristics of the Roman Church. This, no less

than the austere religious orders which she has
founded, shows in what sense she receives the beatitude, "Blessed are the poor in spirit." And the same
kind spirit of equality may be seen in her churches
and cathedrals, where rich and poor kneel upon the
same pavement, before their common God and
Saviour, and in her cloisters, and universities, and
schools, where social distinctions cannot enter.

When I walk through the cloisters of these venerable institutions of learning, or gaze upon the ancient
city from *Monte Mario,* or the Janiculum, it seems
to me that never until now did I appreciate the
world's indebtedness to Rome. Dislike it as we may,
we cannot disguise the fact, that to her every Christian nation owes, in a great measure, its civilization,
its literature, and its religion. The endless empire
which Virgil's muse foretold, is still hers; and, as one
of her ancient Christian poets said, those lands which
were not conquered by her victorious arms are held
in willing obedience by her religion. When I think
how all our modern civilization, our art, letters, and
jurisprudence, sprang originally from Rome, it appears to me that a narrow religious prejudice has
prevented our forming a due estimate of her services
to humanity. To some, the glories of the ancient
empire, the memory of the days when her sover-
eignty extended from Britain to the Ganges, and her
capital counted its inhabitants by millions, seem to
render all her later history insignificant and dull; but
to my mind the moral dignity and power of Christian
Rome is as superior to her old military omnipotence
as it is possible for the human intellect to conceive.
The ancient emperors, with all their power, could

not carry the Roman name much beyond the limits of Europe; the rulers who have succeeded them have made the majestic language of Rome familiar to two hemispheres, and have built up, by spiritual arms, the mightiest empire that the world has ever seen. For me, Rome's most enduring glories are the memories of the times when her great missionary orders civilized and evangelized the countries which her arms had won, when her martyrs sowed the seed of Christianity with their blood, and her confessors illumined the world with their virtues; when her pontiffs, single-handed, turned back barbarian invasions, or mitigated the severities of the feudal age, or protected the people by laying their ban upon the tyrants who oppressed them, or defended the sanctity of marriage, and the rights of helpless women against divorce-seeking monarchs and conquerors. These things are the true fulfilment of the glowing prophecy of Rome's greatness, which Virgil puts into the mouth of Anchises, when Æneas visits the Elysian Fields, and hears from his old father that the mission of the government he is about to found is to rule the world by moral power, to make peace between opposing nations, to spare the subject, and to subdue the proud:

> "Tu regere imperio populos, Romane, memento;
> Hæ tibi erunt artes, pacisque imponere morem,
> Parcere subjectis, et debellare superbos."

ROME TO MARSEILLES

THE weather was fearfully hot the day of my departure from Rome. The sun was staring down, without winking, upon that wonderful old city, as if he loved the sight. The yellow current of old Father Tiber seemed yellower than ever in the glare. Except from sheer necessity, no person moved abroad; for the atmosphere, which early in the morning had seemed like airs from heaven, before noon had become most uncomfortably like a blast from the opposite direction. The Piazza di Spagna was like Tadmor in the wilderness. Not a single English tourist, with his well-read Murray under his arm, was to be seen there; not a carriage driver broke the stillness of the place with his polyglot solicitations to ride. The great staircase of *Trinità de' Monti* seemed an impossibility; to have climbed up its weary ascent under that broiling sun would have been poor entertainment for man or beast. The squares of the city were like furnaces, and made one mentally curse architecture, and bless the narrow, shady streets. The soldiers on guard at the gates and in the public places looked as if they could n't help it. Now and then a Capuchin monk, in his heavy, brown habit, girded with the knotted cord, toiled along on some errand of benevolence, and made one marvel at his endurance. Occasionally a cardinal rolled by in scarlet state, looking as if he gladly would have exchanged the bondage of his dignity and power for a single day of virtuous liberty in linen pantaloons.

Traffic seemed to have departed this life; there were no buyers, and the shopkeepers slumbered at their counters. The *cafés* were shrouded in their long, striped awnings, and seemed to invite company by their well-wet pavement. A few old Romans found energy enough to call for an occasional ice or lemonade, and talked in the intervals about *Pammerstone,* and his agent, Mazzini. How the sun blazed down into the Coliseum! Not a breath of air stirred the foliage that clothes that mighty ruin. Even the birds were mute. To have crossed that broad arena would have perilled life as surely as in those old days when the first Roman Christians there confessed their faith. On such a day, one's parting visits must necessarily be brief; so I left the amphitheatre, and walked along the dusty *Via Sacra,* pausing a moment to ponder on the scene of Cicero's triumphs, and of so many centuries of thrilling history, and coming to the conclusion that, if it were such a day as that when Virginius in that place slew his dear little daughter, the blow was merciful indeed. The market-place in front of the Pantheon, usually so thronged and lively, was almost deserted. The fresh, bright vegetables had either all been sold, or had refused to grow in such a heat. But the Pantheon itself was unchanged. There it stood, in all its severe grandeur, majestic as in the days of the Cæsars, the embodiment of heathenism, the exponent of the worship of the old, inexorable gods,—of justice without mercy, and power without love. Its interior seemed cool and refreshing, for no heat can penetrate that stupendous pile of masonry,—and I gathered new strength from my short visit. It was a fine thought in the old Romans to adapt the temples of heathenism to the uses of Christianity. The contrasts suggested to our minds by this practice are very striking. When we see that the images of the old revengeful and impure divinities have given place to those of the humble and self-denying heroes of Christianity, that the Saviour of the world stretches out His arms upon the cross, in the place from which the haughty Jupiter once hurled his thunderbolts, we are borne at once to a conclusion more irresistible than any that the mere force of language could produce. One of our own poets felt this in Rome, and expressed this same idea in graceful verse:—

"The goddess of the woods and fields,
The healthful huntress undefiled,
Now with her fabled brother yields
To sinless Mary and her Child."

But I must hurry on towards St. Peter's. There are three places in Rome which every one visits as soon as possible after he arrives, and as short a time as may be before his departure—the Coliseum, the Pantheon, and St. Peter's. The narrow streets between the Pantheon and the Bridge of St. Angelo were endurable, because they were shady. It was necessary to be careful, however, and not trip over any of the numerous Roman legs whose proprietors were stretched out upon the pavement in various picturesque postures, sleeping away the long hours of that scorching day. At last the bridge is reached.

Bernini's frightful statues, which deform its balus-
trades, seem to be writhing under the influence of the
sun. I am quite confident that St. Veronica's napkin
was curling with the heat. The bronze archangel
stood as usual upon the summit of the Castle of St.
Angelo. I stopped a few moments, thinking that he
might see the expediency of sheathing his sword and
retreating, before he should be compelled, in the con-
fusion of such a blaze as that, to *run* away; but it was
useless. I moved on towards St. Peter's, and he still
kept guard there as brazen-faced as ever. The great
square in front of the basilica seemed to have
scooped up its fill of heat, and every body knows that
it is capable of containing a great deal. The few
persons whom devotion or love of art had tempted
out in such a day, approached it under the shade of
its beautiful colonnades. I was obliged to content
myself with the music of one of those superb fountains only, for the workmen were making a new
basin for the other. St. Peter's never seemed to me
so wonderful, never filled me up so completely, as it
did then. The contrast of the heat I had been
in with that atmosphere of unchangeable coolness,
the quiet of the vast area, the fewness of people moving about, all conspired to impress me with a new
sense of the majesty and holiness of the place. The
quiet, unflickering blaze of the numerous lamps that
burn unceasingly around the tomb of the Prince of
the Apostles seemed a beacon of immortality. To one
who could at that hour recall the bustle and turmoil
of the Boulevards of Paris, or of the Strand, or of
Broadway, the vast basilica itself seemed to be an
island of peace in the tempestuous ocean of the

world. I am not so blind a lover of Gothic architecture that I can find no beauty nor religious feeling in the Italian churches. I prefer, it is true, the "long-drawn aisle and fretted vault," and the "storied windows richly dight"; but I cannot for that reason sneer at the gracefully turned arches, the mosaic walls and domes rich in frescoes and precious marbles, that delight one's eyes in Italy. Both styles are good in their proper places. The Gothic and Norman, with their high-pitched roofs, are the natural growth of the snowy north, and to attempt to transplant them to a land where heat is to be guarded against, were as absurd as to expect the pine and fir to take the place of the fig tree and the palm. Talk as eloquently as we may about being superior to external impressions, I defy any man to breathe the quiet atmosphere of any of these old continental churches for a few moments, without feeling that he has gathered new strength therefrom to tread the thorns of life. Lamartine has spoken eloquently on this theme: "Ye columns who veil the sacred asylums where my eyes dare not penetrate, at the foot of your immovable trunks I come to sigh! Cast over me your deep shades, render the darkness more obscure, and the silence more profound! Forests of porphyry and marble! the air which the soul breathes under your arches is full of mystery and of peace! Let love and anxious cares seek shade and solitude under the green shelter of groves, to soothe their secret wounds. O darkness of the sanctuary! the eye of religion prefers thee to the wood which the breeze disturbs! Nothing changes thy foliage; thy still shade is the image of motionless eternity!"

There was not time to linger long. The pressure of worldly engagements was felt even at the shrine of the apostles. I walked about, and tried to recall the many splendid religious pageants I had there witnessed, and wondered sorrowfully whether I should ever again listen to that matchless choir, or have my heart stirred to its depths by the silver trumpets that reëcho under that sonorous vault in the most solemn moment of religion's holiest rite. Once more out in the clear hot atmosphere which seemed hotter than before. The Supreme Pontiff was absent from his capital, and the Vatican was comparatively empty. The Swiss guards, in their fantastic but picturesque uniform, were loitering about the foot of the grand staircase, and sighing for a breath of the cool air of their Alpine home. I took a last long gaze at that grand old pile of buildings,—the home of all that is most wonderful in art, the abode of that power which overthrew the old Roman empire, inaugurated the civilization of Europe, and planted Christianity in every quarter of the globe,—and then turned my unwilling feet homewards. In my course I passed the foot of the Janiculum Hill: it was too hot, however, to think of climbing up to the convent of Sant' Onofrio—though I would gladly have paid a final visit to that lovely spot where the munificence of Pius IX. has just completed a superb sepulchre for the repose of Tasso. So I crossed the Tiber in one of those little ferry boats which are attached to a cable stretched over the river, and thus are swung across by the movement of the current,—a labour-saving arrangement preëminently Roman in its character,—and soon found myself in my lodgings

ROME TO MARSEILLES

However warm the weather may be in Rome, one can keep tolerably comfortable so long as he does not move about,—thanks to the thick walls and heavy wooden window shutters of the houses,—so I found my room a cool asylum after my morning of laborious pleasure.

At last, the good byes having all been said, behold me, with my old portmanteau, (covered with its many-coloured coat of baggage labels, those trophies of many a hard campaign of travel,) at the office of the diligence for Civita Vecchia. The luggage and the passengers having been successfully stowed away, the lumbering vehicle rolled down the narrow streets, and we were soon outside the gate that opens upon the old Aurelian Way. Here the passports were examined, the postilions cracked their whips, and I felt indeed that I was "banished from Rome." It is a sad thing to leave Rome. I have seen people who have made but a brief stay there shed more tears on going away than they ever did on a departure from home; but for one who has lived there long enough to feel like a Roman citizen—to feel that the broken columns of the Forum have become a part of his being—to feel as familiar with St. Peter's and the Vatican as with the King's Chapel and the Tremont House—it is doubly hard to go away. The old city, so "rich with the spoils of time," seems invested with a personality that appeals most powerfully to every man, and would fain hold him back from returning to the world. The lover of art there finds its choicest treasures ever open to him; the artist there finds an abundance of employment for his chisel or his brush; the man of business there finds an asylum from the vexing cares of a commercial career; the student of antiquity or of history can there take his fill amid the "wrecks of a world whose ashes still are warm," and listen to the centuries receding into the unalterable past with their burdens of glory or of crime; the lover of practical benevolence will there be delighted by the inspection of establishments for the relief of every possible form of want and suffering; the enthusiast for education finds there two universities and hundreds of public schools of every grade, and all as free as the bright water that sparkles in Rome's countless fountains; the devout can there rekindle their devotion at the shrines of apostles and martyrs, and breathe the holy air of cloisters in which saints have lived and died, or join their voices with those that resound in old churches, whose pavements are furrowed by the knees of pious generations; the admirer of pomp, and power, and historic associations can there witness the more than regal magnificence of a power, compared to which the houses of Bourbon or of Hapsburg are but of yesterday; the lover of republican simplicity can there find subject for admiration in the facility of access to the highest authorities, and in the perfection of his favourite elective system by which the supreme power is perpetuated. There is, in short, no class of men to whom Rome does not attach itself. People may complain during their first week that it is dull, or melancholy, or dirty; but you generally find them sorry enough to go away, and looking back to their residence there as the happiest period of their existence. Somebody has said,—and I wish that I could recall the exact words, they are so true,—that when we leave Paris, or Naples, or Florence, we feel a natural sorrow, as if we were parting from a cherished friend; but on our departure from Rome we feel a pang like that of separation from a woman whom we love!

At last Rome disappeared from sight in the dusk of evening, and the discomforts of the journey began to make themselves obtrusive. The night air in Italy is not considered healthy, and we therefore had the windows of the diligence closed. Like Charles Lamb after the oyster pie, we were "all full inside," and a pretty time we had of it. As to respiration, you might as well have expected the performance of that function from a mackerel occupying the centre of a well-packed barrel of his finny comrades, as of any person inside that diligence. Of course there was a baby in the company, and of course the baby cried. I could not blame it, for even a fat old gentleman who sat opposite to me would have cried if he had not known how to swear. But it is useless to recall the anguish of that night: suffice it to say that for several hours the only air we got was an occasional vocal performance from the above-mentioned infant. At midnight we reached Palo, on the sea coast, where I heard "the wild water lapping on the crag," and felt more keenly than before that I had indeed left Rome behind me. The remainder of the journey being along the coast, we had the window open, though it was not much better on that account, as we were choking with dust. It was small comfort to see the cuttings and fillings-in for the railway which is destined soon to destroy those beastly diligences, and place Rome within two or three hours of its seaport.

At five o'clock in the morning, after ten toilsome hours, I found myself, tired, dusty, and hungry, in Civita Vecchia, a city which has probably been the cause of more profanity than any other part of the world, including Flanders. I was determined not to be fleeced by any of the hotel keepers; so I staggered about the streets until I found a barber's shop open. Having repaired the damage of the preceding night, I hove to in a neighbouring *café* long enough to take in a little ballast in the way of breakfast. Afterwards I fell in with an Englishman, of considerable literary reputation, whom I had several times met in Rome. He was one of those men who seem to possess all sorts of sense except common sense. He was full of details, and could tell exactly the height of the dome of St. Peter's, or of the great pyramid,—could explain the process of the manufacture of the Minié rifle or the boring of an artesian well, and could calculate an eclipse with Bond or Secchi,—but he could not pack a carpet-bag to save his life. That he should have been able to travel so far from home alone is a fine commentary on the honesty and good nature of the people of the continent. I could not help thinking what a time he would have were he to attempt to travel in America. He would think he had discovered a new nomadic tribe in the cabmen of New York. He had come down to Civita Vecchia in a most promiscuous style, and when I discovered him he was trying to bring about a union between some six or eight irreconcilable pieces of luggage. I aided him successfully in the work, and his look of perplexity and despair gave way to one of gratitude and admiration for his deliverer. Delighted at this escape from the realities of his situation, he launched out into a profound dissertation on the philosophy of language and the formation of provincial dialects, and it was some time before I could bring him down to the common and practical business of securing his passage in the steamer for Marseilles. Ten o'clock, however, found us on board one of the steamers of the *Messageries Imperiales,* and we were very shortly after under way. We were so unfortunate as to run aground on a little spit of land in getting out of port, as we ran a little too near an English steamer that was lying there. But a Russian frigate sent off a cable to us, and thus established an alliance between their flag and the French, which drew the latter out of the difficulty in which it had got by too close a proximity to its English neighbour.

It was a beautiful, cloudless day, and reminded me of many halcyon days I had spent on that blue Mediterranean in other times. It reminded me of some of my childhood's days in the country in New England,—days described by Emerson where he says that we "bask in the shining hours of Florida and Cuba,"—when "the day, immeasurably long, sleeps over the broad hills and warm, wide fields,"—when "the cattle, as they lie on the ground, seem to have great and tranquil thoughts." It was on such a day that I used to delight to pore over my Shakspeare, undisturbed by any sound save the hum of the insect world, or the impatient switch of the tail, or movement of the feet, of a horse who had sought the same shade I was enjoying. To a man who has been rudely used by fortune, or who has drunk deep of sorrow or disappointment, I can conceive of nothing more grateful or consoling than a summer cruise in the Mediterranean. "The sick heart often needs a warm climate as much as the sick body."

My English friend, immediately on leaving port, took some five or six prescriptions for the prevention of seasickness, and then went to bed, so that I had some opportunity to look about among our ship's company. There were two men, apparently companions, though they hardly spoke to each other, who amused me very much One was a person of about four feet and a half in height, who walked about on deck with that manner which so many diminutive persons have, of wishing to be thought as tall as Mr. George Barrett. He boasted a deportment that would have made the elder Turveydrop envious, while it was evident that under that serene and dignified exterior lay hidden all the warm-heartedness and geniality of that eminent philanthropist who was obliged to play a concerto on the violin to calm his grief at seeing the conflagration of his native city. The other looked as if "he had not loved the world, nor the world him"; he was a thin, bilious-looking person, and seemed like a whole serious family rolled into one individuality. I felt a great deal of curiosity to know whether he was reduced to that pitiable condition by piety or indigestion. I felt sure that he was meditating suicide as he gazed upon the sea, and I stood by him for some time to prevent his accomplishing any such purpose, until I became convinced that to let him take the jump, if he pleased, would be far the more philanthropic course of action. There was a French bishop, and a colonel of the French staff at Rome, among the passengers, and by their genial urbanity they fairly divided between them the affections of the whole company. Either of them would have made a fog in the English Channel seem like the sunshine of the Gulf of Egina. I picked up a pleasant companion in an Englishman who had travelled much and read more, and spent the greater part of the day with him. When he found that I was an American, he at once asked me if I had ever been to Niagara, and had ever seen Longfellow and Emerson. I am astonished to find so many cultivated English people who know little or nothing about Tennyson; I am inclined to think he has ten readers in America to one in England, while the English can repeat Longfellow by pages.

After thirty hours of pleasant sailing along by Corsica and Elba, and along the coast of France, until it seemed as if our cruise (like that of the widow of whom we have all read) would never have an end, we came to anchor in the midst of a vast fleet of steamers in the new port of Marseilles. The bustle of commercial activity seemed any thing but pleasant after the classical repose of Rome; but the landlady of the hotel was most gracious, and when I opened the window of my room looking out on the Place Royale, one of those peripatetic dispensers of melody, whose life (like the late M. Mantalini's after he was reduced in circumstances) must be "one demnition horrid grind," executed "Sweet Home" in a manner that went entirely home to the heart of at least one of his accidental audience.

MARSEILLES, LYONS, AND
AIX IN SAVOY

IF the people of Marseilles do not love the Emperor of the French, they ought to be ashamed of themselves. He has so completely changed the aspect of that city by his improvements, that the man who knows it as it existed in the reign of Louis Philippe, would be lost if he were to revisit it now. The completion of the railway from Paris to Marseilles is an inestimable advantage to the latter city, while the new port, in magnitude and style of execution, is worthy of comparison with the splendid docks of London and Liverpool. The flags of every civilized nation may be seen there; and the variety of costumes and languages, which bewilder one's eyes and ears, assure him that he is in the commercial metropolis of the Mediterranean. The frequency of steam communication between Marseilles and the various ports of Spain, Italy, Africa, and the Levant, draws to it a large proportion of the travellers in those directions. I believe that Marseilles is only celebrated for having been colonized by the Phocæans, or some such people, for having several times been devastated by the plague, and for having been very perfectly described by Dickens in his Little Dorrit. The day on which I arrived there was very like the one described by Dickens; so if any one would like further particulars, he had better overhaul his Little Dorrit, and, "when found, make note of it."

The day after my arrival I saw a grand religious procession in the streets of the city. The landlady of my hotel had told me of it, but my expectations were not raised very high, for I thought that after the grandeur of Rome, all other things in that way would be comparatively tame. But I was mistaken; the procession fairly rivalled those of Rome. There were the same gorgeous vestments, the same picturesque groupings of black robes and snowy surplices, of mitres and crosiers and shaven crowns, of scarlet and purple and cloth of gold, the same swinging censers and clouds of fragrant incense, the same swelling flood of almost supernatural music. The municipal authorities of the city, with the staff of the garrison, joined in the procession, and the military display was such as can hardly be seen out of France. I have often been struck with the facility with which the Catholic religion adapts itself to the character of every nation. I have had some opportunity of observation; I have seen the Catholic Church on three out of the four continents, and have every where noticed the same phenomenon. Mahometanism could never be transplanted to the snowy regions of Russia or Norway; it needs the soft, enervating atmosphere of Asia to keep it alive; the veranda, the bubbling fountain, the noontide repose, are all parts of it. Puritanism is the natural growth of a country where the sun seldom shines, and which is shut out by a barrier of water and fog from kindly intercourse with its neighbours. It could never thrive in the bright south. The merry vine-dressers of Italy could never draw down their faces to the proper length, and would be very unwilling to exchange their blithesome *canzonetti* for Sternhold and Hopkins's version. But the Catholic Church, while it unites its professors in the belief of the same inflexible creed, leaves them entirely free in all mere externals and national peculiarities. When I see the light-hearted Frenchman, the fiery Italian, the serious Spaniard, the cunning Greek, the dignified Armenian, the energetic Russian, the hard-headed Dutchman, the philosophical German, the formal and "respectable" Englishman, the thrifty Scotchman, the careless and warm-hearted Irishman, and the calculating, go-ahead American, all bound together by the profession of the same faith, and yet retaining their national characteristics,—I can compare it to nothing but to a similar phenomenon that we may notice in the prism, which, while it is a pure and perfect crystal, is found on examination to contain, in their perfection, all the various colours of the rainbow.

The terminus of the Lyons and Mediterranean Railway is one of the best things of its kind in the world. I wish that some of our American railway directors could take a few lessons from the French. The attention paid to securing the comfort and safety of the passengers and the regularity of the trains would quite bewilder him. Instead of finding the station a long, unfinished kind of shed, with two small, beastly waiting rooms at one side, and a stand for a vender of apples, root beer, and newspapers, he would see a fine stone structure, several hundred feet in length, with a roof of iron and glass. He would enter a hall which would remind him of the Doric hall of the State House in Boston, only that it is several times larger, and is paved with marble. He would choose out of the three ticket offices of the three classes, where he would ride, and he would be served with a promptness and politeness that would remind him of Mr. Child in the palmy days of the old Tremont Theatre, while he would notice that an officer stood by each ticket office to see that every purchaser got his ticket and the proper change, and to give all necessary information. Having booked his luggage, he would be ushered into one of the three waiting rooms, all of them furnished in a style of neatness and elegance that would greatly astonish him. He might employ the interval in the study of geography, assisted by a map painted on one side of the room, giving the entire south of France and Piedmont, with the railways, &c., and executed in such a style that the names of the towns are legible at a distance of fifteen or twenty feet. Two or three minutes before the hour fixed for the starting of the train, the door would be opened, and he would take his seat in the train with the other passengers. The whole affair would go on so systematically, with such an absence of noise and excitement, that he would doubt whether he had been in a railway station at all, until he found himself spinning along at a rapid rate, through long tunnels, and past the beautiful panorama of Provençal landscape.

The sun was as bright as it always is in fair Provence, the sky as blue. The white dusty roads wound around over the green landscape, like great serpents seeking to hide their folds amid those hills. The almond, the lemon, and the fig attracted the at-

tention of the traveller from the north, before all
other trees,—not to forget however, the pale foliage
of that tree which used to furnish wreaths for Minerva's brow, but now supplies us with oil for our
salads. Arles, with its old amphitheatre (a broken
shadow of the Coliseum) looming up above it, lay
stifled with dust and broiling in the sun, as we hurried
on towards Avignon. It does not take much time to
see that old city, which, from being so long the abode
of the exiled popes, seems to have caught and retained something of the quiet dignity and repose of
Rome itself. That gloomy old palace of the popes,
with its lofty turrets, seems to brood over the town,
and weigh it down as with sorrow for its departed
greatness. Centuries have passed, America has been
discovered, the whole face of Europe has changed,
since a pontiff occupied those halls; and yet there it
stands, a monument commemorating a mere episode
in the history of the see of St. Peter.

Arriving at Lyons, I found another palatial station, on even a grander scale than that of Marseilles.
The architect has worked the coats of arms of the
different cities of France into the stone work of the
exterior in a very effective manner. Lyons bears
witness, no less than Marseilles, to the genius of the
wonderful man who now governs France. It is a
popular notion in England and America, that the
enterprise of Napoleon III. has been confined to the
improvement of Paris. If persons who labour under
this error would extend their journeyings a little beyond the ordinary track of a summer excursion, they
would find that there is scarcely a town in the empire
that has not felt the influence of his skill as a states-

man and political economist. The *Rue Imperiale* of
Lyons is a monument of which any sovereign might
be justly proud. The activity of Lyons, the new
buildings rising on every side, and its look of prosperity, would lead one to suppose that it was some
place that had just been settled, instead of a city
with twenty centuries of history. The Sunday, I was
glad to see, was well observed; perhaps not exactly
in the style which Aminadab Sleek would commend,
but in a very rational, Christian, un-Jewish manner.
The shops were, for the most part, closed, the
churches were crowded with people, and in the afternoon and evening the entire population was abroad
enjoying itself—and a cleaner, better-behaved, hap-
pier-looking set of people I never saw. The exces-
sive heat still continues. It is now more than two
months since I opened my umbrella; the prospects of
the harvest are good, but they are praying hard in
the churches for a little rain. During my stay at
Lyons, I lived almost entirely on fresh figs, and
plums and ices. How full the *cafés* were those sultry
evenings! How busy must the freezers have been
in the cellars below! I read through all the newspapers I could lay my hands on, and then amused
myself with watching the gay, chattering throng
around me. How my mind flew across the ocean
that evening to a quiet back parlour at the South
End! I could see the venerable Baron receiving a
guest on such a night as that, and making the weather
seem cool by contrast with the warmth of his hospitality. I could see him offering to his perspiring
visitor a release from the slavery of broadcloth, in
the loan of a nankeen jacket, and then busying him-

self in the preparation of a compound of old Co-
chituate, (I had almost said old Jamaica,) of ice, of
sugar, yea, of lemons, and commending the grateful
chalice to the parched lips of his guest. Such an
evening in the Baron's back parlour is the very
ecstasy of hospitality. It is many months since that
old nankeen jacket folded me in its all-embracing
arms, but the very thought of it awakes a thrill of
pleasure in my heart. When I last saw it, "decay's
effacing fingers" had meddled with the buttons
thereof, and it was growing a trifle consumptive in
the vicinity of the elbows; but I hope that it is good
for many a year of usefulness yet, before the epitaph
writer shall commence the recital of its merits with
those melancholy words, *Hic jacet!* Pardon me,
dear reader, for this digression from the recital of
my wanderings; but this jacket, the remembrance of
which is so dear to me, is not the trifle it may seem
to you. It is, I believe, the only institution in the
world of the same age and importance, which has
not been apostrophized in verse by that gifted bard,
Mr. Martin Farquhar Tupper. If this be not celebrity, what is it?

In one of the narrow streets of Lyons I found a
barber named Melnotte. He was a man somewhat
advanced in life, and I feel sure that he addressed a
good-looking woman in a snowy white cap, who
looked in from a back room while I was having my
hair cut, as Pauline. Be that as it may, when he had
finished his work, and I walked up to the mirror to
inspect it, he addressed to me the language of Bulwer's hero, "Do you like the picture?" or words to
that effect. I cannot help mistrusting that Sir Ed-

ward may have misled us concerning the ultimate history of the Lady of Lyons and her husband. But the heat was too intolerable for human endurance; so I packed up, and leaving that fair city, with its numerous graceful bridges, and busy looms whose fabrics brighten the eyes of the beauties of Europe and America, and lighten the purses of their chivalry,—leaving Our Lady of Fourvières looking down with outstretched hands from the dome of her lofty shrine, and watching over her faithful Lyonnese,—I turned my face towards the Alpine regions.

The Alps have always been to me what Australia was to the late Mr. Micawber—"the bright dream of my youth, and the fallacious aspiration of my riper years." I remember when I was young, long before the days of railways and steamers, in the times when a man who had travelled in Europe was invested with a sort of awful dignity—I remember hearing a travelled uncle of mine tell about the Alps, and I resolved, with all the enthusiasm of boyhood, thenceforward to "save up" all my Fourth of July and Artillery Election money, until I should be able to go and see one. When the Rev. James Sheridan Knowles (he was a wicked playactor in those days) produced his drama of William Tell, how it fed the flame of my ambition! How I longed to stand with the hero once again among his native hills! How I loved the glaciers! How I doted on the avalanches! But age has cooled the longings of my heart for mountain excursions, and robbed my legs of all their climbing powers, so that if it depends upon my own bodily exertions, the Vale of Chamouni will be entirely unavailable for me, and every mount will be to me a blank. The scenery along the line of railway from Ambérieu to Culoz on the Rhone is very grand. The ride reminded me of the ride over the Atlantic and St. Lawrence road through the White Mountains, only it is finer. The boldness of the cliffs and precipices was something to make one's heart beat quick, and cause him to wonder how the peasants could work so industriously, and the cattle feed so constantly, without stopping to look up at the magnificence that hemmed them in.

At Culoz I went on board one of those peculiar steamers of the Rhone—about one hundred and fifty feet in length by ten or twelve in width. Our way lay through a narrow and circuitous branch of the river for several miles. The windings of the river were such that men were obliged to turn the boat about by means of cables, which they made fast to posts fixed in the banks on either side for that purpose. The scenery along the banks was like a dream of Paradise. To say that the country was smiling with flowers and verdure does not express it—it was bursting into a broad grin of fertility. Such vineyards! Not like the grape vine in your back yard, dear reader, nailed up against a brick wall, but large, luxuriant vines, seeming at a loss what to do with themselves, and festooned from tree to tree, just as you see them in the scenery of Fra Diavolo. And then there were groups of people in costumes of picturesque negligence, and women in large straw hats, and dresses of brilliant colours, just like the chorus of an opera. The deep, rich hue of the foliage particularly attracted my notice. It was as different from the foliage of New England as Winship's Gardens are from an invoice of palm-leaf hats. Beyond the immediate vicinity of the river rose up beautiful hills and cliffs like the Palisades of the Hudson. Let those who will, prefer the wild grandeur of our American mountain scenery; there is a great charm for me in the union of nature and art. The careful cultivation of the fields seems to set off and render more grand and austere the gray, jagged cliffs that overlook them. As the elder Pliny most justly remarks, (lib. iv. cap. xi. 24,) "It requires the lemon as well as the sugar to make the punch."

After about an hour's sail upon the river, we came out upon the beautiful Lake of Bourget. It was stirred by a gentle breeze, but it seemed as if its bright blue surface had never reflected a cloud. All around its borders the trees and vines seemed bending down to drink of its pure waters. Far off in the distance rose up the mighty peaks of the Alps—their snow-white tops contrasting with the verdure of their sides. They seemed to be watching with pleasure over the glad scenes beneath them, like old men whose gray hairs have been powerless to disturb the youthful freshness and geniality of their hearts.

At St. Innocent I landed, and underwent the custom house formalities attendant upon entrance into a new territory. The officials were very expeditious, and equally polite. I at first supposed that the letters V. E., which each of them bore conspicuously on his cap, meant *"very empty,"*—but it afterwards occurred to me that they were the initials of his majesty, the King of Sardinia. A few minutes' ride over the "Victor Emmanuel Railway" brought me to the beautiful village of Aix. It is situated, as my friend

the Lyonnese barber would say, in "a deep vale shut
out by Alpine hills from the rude world." It possesses about 2500 inhabitants; but that number is
considerably augmented at present, for the mineral
springs of Aix are very celebrated, and this is the
height of "the season." There is a great deal of
what is called "society" here, and during the morning the baths are crowded. It is as dull as all water-
ing places necessarily are, and twice as hot. I think
that the French manage these things better than we
do in America. There is less humbug, less display of
jewelry and dress, and a vast deal more of common
sense and solid comfort than with us. The *cafés* are
like similar establishments in all such places—an
abundance of ices and ordinary coffee, and a plentiful
lack of newspapers. I have found a companion,
however, who more than makes good the latter deficiency. He is an Englishman of some seventy years,
who is here bathing for his gout. His light hair and
fresh complexion disguise his age so completely that
most people, when they see us together, judge me,
from my gray locks, to be the elder. He is one of the
most entertaining persons I have ever met—he knows
the classics by heart,—is familiar with English,
French, Italian, German, and Spanish literature,—
speaks nine languages,—and has travelled all over
the world. He is as familiar with the Steppes of
Tartary as with Wapping Old Stairs,—has imbibed
sherbet in Damascus and sherry cobblers in New
York, and seen a lion hunt in South Africa. But his
heart is the heart of a boy—"age cannot wither nor
custom stale" its infinite geniality. He cannot pass
by a beggar without making an investment for eter-

nity, and all the babies look over the shoulders of their nurses to smile at him as he walks the streets. I mention him here for the sake of recording one of his opinions, which struck me by its truth and orig, inality. We were sitting in a *café* last evening, and, after a long conversation, I asked him what he should give as the result of all his reading and ob, servation of men and things, and all his experience, if he were to sum it up in one sentence. "Sir," said he, removing his meerschaum from his mouth, and turning towards me as if to give additional force to his reply, "it may all be comprised in this: the world is composed of two classes of men—natural fools and d—d fools; the first class are those who have never made any pretensions, or have reached a just appreciation of the nothingness of all human acquire- ments and hopes; the second are those whose belief in their own infallibility has never been disturbed; and this class includes a vast number of every rank, from the profound German philosopher, who thinks that he has fathomed infinity, down to that young fop twirling his moustache at the opposite table, and flattering himself that he is making a great impres- sion."

Savoy, as every body knows, was once a part of France, and it still retains all of its original charac- teristics. I have not heard ten words of Italian since I arrived here, and, judging from what I do hear and from the tone of the newspapers, it would like to become a part of France again. The Savoyards are a religious, steady-going people, and they have little love either for the weak and dissolute monarch who governs them, or for the powerful, infidel prime minister who governs their monarch. The high-pitched roofs of the houses here are suggestive of the snows of winter; but the heat reminds me of the coast of Africa during a sirocco. How true is Sydney Smith's remark, "Man only lives to shiver or perspire"! The thermometer ranges any where from 80° to 90°. Can this be the legitimate temperature of these mountainous regions? I am "ill at these numbers," and nothing would be so invigorating to my infirm and shaky frame as a sniff of the salt breezes of Long Branch or Nantasket.

AIX TO PARIS

THERE is no need of telling how disgusted I became with Aix-les-Bains and all that in it is, after a short residence there. How I hated those straw-hatted people who beset the baths from the earliest flush of the aurora! How I detested those fellows who were constantly pestering me with offers (highly advantageous, without doubt) of donkeys whereon to ride, when they knew that I did n't want one! How I abominated the sight of a man (who seemed to haunt me) in a high velvet-collared coat and a bell-crowned hat just overtopping an oily-looking head of hair and bushy whiskers—who looked, for all the world, as if he were made up for Sir Harcourt Courtly! How maliciously he held on to the newspapers in the *café!* How constantly he sat there and devoured all the news out of them through the medium of a double tortoise-shell eye-glass, which always seemed to be just falling off his nose! How I abhorred the sight of those waiters, who looked as if the season were a short one, and time (as B. Franklin said) was money! How stifling was the atmosphere of that "seven-by-nine" room for which I had to pay so dearly! How hot, how dusty, how dull it was, I need not weary you by telling; suffice it to say, that I never packed my trunk more willingly than when I left that village. I am very glad to have been there, however, for the satisfaction I felt at leaving the place is worth almost any effort to obtain. The joy of departure made even the exorbitant bills seem reasonable; and when I thought of the stupidity and discomfort I was escaping from, I felt as if, come what might, my future could only be one of sunshine and content. Aix-les-Bains is one of the pleasantest places to leave that I have ever seen. I can never forget the measureless happiness of seeing my luggage ticketed for Paris, and then taking my seat with the consciousness that I was leaving Aix (not *aches*, alas!) behind me.

The Lake of Bourget was as beautiful and smiling as before—only it did seem as if the sun might have held in a little. He scorched and blistered the passengers on that steamboat in the most absurd manner. He seemed never to have heard of Horace, and was consequently entirely ignorant of the propriety of maintaining a *modus* in his *rebuses*. The scenery along the banks of the Rhone had not changed in the least, but was as romantic and theatrical as ever. At Culoz I was glad to get on shore, for like Hamlet, I had been "too much i' the sun"; so I left the "blue rushing of the arrowy Rhone," (which the late Lord Byron, with his usual disregard of truth, talks about, and which is as muddy as a Medford brick-yard,) and took refuge in the hospitality of a custom house. Here I fell into a meditation upon custom house officers. I wonder whether the custom house officers of France are in their leisure hours given to any of the vanities which delight their American brethren. There was one lean, thoughtful-looking man among those at Culoz who attracted my attention. I tried ineffectually to make out his bent from his physiognomy. I could not imagine him occupying his leisure by putting any twice-told tales on paper—or cultivating Shanghai poultry—or riding on to the tented field amid the roar of artillery at the head of a brigade of militia, —and I was obliged, in the hurry of the examination of luggage, to give him up.

I had several times, during the journey from Aix, noticed a tall, eagle-eyed man, in a suit of gray, and wearing a moustache of the same colour, and while we were waiting for the train at Culoz, I observed that he attracted a great deal of attention: his bearing was so commanding, that I had set him down as being connected with the military interest, before I noticed that he did not bear arms, for the left sleeve of his coat hung empty and useless by his side; so I ventured to inquire concerning him, and learned that I was a fellow-traveller of Marshal Baraguay d'Hilliers. I must do him the justice to say that he did not look like a man who would leave his arms on the field.

We were soon whirling, and puffing, and whistling along through the tame but pleasing landscape of France. Those carefully-tilled fields, those vineyards almost overflowing with the raw material of conviviality, those interminable rows of tall trees which seem to give no shade, those farm-houses, whose walls we should in America consider strong enough for fortifications, those contented-looking cattle, those towns that seem to consist of a single street and an old gray tower, with a dark-coloured conical top, like a candle extinguisher,—all had a good, familiar look to me; and the numerous fields of Indian corn almost made me think that I was on my way to Worcester or Fitchburg. I stopped for a while at Macon, (a town which I respect for its contributions to the good cheer of the world,) and hugely enjoyed a walk through its clean, quiet streets. While I was waiting at the station, the express train from Paris came along; and many of the passengers left their places (like Mr. Squeers) to stretch their legs. Among them was a man whose acquisitive eye, black satin waistcoat, fashionable hat, (such as no man but an American would think of travelling in,) and coat with the waist around his hips, and six or eight inches of skirt, immediately fixed my attention. Before I thought, he had asked me if I could speak English. I set him at his ease by answering that I took lessons in it once when I was young, and he immediately launched out as follows: "Well, this is the cussedest language I ever did hear. I don't see how in *the* devil these blasted fools can have lived so long right alongside of England without trying to learn the English language." The whistle of the engine cut short the declaration of his sentiments, and he was whizzing on towards Lyons a moment after. Whoever that man may have been, he owes it to himself and his country to write a book. His work would be as worthy of consideration as the writings of two thirds of our English and American travellers, who think they are qualified to write about the government and social condition of a country because they have travelled through it. Fancy a Frenchman, entirely ignorant of the English tongue, landing at Boston, and stopping at the Tremont House or Parker's; he visits the State House, the

Athenæum, Bunker Hill, the wharves, &c. Then on Sunday he wishes to know something about the religion of these strange people; so he goes across the street to the King's Chapel, and finds that it is closed; so he walks down the street in the burning sun to Brattle Street, where he hears a comfortable, drony kind of sermon, which seems to have as composing an effect upon the fifty or a hundred persons who are present as upon himself. In the afternoon he finds his way to Trinity Church, (somebody having charitably told him that that is the most genteel place,) and there he hears "our admirable liturgy" sonorously read out to twenty or thirty people, all of whom are so engrossed in their devotions that the responses are entirely neglected. Having had enough of what the Irishman called the English lethargy, he returns to his lodgings, and writes in his note-book that the Americans seldom go to church, and when they do, go there to sleep in comfortable pews. Then he makes a little tour of a fortnight to New Haven, Providence, Springfield, &c., and returns to France to write a book of travels in New England. And what are all his observations worth? I'll tell you. They are worth just as much, and give exactly as faithful a representation of the state of society in New England, as four fifths of the books written by English and American travellers in France, Spain, and Italy, do of the condition of those countries.

I have encountered many interesting studies of humanity here on the continent in my day. I have met many people who have come abroad with a vague conviction that travel improves one, and who

do not see that to visit Europe without some preparation is like going a-fishing without line or bait.
They appear to think that some great benefit is to be
obtained by passing over a certain space of land and
water, and being imposed upon to an unlimited extent by a horde of *commissionnaires, ciceroni,* couriers, and others, who find in their ignorance and lack
of common sense a source of wealth. I met, the
other day, a gentleman from one of the Western
States, who said that he was "putting up" at
Meurice's Hotel, but didn't think much of it; if it
had not been for some English people whom he fell
in with on the way from Calais, he should have gone
to the Hôtel de Ville, which he supposed, from the
pictures he had seen, must be a "fust class house"! I
have within a few hours seen an American, who could
not ask the simplest question in French, but thinks
that he shall stop three or four weeks, and learn the
language! I have repeatedly met people who told
me that they had come out to Europe "jest to see the
place." But it is not alone such ignoramuses as these
who merit the pity or contempt of the judicious and
sensible. Their folly injures no one but themselves.
The same cannot be said, however, of the authors of
the numerous duodecimos of foreign travel which
burden the booksellers' counters. They have supposed that they can sketch a nation's character by
looking at its towns from the windows of an express
train. They presume to write about the social life
of France or Italy, while they are ignorant of any
language but their own, and do not know a single
French or Italian family. Victims of a bitter prejudice against those countries and their institutions,

they are prepared beforehand to be shocked and disgusted at all they see. Like Sterne's Smelfungus, they "set out with the spleen and jaundice, and every object they pass by is discoloured or distorted." Kenelm Digby wisely remarks that one of the great advantages of journeying beyond sea, to a man of sense and feeling, is the spectacle of general travellers: "it will prevent his being ever again imposed upon by these birds of passage, when they record their adventures and experience on returning to the north."

Dijon is a fine old city. Every body knows that it used to be the capital of Burgundy, but to the general reader it is more particularly interesting as being the place to which Mrs. Dombey and Mr. Carker fled after the elopement. There is a fine cathedral and public library, and the whole place has an eminently Burgundian flavour which makes one regret that he got tired so soon when he tried to read Froissart's Chronicles. There is a church there which was desecrated during the old revolution, and is now used as a market-house. It bears an inscription which presents a satirical commentary on its recent history: *"Domine, dilexi decorem domus tuæ!"* The Dijon gingerbread (which the people, in their ignorance and lack of our common school advantages, call *pain d'épice*) would really merit a diploma from that academy of connoisseurs, the Massachusetts House of Representatives. But Dombey and Dijon are all forgotten in our first glimpse of the "gay capital of bewildering France." There lay Paris, sparkling under the noonday sun. The sight of its domes and monuments awoke all my fellow-travellers: shabby caps and handkerchiefs were exchanged for hats and bonnets, which gave their wearers an air of respectability perfectly uncalled for. We were soon inside the fortifications, which have been so outgrown by the city that one hardly notices them; and, after the usual luggage examination, I found myself in an omnibus, and once more on the Boulevards.

And what a good, comfortable home-feeling it was! There were the old, familiar streets, the well-known advertisements, painted conspicuously, in blue, and green, and gold, on what would else have been a blank, unsightly wall, and inviting me to purchase cloths and cashmeres; there were the same ceaseless tides of life ebbing and flowing through those vast thoroughfares, the same glossy beavers, the same snowy caps and aprons, the same blouses, the same polite, *s'il vous-plaît, pardon, m'sieur,* take-it-easy air, that Paris, as seen from an omnibus window, always presents. We rolled through the Rue St. Antoine, and it was hard to realize that it had ever been the theatre of so much appalling history. I tried to imagine the barricades, the street ploughed up by artillery, and that heroic martyr, Archbishop Affre, falling there, and praying that his blood might be the last shed in that fratricidal strife; but it was useless; the lively present made the past seem but the mere invention of the historian. All traces of the frightful scenes of 1848 have been effaced, and the facilities for barricades have been disposed of in a way that must make red republicanism very disrespectful to the memory of MacAdam. As we passed a church in that bloody locality, a wedding party came out; the bridegroom looked as if he had taken chloroform to enable him to get through his difficulties, and the effect of it had not entirely passed off. The bride (for women, you know, have greater power of endurance than men) seemed to take it more easily, and, beaming in the midst of a sort of wilderness of lace, and gauze, and muslin, like a lighthouse in a fog, she tripped briskly into the carriage, with a bouquet in her hand, and happiness in her heart. Before the bridal party got fairly out of sight, a funeral came along. The white pall showed that it was a child who slept upon the bier; for the Catholic church does not mourn over those who are removed from the temptations of life before they have known them. The vehicles all gave way to let the little procession pass, the hum seemed to cease for a moment, every head was uncovered, even the porter held his burden on his shoulder with one hand that he might pay his respects to that sovereign to whom even republicans are obliged to bow, and the many-coloured hats of the omnibus drivers were doffed. I had often before noticed those striking contrasts that one sees in a capital like Paris; but to meet such a one at my very entrance impressed me deeply. Such is Paris. You think it the liveliest place in the world, (and so it is;) but suddenly you come upon something that makes you thoughtful, if it does not sadden you. Life and death elbow and jostle each other along these gay streets, until it seems as if they were rivals striving to drive each other out. I entered a church a day or two since. There was a funeral at the high altar. The black vestments and hangings, the lighted tapers, the solemn chant of the *De profundis* were eloquent of death and what must follow it. I was startled by hearing a child's cry, and looking round into the chapel which served as a baptistery, there stood two young mothers who had just received their infants from that purifying laver which made them members of the great Christian family. I never before had that beautiful thought of Chateaubriand's so forced upon me—"Religion has rocked us in the cradle of life, and her maternal hand shall close our eyes, while her holiest melodies soothe us to rest in the cradle of death."

There are, without doubt, many persons, who can say that in their pilgrimage of life they have truly "found their warmest welcome at an inn." ·My experience outstrips that, for I have received one of my most cordial greetings in a *café*. The establishment in question is so eminently American, that I should feel as if I had neglected a sacred duty, if I did not describe it, for the benefit of future sojourners in the French capital, who are hereby requested to overhaul their memorandum books and make a note of it. It does not boast the magnificence and luxury of the *Café de Paris*, Véry's, the *Trois Frères Provençaux*, nor of Taylor's; nor does it thrust itself forward into the publicity of the gay Boulevards, or of the thronged arcades of the *Palais Royal*. It does not appeal to those who love the noise and dust of fashion's highway; for them it has no welcome. ·But to those who love "the cool, sequestered path of life," it offers a degree of quiet comfort, to which the "slaves of passion, avarice, and pride," who view themselves in the mirrors of the *Maison Dorée*, are strangers. You turn from the *Boulevard des Italiens* into the *Rue de la Michodière*, which you perambulate until you come to number six, where you will stop and take an observation. Perhaps wonder will predominate over admiration. The front of the establishment does not exceed twelve feet in width, and the sign over the door shows that it is a *Crêmerie*. The fact is also adumbrated symbolically by a large brass can, which is set over the portal. In one of the windows may be observed a neatly-executed placard, to this effect:—

AUX AMÉRICAINS
Spécialité.

———

Pumpkin Pie.

"Enter—its vastness overwhelms thee not!" On the contrary, having passed through the little front shop, you stand in a room ten or twelve feet square —just the size of Washington Irving's "empire," in the Red Horse Inn, at Stratford. This little room is furnished with two round tables, a sideboard, and several chairs, and is decorated with numerous crayon sketches of the knights of the aforesaid round tables. You make the acquaintance of the excellent Madame Busque, and order your dinner, which is served promptly and with a motherly care, which will at first remind you of the time when your bib was carefully tied on, and you were lifted to a seat on the family Bible, which had been placed on a chair, to bring the juvenile mouth into proper relations with the table.

Nothing can surpass the home feeling that took
possession of me when I found myself once more in
Madame Busque's little back room at No. 6, *Rue de
la Michodière*. How cordial was that estimable
lady's welcome! She made herself as busy as a cat
with one chicken, and prepared for me a "tired
nature's sweet restorer" in the shape of one of her
famous omelets. The old den had not changed in
the least. Madame Busque used to threaten occasionally to paint it, and otherwise improve and em-
bellish it; but we always told her that if she did any
thing of that kind, or tried to render it less dingy, or
snug, or unpretending, we would never eat another
of her pumpkin pies. Not all the mirrors and magnificence of the resorts of fashion can equal the quiet
cosiness of Madame Busque's back room. You meet
all kinds of company there. The blouse is at home
there, as well as its ambitious cousin, the broadcloth
coat. Law and medicine, literature and art, pleasure
and honest toil, meet there upon equal terms. Our
own aristocratic Washington never dreamed of such
a democracy as his calm portrait looks down upon in
that room. Then we have such a delightful neighbourhood there. I feel as if the charcoal woman of
the next door but one below was some relation to me
—at least an aunt; she always has a pleasant word
and a smile for the frequenters of No. 6; and then it
is so disinterested on her part, for we can none of us
need any of her charcoal. I hope that no person
who reads this will be misled by it, and go to Madame Busque's *crêmerie* expecting to find there the
variety which the restaurants boast, for he will be

disappointed. But he will find every thing there of the best description. My taste in food (as in most other matters) is a very catholic one: I can eat beef with the English, garlic and onions with the French, sauerkraut with the Germans, macaroni with the Italians, pilaf with the Turks, baked beans with the Yankees, hominy with the southerners, and oysters with any body. But as I feel age getting the better of me day by day, I think I grow to be more and more of a pre-Raphaelite in these things. So I crave nothing more luxurious than a good steak or chop, with the appropriate vegetables; and these are to be had in their perfection at Madame Busque's. My benison upon her!

The canicular weather I suffered from in the south followed me even here. I found every body talking about the extraordinary *chaleur*. Shade of John Rogers! how the sun has glared down upon Paris, day after day, without winking, until air-tight stoves are refrigerators compared to it, and even old-fashioned preaching is outdone! How the asphalte sidewalks of the Boulevards have melted under his rays, and perfumed the air with any thing but a Sabæan odour! The fragrance of the linden trees was entirely overpowered. The thought of the helmets of the cavalry was utterly intolerable. Tortoni's and the *cafés* were crowded. Great was the clamour for ices. Greater still was the rush to the cool shades of the public gardens, or the environs of Bougival and Marly. At last, the welcome rain came hissing down upon these heated roofs; and *malheur* to the man who ventures out during these days without his umbrella. It has been a rain of terror. It almost spoilt the great national *fête* of the 15th; but the people made the best of it, and, between the free theatrical performances at sixteen theatres, the superb illuminations, and the fireworks, seemed to have a very merry time. I went in the morning to that fine lofty old church, (whose Lady Chapel is a splendid monument of Couture's artistic genius,) St. Eustache, where I heard a new mass, by one M. L'Hôte. It was well executed, and the orchestral parts were particularly effective. After the mass, the annual *Te Deum* for the Emperor was sung. The effect of the latter was very grand; indeed, when it was finished, I was just thinking that it was impossible for music to surpass it, when the full orchestra and two organs united in a burst of harmony that almost lifted me off my feet. I recognized the old Gregorian anthem that is sung every Sunday in all the churches, and when it had been played through, the trumpets took up the air of the chant, above the rest of the accompaniment, and the clear, alto voice of one of those scarlet-capped choir-boys rang out the words, *Domine, salvum fac imperatorem nostrum, Napoleonem,* in a way that seemed to make those old arches vibrate, and wonderfully quickened the circulation in the veins of every listener. It was like the gradual mounting and heaving up of a high sea in a storm on the Atlantic, which, when it has reached a pitch you thought impossible, curls majestically over, and, breaking into a creamy foam, loses itself in a transitory vision of emerald brilliancy, that for the moment realizes the most gorgeous and improbable fables of Eastern luxury. It made even me, not-

withstanding my prejudices in favour of republicanism, forget the spread eagle, and my free (and
easy) native land, and for several hours I found
myself singing that solemn anthem over in a most
impressive manner. *Vive l'Empereur!*

PARIS

THIS is a wonderful city. It seems to me, as I ride up and down the gay Boulevards on the roof of an omnibus, or gaze into the brilliant shop-windows of the Palais Royal, or watch the happy children in the garden of the Tuileries, or stand upon the bridges and take in as much as I can at once of gardens, palaces, and church towers—it seems to me like a great theatre, filled with gay company, to whom the same grand spectacle is always being shown, and whose faces always reflect something of that brilliancy which lights up the gorgeous, never-ending, last scene of the drama. I know that the play has its underplot of vicious poverty and crime, but they shrink from the glare of the footlights and the radiance of the red fire that lights up the scene. Taken in the abstract—taken as it appears from the outside—Paris is the most perfect whole the world can show. It was a witty remark of a well-known citizen of Boston, touching the materialistic views of many of his friends, that "when good Boston people die, they go to Paris." I know many whose highest idea of heaven would find its embodiment in the sunshine of the Place de la Concorde or the gas light of the Rue de Rivoli. Paris captivates you at once In this it differs from Rome. You do not grow to love it; you feel its charms before you have recov-ered from the fatigue of your journey—before you have even reached your hotel, as you ride along and recognize the buildings and monuments which books and pictures have made familiar. In Rome all is different. Michel Angelo's mighty dome, to be sure, does impress you, as you come to the city; but when you enter, the narrow streets are such a contrast to the broad, free campagna you have just left, that you feel oppressed and cramped as you ride through them. You find one of the old temples kept in repair and serving as a custom house; this is a damper at the outset, and you sigh for something to revive the ancient customs of the world's capital. You walk into the Forum the next day, musing upon the line of the twelve Cæsars, and your progress is arrested, and your sense of the dramatic unities of your position deeply wounded, by an unamusing and prosaic clothes-line. You keep on and try to recall Cicero, and Catiline, and Jugurtha, and Servius Tullius, and Brutus, and Virginius,—but it is useless, for you find a cow feeding there as quietly as if she were on the hills of Berkshire. The whole city seems sad and mouldy, and out of date, and you think you will "do the sights" as rapidly as possible, and then be off. But before many days you find that all is changed. The moss that clothes those broken walls becomes as venerable in your sight as the gray hairs upon your mother's brow; the ivy that enwreathes those old towers and columns seems to have wound itself around your heart and bound it forever to that spot. Clothes-lines, dirt, and all the inconveniences inseparable from the older civilization of Rome, fade away. The Forum, the Palace of the Cæsars, the Appian Way, all become instinct with a new—

[123]

or rather with their old life; and you feel that you are in the Rome of Livy and Sallust,—you have found the Rome of which you dreamed in boyhood, and you are happy. With Paris, as I have said, you are not obliged to serve such an apprenticeship. You have read of Paris in history, in novels, in guide-books, in the lucubrations of the whole tribe of correspondents—you recognize it at once on seeing it, and accept it for all that it pretends to be. And you are not deceived. And this, I apprehend, is the reason why we never feel that deep, clinging affection for Paris that we do for that "goddess of all the nations, to whom nothing is equal and nothing second"—that city which (as one of her prophet-poets said) shall ever be "the capital of the world, for whatever her arms have not conquered shall be hers by religion." You feel that Paris is the capital of Europe, and you bow before it as you would before a sovereign whose word·was law.

I wonder whether every body judges of all new things by the criterion of childhood, as I find myself constantly doing. Whatever it may be, I apply to it the test of my youthful recollections of something similar, and it almost always suffers by the process. Those beautiful architectural wonders that pierce the sky at Strasburg and Antwerp will bear no comparison, in point of height, with the steeple of the Old South as it exists in the memory of my childhood. I have never seen a picture gallery in Europe which awakened any thing like my old feelings on visiting one of the first Athenæum exhibitions many years ago. Those wonderful productions of Horace Vernet, in which one may read the warlike history of

PARIS

France, are nothing compared to my recollections of
Trumbull's "Sortie of Gibraltar," as seen through
an antediluvian tin trumpet which considerably interfered with my vision, but which I thought it was
necessary to use. I have visited libraries which ante-
dated by centuries the discovery of America,—I
have rambled over castles which seemed to reëcho
with the clank of armour and the clarion calls of the
old days of chivalry,—I have walked through the
long corridors and halls of the Vatican with cardi-
nals and kings,—I have mused in church-crypts and
cloisters, in whose silent shade the dead of a thousand years reposed,—but I have never yet been impressed with any thing like the awe which the old
Athenæum in Pearl Street used to inspire into my
boyish heart. Pearl Street in those days was as
innocent of traffic and its turmoil as the quiet roads
around Jamaica Pond are now. A pasture, in which
the Hon. Jonathan Phillips kept a cow, extended
through to Oliver Street, and handsome old-fashioned private houses with gardens around them occupied the place of the present rows of granite
warehouses. The Athenæum, surrounded by horse-
chestnut trees, stood there in aristocratic dignity and
repose, which it seemed almost sacrilegious to disturb with the noise of our childish sports. There
were a few old gentlemen who used to frequent its
reading-room, whose white hair, (and some of them
even wore knee breeches and queues and powder,)
always stilled our boyish clamour as we played on
the grass-plots in the yard. To some of these old
men our heads were often uncovered,—for children
were politer in those days than now,—and to our

young imagination it seemed as if they were sages, who carried about with them an atmosphere of learning and the fragrance of academic groves. They seemed as much a part of the mysterious old establishment as the books in the library, the dusty busts in the entries, or the old librarian himself. Sometimes I used to venture into those still passages, and steal a look into that reading-room whose quiet was never broken, save by the wealthy creak of some old citizen's boots, or by the long breathing of some venerable frequenter of the place, enjoying his afternoon nap. In later years I came to know the Athenæum more familiarly; the old gentlemen lost the character of sages and became estimable individuals of quiet tastes, who were fatiguing the Massachusetts Hospital Life Insurance Company by their long-continued perusal of the Daily Advertiser and the Gentleman's Magazine; but my old impression of the awful mystery of the building remains to this day. I mourned over the removal to the present fine position, and I seek in vain amid the stucco-work and white paint of the new edifice for the charm which enthralled me in the old home of the institution. Some people, carried away by the utilitarian spirit of the age, may think that it is a great improvement; but to me it seems nothing but an unwarrantable innovation on the established order of things, and a change for the worse. Where is the quiet of the old place? Younger and less reverential men have risen up in the places of the old, and have destroyed all that rendered the old library respectable. The good old times when Dr. Bass, the librarian, sat on one side of the fireplace, and the late John Bromfield (with his silk handkerchief spread over his knees) on the other, and read undisturbed for hours, have passed away. A hundred persons use the library now for one who did then; and I am left to feed upon the memory of better times, when learning was a quiet, comfortable, select sort of thing, and mutter secret maledictions on the revolutionary spirits who have made it otherwise.

But pardon me, dear reader,—all this has little to do with Paris, except by way of illustration of my remark that the youthful standard of intellectual weights and measures is the only infallible one we ever know. But Paris is something by itself: it overrides all standards of greatness or beauty, and all preconceived notions of itself, and addresses itself with confidence to every taste. Ladies love Paris as a vast warehouse of jewelry and all the rich stuffs that hide the crinoline from eyes profane. Physicians revel in its hospitals, and talk of "splendid operations," such as make the unscientific change colour.

Paris is a world in itself. Here may the Yankee find his pumpkin-pie and sherry-cobblers, the Englishman his *rosbif*, the German his sauerkraut, the Italian his macaroni. Here may the lover of dramatic art choose his performance among thirty theatres, and he who, with Mr. Swiveller, loves "the mazy," will find at the Jardin Mabille a bower shaded for him. Here the bookworm can mouse about, in more than twenty large public libraries, and spend weeks in the delightful exploration of countless book-stalls. Here the student of art can read the history of France on the walls of Versailles, or, revelling in the opulence of the Louvre, forget his studies, his technicalities, his criticisms, in contemplation of the majestic loveliness of Murillo's "sinless Mother of the sinless Child." Here may "fireside philanthropists, great at the pen," compare their magnificent theories with the works of delicate ladies who have left the wealth they possessed and the society they adorned, for the humble garb of the Sister of Charity and a laborious ministry to the poor, the diseased, and the infirm, and meditate in the cool quadrangles of hospitals and benevolent institutions, founded by saints, and preserved in their integrity by the piety of their disciples. Here may the man who wishes to look beyond this brilliant world, find churches ever open, inviting to prayer and meditation, where he may be carried beyond himself by the choicest strains of Haydn and the solemn grandeur of the Gregorian Chant,—or may be thrilled by the eloquent periods of Ravignan or Lacordaire, until the unseen eternal fills his whole soul, and the visible temporal glories of the gay capital seem to him the transient vanities they really are.

How few people really know Paris! To most minds it presents itself only as a place of general pleasure-seeking and dissipation. I have seen many men whose only recollections of Paris were such as will give them no pleasure in old age, who flattered themselves that they knew Paris. They thought that the whole city was given up to the folly that captivated them, and so they represent Paris as one vast reckless masquerade. I have seen others who, walking through the thronged *cafés* and restaurants, have felt themselves justified in declaring that the

French had no domestic life, and were as ignorant of family joys as their language is destitute of a single word to express our good old Saxon word "home"; not knowing that there are in Paris thousands of families as closely knit together as any that dwell in the smoky cities of Old England, or amid the bustle and activity of our new world. Good people may turn up their eyes, and talk and write as many jeremiads as they will about the vanity and wickedness of Paris; but the truth is, that this great Babel has even for them its cheering side, if they would but keep their eyes open to discover it. Let them visit the churches on the vigils of great feasts, and every Saturday, and see the crowds that throng the confessionals: let them rise an hour or two earlier than usual, and go into any of the churches, and they will find more worshippers there on any common week-day morning than half of the churches in New England collect on Sundays. Let them visit that magnificent temple, the Madeleine, and see the freedom from social distinctions which prevails there: the soldier, the civilian, the rich and the poor, the high-bred lady, the servant in livery, and the negress with her bright yellow and red kerchief wound around her head, are there met, on an equality that free America knows not of.

The observance of the Sunday is a sign of the times which ought not to be overlooked. Only a few years ago, and suspension of business on Sunday was so uncommon that notice was given by a sign to that effect on the front of the few shops whose proprietors indulged in that strange caprice. The signs (like certain similar ones on apothecary shops in

Boston, to the effect that prescriptions are the only business attended to on the first day of the week) used to seem to me like a bait to catch the custom of the godly. But the signs have passed away before this movement, inaugurated by the Emperor, who forbade labour on the public works on Sunday, and preached up by the late Archbishop of Paris and the parish clergy. There are few shops in Paris that do not close on Sunday now—at least in the afternoon. And this is done by the free will of the trades-people: it is not the result of a legislative enactment. The law here leaves all people free in regard to their religious duties. The shops of the Jews, of course, are open on Sunday, for they are obliged to close on Saturday, and of course ought not to be expected to observe two days. Of course, too, the public galleries, and gardens, and places of amusement are all open; God forbid that the hard-faring children of toil should be cheated out of any innocent recreation on the only free day they have by any attempts to judaize the Christian Sunday into a sabbath. It is a great mistake to suppose that people can be made better by diminishing the sources of innocent pleasure. No; if the Sunday be made a hard, uninteresting day, when smiling is a grave impropriety, and a hearty laugh a mortal sin, children will begin by disliking the day, and end by despising the religion that made it gloomy. But provide the people with music in the public parks on Sunday afternoon and evening,—make the day a cheerful, happy time to those who are ingulfed in the carking cares of life all the rest of the week,—make it a day which children shall look forward to with longing, and you will find that the people are better, and happier, and thriftier for the change. You will find that the mechanic or labourer, instead of lounging away his Sunday in a grog-shop, (for the business goes on even though the front door may be barred and the shutters closed,) will be ambitious to take his wife and children to hear the music, and will after a time become as well behaved as the common run of people. It is better to use the merest worldly motives to keep men in the path of decency, than to let them slide away to perdition because they refuse to listen to the more dignified teachings of religion.

I have been much impressed by a visit to a large, but unpretentious-looking house in the Rue du Bac—the "mother-house" of that admirable organization, the Sisters of Charity. It was not much of a visit, to be sure—for not even my gray hairs and respectable appearance could gain for me an admission beyond the strangers' parlour, the courtyard, and the cool, quiet chapel. But that was enough to increase my respect and admiration for those devoted women. The community there consists of *six hundred* Sisters of Charity, whose whole time is occupied in taking care of the sick, and needy, and neglected in the hospitals and asylums, and in every quarter of the city. You see them at every turn, going quietly about their work of benevolence, and presenting a fine contrast to some of our noisy theorists at home. I may be in error, but it strikes me that that community is doing more in its present mode of action to advance the true dignity and "rights" of the sex, than if it were to resolve itself into a convention, after the American fashion. I was somewhat anx-

ious to inquire whether any of the sisters of the community had ever taken to lecturing or preaching in
public; but the modest and unassuming manner of all
those whom I saw, rendered such a question unnec-
essary. I fear that oratory is sadly neglected among
them; with this exception, and perhaps the absence
of a certain strong-mindedness in their characters, I
think that they will compare very favourably with
any of our distinguished female philanthropists.
They wear the same gray habit and odd-shaped
white bonnet that the Sisters of Charity wear in Boston. While we praise the self-forgetful heroism of
Florence Nightingale as it deserves, let us not forget
that France sent out her Florence Nightingales to
the Crimea by fifties and hundreds—young and delicate women, hiding their personality under the common dress of a religious order, casting aside the
names that would recall their rank in the world,
unencouraged in their beneficence by any newspaper
paragraphs, and unrewarded save by the sweet consciousness of duty done. The Emperor Alexander,
struck by the part played in the Crimean campaign
by the Sisters of Charity, has recently asked the
superior of the order to detail five hundred of the
sisters, for duty in the hospitals of Russia. It is
understood that the request will be complied with so
far as the number of the community will permit.

If I were asked to sum up in one sentence the
practical result of my observations of men and manners here on the continent, I should say that it was
this: We have a great deal to learn in America concerning the philosophy of life. I do not mean that
philosophy which teaches us that "it is not all of life

to live," but the philosophy of making ninety-three
cents furnish the same amount of comfort in America that five francs do in Paris. The spirit of cen-
tralization is stronger here than in any American
city: (it is too true, as Heine said, that to speak of
the departments of France having a political opinion
as distinguished from Paris, "is to talk of a man's
legs thinking;") and there is no reason why people
of moderate means should not be able to live as
respectably, comfortably, and economically in our
cities as here, if they will only use a little common
sense. The model-lodging-house enterprise was a
most praiseworthy one, but it seems to have been
confined only to the wants of the most necessitous
class in the community. There is, however, a large
class of salesmen, and book-keepers, and mechanics,
on salaries of six hundred to twelve or fourteen hundred dollars, whose position is no less deserving of
commiseration. When the prices of beefsteak and
potatoes went up so amazingly a few years ago,
there were few salaries that experienced a similar
augmentation. The position of the men on small
salaries therefore became peculiar, not to say unpleasant, as rents rose in the same proportion as
every thing else. Any person, familiar with the rents
of brick houses for small families in most of the
Atlantic cities, will see how difficult it is for such
people as these to live within their means. Now, the
remedy for this evil is a simple one, but it requires
some public-spirited men to initiate it. Suppose that
a few large, handsome houses, on the European
plan, (that is, having a suite of rooms, comprising
a parlour, dining-room, two or three bedrooms, and

a kitchen, on each floor,) were built in any of our great thoroughfares,—the ground floors might be used for shops,—for there is no reason why respectable people should any more object to living over shops there, than on the Boulevards. Such houses, it is easy to see, would be good paying property to their owners, as soon as people got into that way of living; and when salaried men saw that they could get the equivalent, in comfort and available room, to an ordinary five hundred dollar house for half that rent, in a central situation, depend upon it, they would not be long in learning how to live in that style. The advantages of this plan of domestic life are numerous and striking. Housekeeping would be disarmed of half its difficulties; the little kitchen would furnish the coffee and eggs in the morning and the tea and toast at night—the dinner might be ordered from a neighbouring restaurant for any hour —for such establishments would increase with the increase of apartments. The dangers of burglary would be diminished, for the housekeeper would have only the door leading to the staircase to lock up at night. The washing would be done out of the house, and the steam of boiling suds, and all anxiety about clothes-lines, and sooty chimneys, and windy weather would thereby be avoided. Thousands of people would be liberated from the caprice and petty tyranny of the railroad directors, whose action has so often filled our newspapers with resolutions and protests, and, so far as Boston is concerned, its peninsula might be made the home of a population of three hundred thousand instead of a hundred and eighty thousand persons. The most rigidly careless person can hardly fail to become a successful house-keeper, when the matter is made so easy as it is by the European plan. The plan, too, not only simplifies the mysteries of domestic economy, but it snuggifies one's establishment wonderfully, and gives it a home feeling, such as what are called genteel houses nowadays wot not of. The change has got to come —and the sooner it does, the better it will be for our cities, and many of their people, who have been driven into remote and unpleasant suburbs by high rents, or who are held back from marriage by the expenses of housekeeping conducted on the present method.

PARIS

THE LOUVRE AND ART

IT is an inestimable advantage to an idle man to have such a place as the Louvre ever open to him. The book-stalls and print-shops of the quays, those never-failing sources of pleasure and of extravagance in a small way, cannot be visited with any satisfaction under the meridian sun; the shop windows, a perpetual industrial exhibition, grow tiresome at times; the streets are too crowded, the gardens too empty; the reading rooms are close; the newspapers are stupid; and what remains? Why, the Louvre opens its hospitable doors, and, blessing the memory of Francis I., the tired wanderer enters, and drinks in the refreshing coolness of those quiet and spacious halls. If he is an antiquarian, he plunges deep into the arcana of ancient Egypt, and emulates the great Champollion; if he is a student of history, he muses on the sceptre of Charlemagne, or the old gray coat and coronation robes of the first Napoleon; if he is devoted to art, he travels through that wilderness of paintings and statuary, and thinks and talks about *chiaro 'scuro,* "breadth of colour," or "bits of foreshortening." But if he be a man of simple tastes, who detests technicalities, and enjoys all such things in a quiet, general sort of way, without knowing exactly what it is that pleases him,—he goes through room after room, now stopping for an instant before a set of antique china, now speculating

[136]

on the figure he should cut in one of those old suits of armour, and finally settling down in a chair before some landscape by Cuyp or Claude, in which the artist seems to have imprisoned the sunbeams and the warm, fragrant atmosphere of early June; or else he seats himself on that comfortable sofa before Murillo's masterpiece, and contemplates the supernal beauty and holy exaltation of the face of her whom Dante calls the "Virgin Mother, daughter of her Son." He is surrounded by artists, engaged in a work that seems to verify the old maxim, *Laborare est orare,*—each one striving to reproduce on his canvas the effects of the angel-guided pencil of Murillo.

I find it useless for me to attempt to visit the Louvre systematically, as most people do. I have frequently tried to do it, but it has ended by my walking through one or two rooms, and then taking up my position before Murillo's Conception, and holding it until the hour came for closing the gallery. When I was young, I used to think what a glorious thing it would have been to have felt the thrill of joy that filled the heart of the discoverer of America, or the satisfaction of Shakspeare when he had finished Hamlet or Macbeth, or of Beethoven when he had completed his seventh symphony; but all that covetousness of the impossible is blotted out by my envy of the great Spanish painter. What must have been the deep transport of his heart, when he gazed upon the heavenly vision his own genius had created! He must have felt

"—— like some watcher of the skies,
When a new planet sails into his ken,
Or like stout Cortez, when, with eagle eyes,
He stared at the Pacific. ——"

[137]

MY UNKNOWN CHUM

In spite of all my natural New England prejudice, I cannot help admiring and loving that old Catholic devotion to the Blessed Virgin. Its humanizing effects can be seen in the history of the middle ages, and they are felt amid all the bustle and roar of this irreverent nineteenth century. Woman cannot again be thought the soulless being heathen philosophy considered her; she cannot again become a slave, for she is recognized as the sister of her who was chosen to make reparation for the misdeeds of Mother Eve. I am strongly tempted to transcribe here some lines written in pencil on the fly-leaf of an old catalogue of the museum of the Louvre, and found on the sofa before Murillo's picture. The writer seems to have had in mind the beautiful conclusion of the life of Agricola by Tacitus, where the great historian says that he would not forbid the making of likenesses in marble or bronze, but would only remind us that such images, like the forms of their originals, are frail and unenduring, while the beauty of the mind is eternal, and can be perpetuated in the manners of succeeding generations better than by ignoble materials and the art of the sculptor. The lines appear to be a paraphrase of this idea.

O blest Murillo! what a task was thine,
  That Mother to portray whose beauty mild
Combined earth's comeliness with grace divine,—
  To whom our God and Saviour as a child
  Was subject—upon whom so oft He smiled!
Yet not less happy also in my part,—
  For I, though in a world by sin defiled,
Though lacking genius and unskilled in art,
May paint that blessed likeness in a contrite heart.

Art is the surest and safest civilizer. Popular
education may be so perverted as only to minister to
new forms of corruption, but art purifies itself; it has
no Voltaires, and Rousseaus, and Eugene Sues,—for
painting and sculpture, like poetry, refuse to be
made the handmaids of vice or unbelief. Open your
galleries of art to the people, and you confer on them
a greater benefit than mere book education; you give
them a refinement to which they would otherwise be
strangers. The boor, turned loose into civilized
society, soon catches something of its tone of politeness; and those who are accustomed to the contemplation of forms of ideal beauty will not easily be
won by the grossness and deformity of vice. A fine
picture daily looked at becomes by degrees a part of
our own souls, and exerts an influence over us of
which we are little aware. Some English writer—
Hazlitt, I think—has said, that if a man were thinking of committing some wicked or disgraceful action,
and were to stop short and look for a moment at
some fine picture with which he had been familiar,
he would inevitably be turned thereby from his purpose. It is to be hoped that the time is not far distant when each of our great American cities shall
possess its gallery of art, which (on certain days of
the week, at least) shall be as free to all well-behaved persons as the public parks themselves. We
may not boast the artistic wealth of Rome, Florence,
Paris, Dresden, or any of the old capitals of Europe;
but the sooner we make a beginning, the better it will
be for our galleries and our mob. We need some
more effectual humanizer than our educational system. Reading, writing, and ciphering are great

things, but they are powerless to overcome the rudeness and irreverence of our people. Our populace seems to lack entirely the sense of the beautiful or the sublime. As Charles Lamb said, "They have, alas! no passion for antiquities—for the tomb of king or prelate, sage or poet. If they had, they would no longer be the rabble." It is too true that the attempts which have been made to open private gardens to the enjoyment of the public have resulted in the most shameful abuses of privilege, and that flowers are stolen from the graves in our cemeteries; but there is no reason for giving our people up as past praying for, on the score of politeness and common decency. They must be educated up to it: some abuses may occur at first, but a few salutary lessons on the necessity of submission to authority will rectify it all, and our people will, in the course of time, become as well-behaved as the people of France or Italy.

I am no antiquarian. I do not love the antique for antiquity's sake. It must appeal to me through the medium of history, or not at all. Etruscan relics have no other charm for me than their beauty of form. I care but little for Egyptian sarcophagi or their devices and hieroglyphics, and I would not go half a mile to see a wilderness of mummies. Whenever I feel a longing for any thing in the Egyptian or heathen line, I can resort to Mount Auburn, with its gateway—and this thought satisfies me; so that I pass by all such things without feeling that I am a loser. With such feelings, there are many of the halls of the Louvre which I only walk through with an admiring glance at their elegance of arrangement.

A few days since, in wandering about there, I found a room which I had never seen before, and which touched me more nearly than any thing there, except the paintings. It has been opened recently. I had been looking through the relics of royalty with a considerable degree of pleasure,—meditating on the armour of Henry the Great, the breviary of St. Louis, and the worn satin shoe which once covered the little foot of Marie Antoinette,—and was about to leave, when I noticed that a door was open which in past years I had seen closed. I pushed in, and found myself in a vast and magnificent apartment, on the gorgeously frescoed ceiling of which was emblazoned the name—which is a tower of strength to every Frenchman—*Napoleon*. Around the room, in elegant glass cases, were disposed the relics of the saint whom Mr. Abbott's bull of canonization has placed in red letters in the calendar of Young America. Leaving aside all joking upon the attempts to prove that much-slandered monarch a saint, there was his history, written as Sartor Resartus would have written it, in his clothes. There was a crayon sketch of him at the age of sixteen; there was a mathematical book which he had studied, the case of mathematical instruments he had used; there was the coat in which he rode up and down the lines of Marengo, inspiring every heart with heroism, and every arm with vigour; the sword and coat he wore as First Consul; the glittering robes which decked him when he sat in the chair of Clovis and Charlemagne, the idol of his nation, and the terror of all the world besides; the stirrups in which he stood at Waterloo, and saw his brave legions cut up and dispersed; and, though last, not least, there was the old gray coat and hat in which he walked about at St. Helena, and the very handkerchief which in his dying hour wiped the chill dew of eternity from his brow. There were many things besides—there were his table and chair; his camp bed on which he rested during those long campaigns; his gloves, his razor strap, his comb, the clothes of his little son, the "King of Rome," and the bow he played with; the saddles and other presents which he received during his expedition to the East, and his various court dresses—but the old gray coat was the most attractive of all. It was a consolation to notice that it had lost a button, for it showed that though its wearer was an anointed emperor, he was not exempt from the vicissitudes of common humanity. I sat down and observed the people who visited the room, and I noticed that they all lingered around the old coat. It made no difference whether they spoke English, French, German, or any other tongue; there was something which appealed to them all; there was a common ground, where the student and the enthusiastic lover of high art could join in harmonious feeling, even with the practical man, who would not have cared a three-cent piece if Praxiteles and Canova had never sculptured, or Raphael and Murillo had never seen a brush. It required but a slight effort to fill the room up of the absent hero, and to "stuff out his vacant garments with his form," and perhaps this very thing tended to make the entire exhibition a sad one. It was the most melancholy commentary on human glory that can be imagined. It ought to be placed in the vestibule of a church, or in some more public place, and it would purge a community of ambition. What a sermon might Lacordaire preach on the temporal and the eternal, with the sword and the coronation robes of Napoleon I. before him!

The interest which I have seen manifested by so many people in the relics of Napoleon I. has afforded me considerable amusement. I have lately seen so much ridicule cast upon the relics of the saints preserved in many of the churches of Italy, by people of the same class as those who lingered so reverentially before the glass cases of the Napoleon room in the Louvre, that I cannot help thinking how rare a virtue consistency is.

Perhaps it may be owing to some weakness in my mental organization, but I cannot acknowledge the propriety of honouring the burial-places of successful generals, and, at the same time, think the shrines of the saints worthy of nothing but ridicule and desecration. I found myself, a few years ago, looking with grave interest at an old coat of General Jackson's, which is preserved in the Patent Office at Washington; and I cannot wonder at the reverence which some people pay to the garments of a martyr in the cause of religion. I cannot understand how it may be right and proper to celebrate the birthdays of worldly heroes, and "rank idolatry" to commemorate the self-denying heroes of Christianity. I cannot join in the setting-up of statues of generals and statesmen, and condemn a similar homage to the saints by any allusions to the enormity of making a "graven image." In fine, if it is right to adorn and reverence the tomb of the Father of his Country, (and what American heart does not acknowledge its propriety?) it certainly cannot be wrong to beautify and venerate the tomb of the chief apostle, and the shrines of saints and martyrs who achieved for themselves and their fellow-men an independence from a tyranny infinitely worse than that from which Washington liberated America.

I have recently been visiting the three great monuments of the reign of Napoleon III.—the completed Louvre, the Bois de Boulogne, and the Halles Centrales. As to the first, those who remember those narrow, nasty streets, which within six years were the approaches to the Louvre and the Palais Royal, and those rickety old buildings reminding one too strongly of cheese in an advanced stage of mouldiness, that used to intrude their unsightly forms into the very middle of the Place du Carrousel,—those who recollect the junk shops that seemed more fitting to the neighbourhood of the docks than to the entrance to a palace and a gallery of art,—feel in a manner lost, when they walk about the courtyards of the noble edifice which has taken the place of so much deformity. If the new wings of the Louvre had been built in one range instead of quadrangles, they would extend more than half a mile! Half a mile of palace, and a palace, too, which in building has occupied one hundred and fifty sculptors for the past five years! Those who have not visited Paris within five years will recollect the Bois de Boulogne only as a vast neglected tract of woodland, which seemed a great waste of the raw material in a place where firewood is so expensive as it is here. It is now laid out in beautiful avenues and walks, the extent of which is said to be nearly two hundred miles. You are refreshed by the sound of waterfalls and the coolness of grottos, the rocks for the formation of which were brought from Fontainebleau, more than forty miles distant from Paris. You walk on, and find yourself on the shores of a lake, a mile or two in length, with two or three lovely islands in it, and in whose bright blue waters thousands of trout are sporting. That wild waste, the old Bois de Boulogne, which few persons but duellists ever visited, has passed away, and in its place you find the most magnificent park in the world. It is indeed a perfect triumph of landscape gardening. It is nature itself, not in miniature, but on such a scale as to deceive you entirely, and fill you with the same feeling of admiration that is awakened by any striking natural beauty. The old French notions of landscape gardening seem to have been entirely cast aside. The carriage roads and paths go winding about so that the view is constantly changing, and the trees are allowed to grow as they please, without being tortured into fantastic shapes by the pruning knife. The banks of the lake have been made irregular, now steep, now sloping gently to the water's edge, and in some places huge jagged rocks have been most naturally worked in, while ivy has been planted around them, and in their crevices those weeds and shrubs which commonly grow in such places. You would about as readily take Jamaica Pond to be artificial as this lovely sheet of water and its surroundings. The Avenue de l'Impératrice is the road from the Arc de Triomphe to the Bois de Boulogne. It is half or three quarters of a mile in length, and is destined to be one of the most striking features of Paris. It is laid out with spacious grass plots, with carriage ways and ways for equestrians and foot passengers, with regular double rows of trees on either side. Many elegant château-like private residences already adorn it, and others are rapidly rising. An idea of its majestic appearance may be had from the fact that its entire width from house to house is about four hundred feet. The large space around the Arc de Triomphe is already laid out in a square, to be called the Place de l'Europe, and the work has already been commenced of reducing the buildings around it to symmetry. The Halles Centrales, the great central market-house of Paris, has just been opened to the public. It is built mainly of iron and glass. As nearly as I could judge of its size, I should think it would leave but little spare room if it were placed in Union Park, New York. It is about a hundred feet in height, and so well ventilated that it is hard to realize when there that one is under cover. A wide street for vehicles runs through its whole length, crossed by others at equal intervals. I have called these three public improvements the great monuments of the reign of Napoleon III.; not that I would limit his good works to these, but because these may be taken as conspicuous illustrations of his care, no less for the amusements than for the bodily wants of his people, and of his zeal for the promotion of art and the adornment of his capital. But these noble characteristics of the Emperor deserve something more than a mere passing notice, and may well form the subject of my next letter.

NAPOLEON THE THIRD[1]

THERE is a period in the life of almost every man which may justly be termed the romantic period. I do not mean the time when a youth, whose heart is as yet unwarped by the selfishness of the world, and his brow unclouded by its trials and its sorrows, thinks that the performance of his life will fully come up to the glowing programme he then composes for it; neither do I refer to the period when, in hungry expectation, we clutched eagerly at the booksellers' announcements of the last productions of the eloquent Bulwer, or of the inexhaustible James. But I refer to the time when childhood forgets its new buttons in reading how poor Ali Baba relieved his wants at the expense of the wicked thieves; how Whittington heard Bow Bells ring out the prophecy of his greatness; how fierce Blue Beard punished his wife's curiosity; and how good King Alfred merited reproof by his forgetfulness of the herdsman's supper. This is the true period of

[1] The author must plead guilty to a little hesitation (induced by the present aspect of European affairs) about incorporating this paper on the French Emperor, written some three years since, in his work. He feels, however, that, whatever may be the issue of the present contest in Europe, the services of Napoleon III. to France and to civilization are a part of history; and he has no wish to disguise his satisfaction at having been one of the first Americans who confronted the vulgar prejudices of his countrymen against that remarkable man, and publicly recognized the wonderful talents which have placed France at the head of all civilized nations.

romance in the lives of all of us; for then all the romance that we read is clothed with the dignity of history, and all our history is invested with the charm of romance. This happy period does not lose its attractions, even when we outgrow the credulity of childhood; for the romance of history captivates us when we no longer are subject to the sway of the novelist; and we leave Mr. Thackeray's last uncut, until we can finish a newspaper chapter in the history of these momentous times.

We know how eagerly we pursue the vicissitudes of fortune which have marked the career of so many of the world's heroes; and this will teach us how future generations will read the history of the pres-ent century. Surely the whole range of romance presents no parallel to the simple history of the won-derful man who now governs France. It is easy to see that his varied fortunes will one day perform a conspicuous part in that juvenile classical literature of which I have spoken; and perhaps it may not be unprofitable, dear reader, for us to endeavour to raise ourselves above the excitement of partisanship and the influences of old prejudices, and look upon his career as may the writers of the twenty-fifth cen-tury.

It is a popular error in America to regard Louis Napoleon as a singular combination of knavery and half-wittedness. Even Mr. Emerson, in his *English Traits,* so far forgets the kindliness of his nature as to call him a "successful thief." The English jour-nalists once delighted to ridicule him as the "nephew of his uncle," and the shadow of a great name, and Punch used to represent him as a pygmy standing

upon the brim of his uncle's hat, and wondering how
he could ever fill it; but he has lived down ridicule,
and they have long since learned that there is such a
thing as the possibility of a mistake in judgment,
even among journalists and politicians. It is time
that we Americans got over a notion which has long
since been exploded on this side of the Atlantic. I
know that I am flying in the face of those who believe
in the plenary inspiration of the New York Tribune,
when I claim for the Emperor any thing like patriotism or capacity as a statesman. I know that the
Greeleian, "philanthropic" code exacts that we
should *not* "give the prisoner the benefit of the
doubt," and that when any one whom we dislike does
any good, we should attribute it to nothing but a
selfish or ambitious motive. I know that this new-
fangled love of all mankind requires us to hate those
who differ from us politically, and never to lose an
opportunity to blacken their characters and diminish
their reputation; and therefore I make all due allow-
ances for the refusal of the Tribune, and journals of
the same amiable family, to see the truth. In April,
1856, I was waiting for a train in a way station on
the Worcester Railroad. A sun-burned, hard-work-
ing man was reading the news of the proclamation of
peace at Paris from a penny paper, and he com-
mented upon it to two or three others who were present, as follows: "Well, I don't know how 'tis, but it
seems to *me* that we've been most almightily mistaken about this 'ere *Lewis* Napoleon. We used to
think he was a shaller kind o' feller any how, but it
really looks now, judging from the *position* of
France in European affairs, as if he was turning out

to be altogether the *biggest dog in that tanyard!*"
The old fellow's conclusion was a true one, though
his rhetoric would not have been commended at
Cambridge; and it is to prevent this conclusion forcing itself upon the public sense, that the sym-
pathizers with socialism have been labouring ever
since. We are told that it is our duty as Americans
and republicans to wish for the overthrow of Napoleon and his empire, and the establishment of the
république démocratique et sociale. Now, having
received my political principles from another source
than the Tribune, I may be pardoned for having a
prejudice in favour of allowing the people of France
to govern France; and, as they elected Louis Napoleon President in 1848 by more than five millions
of votes, and in 1851 chose him dictator (in their
fear of the very party which the Tribune wishes to
see in power) by more than *seven* millions of votes,
and finally, in 1852, made him their Emperor by a
vote of more than seven millions against a little more
than three hundred thousand, we may suppose
France to have expressed a pretty decided opinion
on this matter. The French empire rests upon the
very principle that forms the basis of true republicanism—universal suffrage. Louis Napoleon restored that principle after it had been suppressed or
restricted, and proved himself a truer republican
than his opponents. For nine years, Napoleon has
been sustained by the people of France with a
unanimity such as the United States never knew, except in the election of Washington as first President,
and his majority has increased every time that he has
appealed to the people. It is idle to say that there are

parties here that are opposed to him; it would be a remarkable phenomenon if there were not. But there is a more united support here for the Emperor than there is in our own country for the constitution of the United States, and any right-minded man would regret a revolutionary movement in one country as much as in the other.

If there was ever a position calculated to test the capabilities of its occupant, it was that in which Louis Napoleon found himself when he obeyed the voice of the French people, and accepted the presidency of the French republic. Surrounded by men holding all kinds of political opinions, from the agrarian Proudhon to the impracticable Louis Blanc, and men of no political opinions whatever,—he found himself obliged to use all the power reposed in him by the constitution, to keep the government from falling asunder. History bears witness to the fact that republican governments deteriorate more rapidly than those which are based upon a less changeable foundation than the popular will. But there was little danger of the French republic deteriorating, for it was about as weak and unprincipled as it could be in its very inception. There were a few men of high and patriotic character in the Assembly, but (as is generally the case) their voices were drowned amid the clamourings of a crowd of radical journalists and ambitious *littérateurs*, whose only bond of union was a fierce hatred of law and religion, and a desire for the spoils of office. These were the men with whom Napoleon had to deal. They had favoured his election to the presidency, for, in their misapprehension of his character, they thought him the mere shadow of a name, and expected under his government to have all things their own way. But they were not long in discovering their mistake.

His conduct soon showed that he was the proper man for the crisis. That unflinching republican, General Cavaignac, had before pointed out the dangers to all European governments, and to civilization itself, that would spring from the continuance of the sanguinary and sacrilegious Roman Republic; and Napoleon, accepting his suggestions, took immediate measures to put an end to the atrocities which marked the sway of Mazzini and his assassins in the Roman States.[1] The success which attended these measures is now a part of history. There is a kind of historical justice in this part of Napoleon's career which must force itself upon every reflecting mind. From the day when St. Remy told his royal convert, Clovis, to "burn what he had adored, and adore what he had burned," the monarch of France had always been considered the "eldest son of the Church." The Roman Pontiff was indebted to Pepin and Charlemagne for those possessions which rendered him independent of the secular power. In the

[1] Lest I should be thought guilty of speaking rashly with regard to the anarchy which Napoleon destroyed in 1849 at Rome, I take the liberty to transcribe a few extracts from the constitution of the Society of "Young Italy," which will give some idea of the principles upon which the Roman Republic rested. I translate from the edition published at Naples, by Benedetto Cantalupo.

"ARTICLE I. The Society is established for the entire destruction of all the governments of the peninsula, and for the forming of Italy into a single state, under a republican government.

"ART. II. In consequence of the evils attendant upon absolute government, and the still greater evils of constitutional monarchy, we ought to join all our efforts to establish a single and indivisible republic.

"ART. XXX. Those members who shall disobey the commands of

hour of need it was always to the Kings of France
that he looked for aid; and whether he sought aid
against the oppressors of the Holy See or the infidel
possessors of the Holy Sepulchre, he seldom appealed to them in vain. It was meet, therefore, that
Napoleon should inaugurate his power by thus re-
viving the ancient traditionary spirit of the French
monarchy; for he could not better prove his worthi-
ness to sit on the throne which had been occupied by
so many generous and heroic spirits, than by fighting the battles of the Church they loved so well.

The foreign and domestic policy which the Prince-
President pursued excited at the same time the anger
of the ultra republican faction, and the hopes of the
religious and conservative portion of society. Order
was restored, and an impetus was given to commercial enterprise and to the arts of peace such as France
had not known since the outbreak of 1848. Still the
discordant elements of which the Assembly was composed, were a just cause of alarm to all friends of
good order, and all parties, conservative and radical,

the Society, or who shall reveal its mysteries, shall be poniarded without
remission.

" Art. XXXI.   The secret tribunal shall pronounce sentence in such
cases as the preceding, and shall designate one or more of the brethren
to carry it into instant execution.

" Art. XXXII.   The brother who shall refuse to execute a sentence
thus pronounced shall be considered as a perjurer, and as such shall be
immediately put to death.

' " Art. XXXIII.   If the victim condemned to punishment should
succeed in escaping, he shall be pursued unremittingly into any place whatever, and shall be struck as by an invisible hand, even if he shall have
taken refuge on the bosom of his mother, or in the tabernacle of Christ.

" Art. XXXIV.   Each secret tribunal shall be competent not only
to condemn the guilty to death, but also to put to death all persons so
sentenced."

regarded the existing state of affairs as a temporary one. Napoleon saw that the only obstacle in the path of the nation to peace and prosperity was the Assembly—the radicals of the Assembly that the Prince-President was the only obstacle to their plans of disorganization and anarchy; and they also saw that, if the question were allowed to go to the people at the expiration of Napoleon's term of office, he would surely be reëlected, and that his policy would be triumphantly confirmed. So, as the time drew near for the new election, the struggle between the President and the Assembly—between order and anarchy—grew more and more severe. Plots were formed against Napoleon, and were just ripening for execution, when, on the second of December, 1851, he terminated the suspense of the nation by seizing and throwing into prison all the chief conspirators against the public peace, and then appealed to the people to sustain him in his efforts to preserve his country from the state of anarchy towards which it seemed to be hastening. The people answered promptly and with good will to the call, and Napoleon gained an almost bloodless victory.

But we are told that by the *coup d'état,* "Napoleon violated his oath to sustain the constitution of the republic—that he is a perjurer, and all his success cannot diminish his crime." So might one of the old loyalists have said about our own Washington. "He was a British subject—by accepting a commission under Braddock, he formally acknowledged his allegiance to the crown—by drawing his sword in the revolution, he violated not only his fidelity as a subject, but his honour as a soldier." And what would any American reply to this? He would say that Washington never bound himself to violate his conscience, and that conscientiously he felt bound to defend the old English principles of free government even against the encroachments of his own rightful sovereign. And so, with equal reason, it may be said of Louis Napoleon, when the term of his presidency was approaching, and the radical members of the Assembly were forming conspiracies to dispose of him so as to prevent his reëlection, he was bound in conscience, as the chief ruler of his country, to prevent the anarchy that must result from such a movement. And how could he do this save by dissolving the Assembly and appealing to the people as he did? The constitution was nullified by the plots of the Assembly, and France in 1851 was really without a government, until the *coup d'état* inaugurated the present reign of public prosperity and peace. The *coup d'état* was not only justifiable—it was praiseworthy. When the prejudices and party spirit of the present time shall have passed away, the historian will grow eloquent in speaking of that fearless and far-sighted statesman, who, when his country was threatened with a repetition of the civil strife which had too often shaken her to her centre, threw himself boldly upon the patriotism of the people with those noble words, "The Assembly, instead of being what it ought to be, the support of public order, has become a nest of conspiracies. It compromises the peace of France. I have dissolved it; and I call upon the whole people to judge between it and myself."—The *coup d'état* excited the anger only of the socialists and of those partisans of the houses of Bourbon and Orléans who loved those families more than they loved their country's welfare; for they saw, by the revival of business, that confidence in the stability of the government was established, and that Napoleon had obtained a place in the affections of the French people from which he could not easily be dislodged.

From this dictatorship, which the dangers of the time had rendered necessary, it was an easy transition to the empire, and Louis Napoleon found his succession to the throne of his uncle confirmed by almost the unanimous vote of the French people. It was a tribute to the man, and to his public policy, such as no ruler in modern times has ever received, and for unanimity is unparalleled in the history of popular elections. His marriage followed quickly upon the proclamation of the empire; and in this, as in all his acts, we can discern his manly and independent spirit. He sought not to ally himself with any of the royal families of Europe, for he felt himself to be so sure of his position, that he could without risk consult his affections rather than policy or ambition.

The skilful diplomacy which led to the alliance with England, the campaign in the Crimea, and the repulse of Russia, are too fresh in every body's recollection to bear any repetition. So far as they concern Napoleon III., the world is a witness to his matchless coolness and determination. What could be grander than the heroic inflexibility he displayed in the face of the accumulated disasters of that campaign, and the murmurs of his allies! Misfortune only seemed to nerve him to more vigorous effort.

During that terrible winter of 1854-5, he appeared more like a fixed, unvarying law of nature than a man,—so immovable was he in his opposition to those who, pressed by the unlooked-for difficulties of the time, counselled a change of policy. The successful termination of the siege of Sebastopol, however, proved the justice of his calculations, and, while conquering monarchs in other times have been content to see the negotiations for peace made in some provincial town, or in a city of some neutral state, the proud satisfaction was conceded to him by Russia of having the peace conferences held in his own capital.

But while commemorating the success of his efforts to raise his country to a commanding position among the nations, we must not forget the great enterprises of internal improvement which he has set on foot within his empire. Who can recall what Paris was under Louis Philippe, or the time of the republic, and compare it with the Paris of to-day, without admiring the genius of Napoleon III.? Who does not recognize a wonderful capacity for the administration of government in the Emperor, when he sees that nearly all of these great improvements (unlike those of Louis XIV., which impoverished the nation) will gradually but surely pay for themselves by increasing the amount of taxable property? Indeed, the improvements in the city of Paris alone are on so vast a scale as to be incomprehensible to any one unacquainted with that capital. If Napoleon were to-day to fall a victim to that organization of republican assassins which is known to exist in France, as well as in the other states of Europe, he would leave, in the Louvre, in the Bois de Boulogne, in the new

Boulevards, and the extension of the Rue de Rivoli, together with the countless other public works which now adorn Paris, testimonials to the splendour of his brief reign, such as no monarch ever left before: of him, as of Sir Christopher Wren, it might be truly said, *"Si quæris monumentum, circumspice."*

But we must not think that Napoleon has confined his exertions to the improvement of Paris alone. Not a single province of his empire has been neglected by him, and there is scarcely a town that has not felt the influence of his policy. The foreign commerce of France has been wonderfully increased by him, and his favourite project for a ship canal through the Isthmus of Suez is now numbered among the probabilities of the age. When it is considered what a narrow strip of land separates the Red Sea from the Mediterranean, and what an immense advantage such a canal would be to all the countries bordering on the latter, it is not wonderful that Napoleon should find so many friends among the sovereigns of Europe. He has not built the magnificent new port of Marseilles merely for the accommodation of the Mediterranean coasting trade of his empire. His far-seeing eye looks upon those massive quays covered with merchandise from every quarter of the Orient, brought, not around the stormy Cape, nor by the toilsome caravan over the parching desert, but by the swift steamers of the *Messageries Impériales* from every port of India, through the waters which, centuries ago, rolled back and opened a path of safety to the chosen people of God.

If the old proverb be true, that a man is known by

the company he keeps, it is equally true, on the other hand, that a statesman may be rightly known by examining the character of his opponents. And who are the opponents of Napoleon III.? With the exception of a few partisans of the Bourbons, (whose opposition to the Napoleon dynasty is an hereditary complaint,) they are radical demagogues, who delight to mislead the fickle multitude with the words, "Liberty, Equality, and Fraternity," on their lips, but the designs of anarchy and bloodshed in their hearts. Their ranks are swelled by a number of visionary "philanthropists," and a large number of newspaper scribblers deprived of their occupation by Napoleon's salutary laws against abuse of the liberty of the press, and lacking ambition to earn an honest livelihood. Among them may be found a few literary men of high reputation, who have espoused some impracticable theory of government, and would blindly throw away their well-earned fame, and shed the last drop of their ink in forcing it upon an unwilling nation.

Slander, like Death, loves a shining mark. The fact cannot be doubted, if we look at the lives of the greatest and best men the world has ever seen. In truth, a large part of the heroism of the noblest patriots, and the purest philanthropists, has been created by the necessity they have been under to bear up against the obloquy with which enmity or envy has assailed them. The Emperor Napoleon is, beyond a doubt, the best abused man in Christendom. There probably never existed a man whose every act and every motive have been more studiously misrepresented and systematically lied about than his.

It cannot be wondered at, either; for he exercises too much power in the state councils of Europe, and fills too large a space in the public eye, not to be assailed by those whose evil prophecies have been falsified by his brilliant reign, and whose lawless schemes have been frustrated by his unexampled prudence and firmness.

And what right has he to complain? If St. Gregory VII. were obliged to submit for centuries to being represented as an ambitious self-seeker and unscrupulous politician, instead of a wise and far-seeing pontiff, a vanquisher of tyrants, and a self-denying saint; if St. Thomas of Canterbury be held up, in hundreds of volumes, as a monster of ingratitude towards a beneficent sovereign, and a haughty and overbearing supporter of prelatical tyranny, instead of a martyr, in defence of religious liberty against the encroachments of the civil authority; if Cardinal Wolsey be held up to public scorn as a proud and selfish prince of the Church, a glutton, and a wine-bibber, instead of a skilful administrator of government, a liberal patron of learning, and all good arts, and the sole restrainer of the evil passions of the most shameless tyrant who ever sat upon the English throne; if Cardinal Richelieu be handed down from generation to generation, painted in the blackest colours, as a scheming politician, in whose heart, wile and cruelty were mixed up in equal parts, instead of a sagacious and inflexible statesman, and a patriot who made every thing (even his religion) bend to his devotion to the glory of his beloved France; if these great men have been thus misrepresented in that history which De Maistre aptly calls "a conspiracy against truth," I do not think that Napoleon III. can reasonably complain of finding himself denounced as a tyrant, a perjurer, and a victim of all the bad passions that vex the human heart, instead of a liberator of his country from that many-headed monstrosity, miscalled the *République Française*, an unswerving supporter of the cause of law and religion, and the architect of the present glory and prosperity of France. It must be a great consolation to the Emperor, under the slanders which have been heaped upon him, to reflect that their authors and the enemies who hate him worst, are, for the most part, infidels and assassins, and enemies of social order. Whatever errors a man may commit, he cannot be far from the course of right so long as he is hated and feared by people of that desperate stamp. The ancient adage tells us that "a cat may look at a king"; and it is, perhaps, a merciful provision of the law of compensation that the base reptiles which fatten on the offal of slander are permitted to trail their slime over a name which is the synonyme of the power and glory of France.

When the prejudices of the present day shall have died out, the historian will relate how devoted Napoleon III. was to every thing that concerned his country's welfare. He will tell of his ceaseless care for the most common wants of his people, and of his vigilance in enforcing laws against those who wronged the poor by their dishonest dealings in the necessaries of life. He will relate how promptly he turned his back upon nobles and ambassadors to visit some of his people who had been overwhelmed by a terrible calamity. and will describe the kind, fatherly

manner in which he went among them, carrying suc-
cour and consolation to all. He will not compare the
Emperor to his great warrior-uncle; he will *contrast*
the two. He will show how the uncle made all
Europe fear and hate him, and how the nephew con-
verted his enemies into allies; how the uncle manured
the soil of Europe with the bones of his soldiers, and
the nephew, having given splendid proofs of his
ability to make war, won for himself the title of "the
Pacificator of Europe"; how the uncle, through his
hot-headed ambition, finally made France the prey of
a hostile alliance, and the nephew brought the representatives of all the European powers around him in
his capital to make peace under his supervision.

The man who, after thirty years of exile and six
years of close imprisonment, can take a country in
the chaotic condition in which France found itself
after the revolution of 1848, and reorganize its government, place its financial affairs on a better footing
than they have been before within the memory of
man, double its commerce, and raise it to the highest
place among the states of Europe, cannot be an ordinary man. In 1852, the Emperor said, "France, in
crowning me, crowns herself;" and he has proved
the literal truth of his words. He has given France
peace, prosperity, and a stable government. He has
imitated Napoleon I. in every one of his great and
praiseworthy actions in his civil capacity, while he
has not made a single one of his mistakes. And if
"he that ruleth his own spirit is greater than he that
taketh a city," this remarkable man, whose self-con-
trol is undisturbed by his most unparalleled success,
is destined to be known in history as Napoleon the
Great.

NAPOLEON THE THIRD

The character of Napoleon III. is marked by a unity and a consistency such as invariably have distinguished the greatest men. We can see this consistency in his fidelity to the cause of law and order, whether it be manifested in his services as a special constable against the Chartists of England, or as the chief magistrate of his nation against the Chartists of France. And to this conspicuous virtue of steadfastness he adds a wonderful universality of acquirements and natural genius. We see him contracting favourable loans and averting impending dangers in the monetary affairs of France, and it would seem as if his early life had been spent amid the clamours of the Bourse; we see him concentrating troops in his capital against the threats of the revolutionists, or designing campaigns against the greatest military powers of Europe; we see him maintaining a perfect composure in the midst of deadly missiles which were expected to terminate his reign and dynasty, and it would seem as if the camp had always been his home, and the dangers of the battle-field his familiar associations; we see him buying up grain to prevent speculators from oppressing his people during a season of scarcity, or imprisoning bakers for a deficiency in the weight of their loaves, or regulating the sales of meats and vegetables,—and it would seem as if he always had been a prudent housekeeper and a profound student of domestic economy; we see him laying out parks, projecting new streets and public buildings, and we question whether he has paid most attention to architecture, engineering, or landscape-gardening; we see him visiting his subjects when they have been overwhelmed by a great calamity, and he would seem to have been a disciple of St. Thomas

of Villanueva, or of St. Vincent of Paul; we see him
taking the lead amid the chief statesmen and diplo-
matists of the world, we read his powerful state
papers and speeches, and we wonder where he acquired his experience; we see him, in short, under all
circumstances, and it appears that there is nothing
that concerns his country's welfare or glory too difficult for him to grapple with, nor any thing affecting
the happiness of his poorest subject trivial enough
for him to overlook. By his advocacy of the cause
of the Church, he has won a place in history by the
side of Constantine and Charlemagne; by his internal policy and care for the needs of his subjects, his
name deserves to be inscribed with those of St. Louis
and Alfred. The language which Bulwer has put
into the mouth of Cardinal Richelieu might be used
by Napoleon III., and would from him be only the
language of historical truth :—

> "I found France rent asunder,
> Sloth in the mart and schism within the temple,
> Brawls festering to rebellion, and weak laws
> Rotting away with rust— * * * *
> *I have re-created France,* and from the ashes
> Civilization on her luminous wings
> Soars phœnix-like to Jove!"

THE PHILOSOPHY OF
FOREIGN TRAVEL

FOREIGN travel is one of the most useful branches of our education, but, like a great many other useful branches, it appears to be "gone through with" by many persons merely as a matter of course. It is astonishing how few people out of the great number constantly making the tour of Europe really carry home any thing to show for it except photographs and laces. Foreign travel ought to rub the corners off a man's character, and give him a polish such as "home-keeping youth" can never acquire; yet how many we see who seem to have increased their natural rudeness and inconsiderateness by a continental trip! Foreign travel ought to soften prejudices, religious or political, and liberalize a man's mind; but how many there are who seem to have travelled for the purpose of getting up their rancour against all that is opposed to their notions, making themselves illustrations of Tom Hood's remark, that "some minds resemble copper wire or brass, and get the narrower by going farther." Foreign travel, while it shows a man more clearly the faults of his own country, ought to make him love his country more dearly than before; yet how often does it have the effect of making a man undervalue his home and his old friends! There must be some

general reason why foreign travel produces its legitimate fruits in so few instances; and I have, during
several European tours, endeavoured to ascertain it.
I am inclined to think that it is a general lack of
preparation for travel, and a mistaken notion that
"sight-seeing" is the chief end of travelling. The
expenses of the passage across the Atlantic are diminishing every year, and when the motive power in
electricity is discovered and applied, the expense of
the trip will be a mere trifle; and in view of these
considerations, I feel that, though I might find a
more entertaining subject for a letter, I cannot find a
more instructive one than the philosophy of European
travel.

Concerning the expense of foreign travel, there
are many erroneous notions afloat. There are hundreds of persons in America—artists, and students,
and persons of small means—who are held back
from what is to them a land of promise, by the mistaken idea that it is expensive to travel in Europe.
They know that Bayard Taylor made a tour on an
incredibly small sum, and they think that they have
not his tact in management, nor his self-denial in
regard to the common wants of life; but if they will
put aside a few of their false American prejudices,
they will find that they can travel in Europe almost
as cheaply as they can live at home. In America, we
have an aristocracy of the pocket, which is far more
tyrannical, and much less respectable, than any aristocracy of blood on this side of the water; for every
man feels an instinctive respect for another who can
trace his lineage back to some brave soldier whose
deeds have shone in his country's history for cen-

turies; but it requires a peculiarly constituted mind to bow down to a man whose chief claim to respect is founded in the fact of his having made a large fortune in the pork or dry goods line. Jinkins is a rich man; he lives in style, and fares sumptuously every day. Jones is one of Jinkins's neighbours; he is not so rich as Jinkins, but he feels a natural ambition to keep up with him in his establishment, and he does so; the rivalry becomes contagious, and the consequence is, that a score of well-meaning people find, to their dismay, at the end of the year, that they have been living beyond their means. Now, if people wish to travel reasonably in Europe, the first thing that they must do is to get rid of the Jones and Jinkins standard of respectability. I have seen many people who were content to live at home in a very moderate sort of way, who, when they came to travel, seemed to require all the style and luxury of a foreign prince. Such people may go all over Europe, and see very little of it except the merest outside crust. They might just as well live in a fashionable hotel in America, and visit Mr. Sattler's cosmoramas. They resemble those unfortunate persons who have studied the classics from Anthon's text-books—they have got a general notion, but of the mental discipline of the study they are entirely ignorant. But let me go into particulars concerning the expenses of travelling. I know that a person can go by a sailing vessel from Boston to Genoa, spend a week or more in Genoa and on the road to Florence, pass two or three weeks in that delightful city, and two months in Rome, then come to Paris, and stay here two or three weeks, then go to London for a month or more, and home by way of Liverpool in a steamer, for less than four hundred dollars; for I did it myself several years ago. During this trip, I lived and travelled respectably all the time—that is, what is called respectably in Europe. I went in the second class cars, and in the forward cabins of the steamers. Jones and Jinkins went in the first class cars and in the after cabins, and paid a good deal more money for the same pleasure that cost me so little. I know, too, that a person can sail from Boston to Liverpool, make a summer trip of two months and a half to Paris, *via* London and the cities of Belgium, and back to Boston *via* London and Liverpool, for a trifle over two hundred and fifty dollars. A good room in London can be got for two dollars and a half a week, in Paris for eight dollars a month, in Rome and Florence for four dollars a month, and in the cities of Germany for very considerably less. And a good dinner costs about thirty cents in London, thirty-five in Paris, fifteen to twenty-five in Florence or Rome, and even less in Germany. Breakfast, which is made very little of on the continent, generally damages one's exchequer to the extent of five to ten cents. It will be seen from this scale of prices that one can live very cheaply if he will; and, as the inhabitants of a country may be supposed to know the requirements of its climate better than strangers, common sense would dictate the adoption of their style of living.

I need not say that some knowledge of the French language is absolutely indispensable to one who would travel with any satisfaction in Europe. This is the most important general preparation that can be made for going abroad. Next after it, I should place a review of the history of the countries about to be visited. The outlines of the history of the different countries of Europe, published by the English *Society for the Diffusion of Useful Knowledge*, are admirably adapted to this purpose. This gives a reality to the scenes you are about to visit that they would not otherwise possess; it peoples the very roadside for you with heroes. And not only does it impart a reality to your travels, but history itself becomes a reality to you, instead of being a mere barren record of events, hard to be remembered. At this time, when the neglect of classical studies is apparent in almost every book, newspaper, and magazine, I am afraid that I shall be thought somewhat old-fashioned and out of date, if I say that some acquaintance with the Latin classics is necessary before a man can really enjoy Italy. Yet it is so; and it will be a great satisfaction to any man to find that Horace and Virgil, and Cicero and Livy, are something more than the hard tasks of childhood. Should a man's classical studies, however, be weak, the deficiency can be made up in some measure by the judicious use of translations, and by Eustace's Classical Tour. Murray's admirable hand-books of course will supply a vast amount of information; but it will not do to trust to reading them upon the spot. Some preparation must be made beforehand,—some capital is necessary to start in business. "If you would bring home the wealth of the Indies, you must carry out the wealth of the Indies." It would be well, too, for a person about to visit Europe to prepare himself for a quieter life than he has been leading at home. I mean, to tone himself down so as to be able to enjoy the freedom from excitement which awaits him here. It is now more than a year since I left America, and likewise more than a year since I have seen any disorderly conduct, or a quarrel, or even have heard high words between two parties in the street, or have known of an alarm of fire. In the course of the year, too, I have not seen half a dozen intoxicated persons. When we reflect what a fruitful source of excitement all these things are in America, it will be easy to see that a man may have, comparatively, a very quiet life where they are not to be found. It will not do any harm, either, to prepare one's self by assuming a little more consideration for the feelings of others than is generally seen among us, and by learning to address servants with a little less of the imperious manner which is so common in America. Strange as it may seem, there is much less distinction of classes on the continent, than in republican America. You are astonished to find the broadcloth coat and the blouse interchanging the civilities of a "light" in the streets, and the easy, familiar way of servants towards their masters is a source of great surprise. You seldom see a Frenchman or an Italian receive any thing from a servant without thanking him for it. Yet there appears to be a perfectly good understanding between all parties as to their relative position, and with all their familiarity, I have never seen a servant presume upon the good nature of his employer, as they often do with us. We receive our social habits in a great measure from England, and therefore we have got that hard old English way of treating servants, as if our object was to make them feel that they are inferiors. So the sooner a man who is going to travel on the continent, can get that notion out of his head, and replace it with the continental one, which seems to be, that a servant, so long as he is faithful in the discharge of his duties, is quite as respectable a member of society as his employer, the better it will be for him, and the pleasanter will be his sojourn in Europe.

One of the first mistakes Americans generally make in leaving for Europe is, to take too much luggage. Presupposing a sufficiency of under-clothing, all that any person really needs is a good, substantial travelling suit, and a suit of black, including a black dress coat, which is indispensable for all occasions of ceremony. The Sistine Chapel is closed to frock coats, and so is the Opera—and as for evening parties, a man might as well go in a roundabout as in any thing but a dress coat. Clothing is at least one third cheaper in Europe than it is with us, and any deficiency can be supplied with ease, without carrying a large wardrobe around with one, and paying the charges for extra luggage exacted by the continental railways.

Let us now suppose a person to have got fairly off, having read up his classics and his history, and got his luggage into a single good-sized valise,—let us suppose him to have got over the few days of seasickness, which made him wish that Europe had been submerged by the broad ocean (as Mr. Choate would say) or ever he had left his native land,—and to have passed those few pleasant days, which every one remembers in his Atlantic passage, when the ship was literally getting along "by degrees" on her course,—and to have arrived safely in some European port. The custom house officers commence the examination of the luggage, looking especially for tobacco; and if our friend is a wise man, he will not attempt to bribe the officers, as in nine cases out of ten he will increase his difficulties by so doing, and cause his effects to be examined with double care; but he will open his trunk, and, if he have any cigars, will show them to the examiner, and if he have not, he will undoubtedly be told to close it again, and will soon be on his way to his hotel. I suppose him to have selected a hotel before arriving in port—which would be done by carefully avoiding those houses which make a great show, or are highly commended in Murray's guide-books. He will find a neat, quiet European hotel a delightful place, after the gilding and red velvet of the great caravanseries of his native country. If he is going to stop more than a single night, he will ask the price of the room to which he is shown, and if it seems too expensive, will look until he finds one that suits him. When he has selected a room, and his valise has been brought up, he will probably observe that the servant (if it is evening) has lighted both of the candles on the mantel-piece. He will immediately blow one of them out and hand it to the waiter, with a look that will show him that he is dealing with an experienced traveller, who knows that he has to pay for candles as he burns them. When he leaves the hotel, he will make it a principle always to carry the unconsumed candle or candles with him, for use as occasion may require; for it is the custom of the country, and will secure him against the little impositions which are always considered fair play upon outsiders. It is possible that he will find, when he goes to wash his hands, that there is no soap in the wash stand, and will thank me for having reminded him to carry a cake with him rolled up in a bit of oiled silk. When he wishes to take lodgings in any city, he will be particular to avoid that part of the town where English people mostly do inhabit, and will be very shy of houses where apartments to let are advertised on a placard in phrases which the originator probably intended for English. He will look thoroughly before he decides, and so will save himself a great deal of dissatisfaction which he might feel on finding afterwards that others had done much better than he. Besides, "room-hunting" is not the least profitable, nor least amusing part of a traveller's experience. He will, when settled in his rooms, attend in person to the purchase of his candles and his fuel, and to the delivery of the same in his apartments; for by so doing he will save money, and will see more of the common people of the place.

Of course he will see all the "sights" that every stranger is under a sort of moral obligation to see, however much it may fatigue him; but he must not stop there. He must not think, as so many appear to, that, when he has seen the palaces, and picture galleries, and gardens, and public monuments of a country, he knows that country. He must try to see and know as much as he can of the people of the country, for they (Louis Quatorze to the contrary, notwithstanding) are the state. Let him cultivate the habit of early rising, and frequent market places and old parish churches in the twilight of the morning, and he will learn more of the people in one month than a year of reading or ordinary sight-seeing could teach him. Let him choose back alleys, instead of crowded and fashionable thoroughfares for his walks; when he falls in with a wandering musician and juggler, exhibiting in public, let him stop, not to see the exhibition, but the spectators; when he goes to the theatre, let him not shut himself up in the privacy of a box, but go into the pit, where all he will see and hear around him will be full as amusing as the performance itself; and when he uses an omnibus, let him always choose a seat by the driver, in preference to one inside. I have learnt more of the religious character of the poorer class in Paris, by a visit to a little out-of-the-way church at sunrise, than could be acquired by hours of conversation with the people themselves. And I have learned equally as much of the brutality and degradation of the same class in England, by going into a gin-shop late at night, calling for a glass of ale, and drinking it slowly, while I was inspecting the company. There is many a man who travels through Europe, communicating only with hotel keepers, couriers, and ciceroni, and learning less of the people than he could by walking into a market-place alone, and buying a sixpence worth of fruit. Yet such men presume to write books, and treat not merely of the governments of these countries, but of the social condition of the people! I once met a man in Italy, who could not order his breakfast correctly in Italian, who knew only one Italian, and he was the waiter who served him in a restaurant; and yet this man was a correspondent of a respectable paper in Boston, and had the effrontery to write column after column upon Italian social life, and to speak of political affairs as if he were Cardinal Antonelli's sole confidant. There are such people here in Paris now, who send over to America, weekly, batches of falsehood about the household of the Tuileries, which the intelligent public of America accepts as being true; for it seems to be a part of some people's republicanism to believe nothing but evil of a ruler who wears a crown. I need not say in this connection, that the traveller who wishes to enjoy Europe must put away the habit (if he be so unfortunate as to have it) of looking upon every thing through the green spectacles of republicanism, and regarding that form of government as the only one calculated to benefit mankind. He must remember that the government of his own country is a mere experiment, compared with the old monarchies of Europe, and he must try to judge impartially between them. He must judge each system by its results, and if on comparison he finds that there is really less slavery in his own country than in Europe; that the government is administered more impartially; that the judiciary is purer; that there is less of mob law and violence, and less of political bargaining and trickery, and that life and property are more secure in his own country than they are here,—why, he will return to America a better republican than before, from the very fact of having done justice to the governments of Europe.

As I have before said, it is better for a traveller to endeavour to live as nearly as possible in the manner of the inhabitants of the country in which he is sojourning. I do not mean that he should feel bound to make as general a use of garlic as some of the people of Europe do, for in some places I verily believe that a custard or a blanc mange would be thought imperfect if they were not seasoned with that savory vegetable; but, *ceteris* being *paribus,* if the general manner of living were followed, the traveller would find it conducive to health and to economy. The habits of life among every people are not founded on a mere caprice; and experience proves that under the warm sun of Italy, a light vegetable diet is healthier and more really invigorating than all the roast beef of Old England would be.

In Europe, no man is ever ashamed of economy. Few Englishmen even shrink from acknowledging that they cannot afford to do this or that, and on the continent profuseness in the use of money is considered the sure mark of a *parvenu.* Every man is free to do as he pleases; he can travel in the first, second, or third class on the railways, and not excite the surprise of any body; and whatever class he may be in, he will be treated with equal respect by all. It is well to bear this in mind, for, taken in connection with the principle of paying for one's room and meals separately according to what one has, it puts it within one's power to travel all over Europe for a ridiculously small sum. You can live in Paris, by going over into the Latin quarter, on thirty cents a day, and be treated by every body, except your own countrymen, with as much consideration as if you abode among the mirrors and gilding of the Hôtel de Louvre. Not that I would advise any one to go over there for the sake of saving money, and live on salads and meats in which it is difficult to have confidence, when he can afford to do better. I only wish to encourage those who are kept from visiting Europe by the idea that it requires a great outlay of money. You can live in Europe for just what you choose to spend, and in a style of independence to which America is a total stranger. Every body does not know here what every body else has for dinner. You may live on the same floor with a man for months and years, and not know any more of him than can be learned from a semi-occasional meeting on the staircase, and an interchange of hat civilities. This seems so common to a Frenchman, that it would be considered by him hardly worth notice; but to any one who knows what a sharp look-out neighbours keep over each other in America, it is a most pleasing phenomenon. It is indeed a delightful thing to live among people who have formed a habit of minding their own business, and at the same time have a spirit of consideration for the rights and feelings of their neighbours.

If, in the above hints concerning the way to travel pleasantly and cheaply in Europe, I have succeeded in removing any of the bugbear obstacles which hold back so many from the great advantages they might here enjoy, I shall feel that I have not tasked my poor eyes and brain for nothing. We are a long way behind Europe in many things, and it is only by frequent communication that we can make up our deficiencies. It cannot be done by boasting, nor by claiming for America all the enterprise and enlightenment of the nineteenth century. Neither can it be done by setting up the United States as superior to every historical precedent, and an exception to every rule. Most men (as the old French writer says) are mortal; and we Americans shall find that our country, with all its prosperity and unequalled progress, is subject to the same vicissitudes as the countries we now think we can afford to despise; and that our history is

"—— but the same rehearsal of the past—
First Freedom, and then Glory; when that fails,
Wealth, vice, corruption,—barbarism at last."

No, we cannot safely scorn the lesson which Europe teaches us; for if we do, we shall have to learn it at the expense of much adversity and wounding of our pride. Every American who comes abroad, if he knows how to travel, ought to carry home with him a new idea of the amenities of life, and of moderation in the pursuit and the use of wealth, such as will make itself felt in the course of time, and make the fast living and recklessness of authority and tendency to bankruptcy of the present day, give way to a spirit of moderation and obedience to law such as always produces private prosperity and public stability.

PARIS TO BOULOGNE

IT was a delicious morning when I packed my trunk to leave Paris. Indeed it was so bright and cloudless that it seemed wrong to go away and leave so fine a combination of perfections. It was more than the "bridal of the earth and sky"; it was the bridal of all the created beings around one and their works with the sky. The deep blue of the heavens, the glittering sunbeams, the clean streets, the fair house fronts, the gay shop windows, the white caps, and shining morning faces of the *bonnes* and market women, the busy, prosperous look of the passers by, were all blended together in one harmonious whole, more touching and poetical than any scene of mere natural beauty that the dewy morn, "with breath all incense and with cheek all bloom," ever looked upon. "Earth hath not any thing to show more fair." Others may delight in communing with solitary nature, and may rave in rhyme about the glories of woods, lakes, mountains, and Ausonian skies; but what is all that compared to the awakening of a great city to the life of day? What are the floods of golden light that every morning bathe the mountain tops, and are poured down into the valleys and fields below, compared to the playing of the sunbeams in the smoke from ten thousand chimneys, and the din of toil displacing the silence of night? I have seen the sunsets of the Archipelago—I have seen Lesbos

and Egina clad in those robes of purple and gold,
which till then I had thought were a mere figment of
the painter's brain—I have enjoyed that "hush of
world's expectation as day died"—I have often
drunk in the glory of a cloudless sunrise on the Atlantic, and even now my heart leaps up at the remembrance of it; but after all, commend me to the deeper
and more sympathetic feelings inspired by the dingy
walls and ungraceful chimney-pots of a metropolis.
Thousands of human hearts are there, throbbing
with hope, or joy, or sorrow,—weighed down perchance by guilt; and humanity with all its imperfec-
tions is a noble thing. A single human heart, though
erring, is a grander creation than the Alps or the
Andes, for it shall outlive them. It is moved by aspi-
rations that outrun the universe, and possesses a
destiny that shall outlive the stars. It is the better
side of human nature that we see in the early morning in large cities. Vice flourishes best under the
glare of gas-lights, and does not salute the rising sun.
The bloated form, the sunken eye, the painted cheek,
shrink from that which would make their deformity
more hideous, and hide themselves in places which
their presence makes almost pestilential. Honest,
healthful labour meets us at every step, and imparts
to us something of its own hopefulness and activity.
We miss the dew-drops glittering like jewels in the
grass, but the loss is more than made up to us by the
bright eyes of happy children, helping their parents
in their work, or sporting together on their way to
school.

There was a time when I thought it very poetical
to roam the broad fields in that still hour when the

golden light seems to clasp every object that it meets, as if it loved it; but of late years a comfortable sidewalk has been more suggestive of poetry and less productive of wet feet. Give me a level pavement before all your groves and fields. The only *rus* that wears well in the long run is *Russ in urbe*. Nine tenths of all the fine things in our literature concerning the charms of country life, have been written, not beneath the shade of overarching boughs, but within the crowded city's smoke-stained walls. Depend upon it, Shakespeare could never have written about the moonlight sleeping on the bank any where but in the city; had the realities of country life been present to him, he would have rejected any such metaphor, for he loved the moonlight too dearly to subject it to the rheumatic attack that would inevitably have followed such a nap as that. It is with country life very much as it is with life at sea. Mr. Choate, who pours out his noblest eloquence on the glories and romance of the sea, seldom sees the outside of his state-room while he is out of sight of land, and all his glowing periods are forgotten in the realities of his position. So, too, the man who wishes to destroy the poetry and romance of country life, has only to walk about in the wet grass or the scorching heat, or to be obliged to pick the pebbles out of his shoes, or a caterpillar off his neck, or to be mocked at by unruly cattle, or pestered by any of the myriads of insect and reptiles which abound in every well-regulated country.

The excellent Madame Busque (*la dame aux pumpkin pies*) had prepared for me a viaticum in the shape of a small loaf of as good gingerbread as

was ever made west of Cape Cod—a motherly attention quite in keeping with her ordinary way of taking
care of her customers. All who frequent the *crêmerie* are her *enfans,* and if she does not show them
every little maternal attention, and tie a bib upon
every one's neck, it is only that we may know better
how to behave when we are beyond the reach of her
kindly hand. Fortified with the gingerbread, I found
myself whirling out of the terminus of the Northern
Railway, and Paris, with its far-stretching fortifications, its domes and towers, and its windmill-crowned
Montmartre, was soon out of sight.

The train was very full, and the weather very
warm. Two of my car-companions afforded me a
good deal of amusement. They were a fat German
and his wife. He was one of the jolliest old gentlemen I ever had the good fortune to travel with. His
silvery hair was cropped close to his head, and he
rode along with his cuffs turned up and his waistcoat
open. He seemed to feel that he was occupying a
good deal of room; but he was the only one there
who felt it. No one of us would have had his circum-
ference reduced an inch, but we should all of us have
delighted to put a thin man who was there out by the
roadside. His wife—a bright-eyed little woman,
whose hair was just getting a little silvery—had a
small box-cage in which she carried a large, intelli-
gent-looking parrot. Before we had gone very far,
the bird began to carry on an animated conversation
with its mistress, but finally disgusted her and surprised us all by swearing in French and German at
the whole company, with all the vehemence of a regiment of troopers. The lady tried hard to stop him,

but it was useless. The old gentleman (like a great many good people who would not swear themselves, but rather like to hear a good round oath occasionally) seemed to enjoy it intensely, and laughed till the tears rolled down his cheeks. At noon the worthy pair made solemn preparations for a dinner. A basket, a carpet-bag, and sundry paper parcels were brought out. The lady spread a large checked handkerchief over their laps for a table cloth, and then produced a staff of life about two feet in length, and cut off a good thick slice for each of them. Cheese was added to it, and also a species of sausage about a foot in length, and three inches in diameter. From these they made a comfortable meal—not eating by stealth, as we Americans should have done—but diving in heartily, and chatting together all the while as cosily as if they had been at home. A bottle of wine was then brought out from the magic carpet-bag, and a glass, also a nice dessert of peaches and grapes. There was a charming at-home-ativeness about the whole proceeding that contrasted strongly with our American way of doing such things, and all the other passengers apparently took no notice of it.

We arrived at Boulogne in the midst of a storm as severe as the morning had been serene. So fair and foul a day I have not seen. An omnibus whisked me to a hotel in what my venerable grandmother used to call a *jiffy*, and I was at once independent of the weather's caprices. A comfortable dinner at the *table d'hôte* repaired the damages of the journey, and I spent the evening with some good friends, whose company was made the more delightful by the months that had separated us. The storm raged without, and we chatted within. The old hotel creaked and sighed as the blast assailed it, and I dreamed all night of close-reefed topsails.

> "'Tis a wild night out of doors;
> The wind is mad upon the moors,
> And comes into the rocking town,
> Stabbing all things up and down:
> And then there is a weeping rain
> Huddling 'gainst the window pane;
> And good men bless themselves in bed;
> The mother brings her infant's head
> Closer with a'joy like tears,
> And thinks of angels in her prayers,
> Then sleeps with his small hand in hers."

Having in former years merely passed through Boulogne, I had never known before what a pleasant old city it is. Its clean streets and well-built houses, and the air of respectable antiquity which pervades it, make a very pleasant impression upon the mind. As you stand on the quay, and look across at the white cliffs on the other side of the Channel, which are distinctly visible on a clear day, the differences in the character of the two nations so slightly separated from one another, strike you more forcibly than ever. The very fish taken on the French side of the channel are different from any that you see in England; and as to the fishwomen, whose sunburnt legs, bare to the knee, are the astonishment of all new-comers,—go over all Europe, and you will find nothing like them. That superb cathedral, the shrine of our Lady of Boulogne, upon which the storm of the first French revolution beat with such fury, is now beginning to wear a look of completion. Its dome, one of the

loftiest and most graceful in the world, is a striking
and beautiful feature in the view of the city. For
more than twelve centuries this has been a famous
shrine. Kings and princes have visited it, not with
the pomp and circumstance of royalty, but in the
humble garb of the pilgrim. Henry VIII. made a
pilgrimage hither in his unenlightened days, before
the pious Cranmer had taught him how wicked it was
to honour the Mother whom his Saviour honoured,
and how godly and just it was to divorce and put to
death the mothers of his children. Here it was that
the heroic crusader, Godfrey, kindled the flame of
that devotion which nerved his arm against the foes
of Christianity, and added a new lustre to his
knightly fame. It is a fashion of the present day to
sneer at the age of chivalry and the crusades, and
some of our best writers have been enticed into the
following of it. While we have so many subjects
deserving the treatment of the satirist, at our very
doors,—while we have the fashionable world to
draw upon,—while we can look around on political
parsons, professional philanthropists and patriots,
politicians who talk of principle, and followers who
are weak enough to believe in them—it would really
seem as if we might allow the crusaders and trou-
badours to rest. Supposing, for the sake of argu-
ment, Christianity to be a true religion,—supposing
it to be a fact that eighteen hundred years ago the
plains of Palestine were trodden by the blessed feet
that were "nailed for our advantage on the bitter
cross"—the redemption of the land which had been
the scene of the sacred history, from the sacrilegious
hands of the Saracens, was certainly an enterprise

creditable to St. Louis, and Richard the lion-hearted, and Godfrey, and the other gentlemen who sacrificed so much in it. It was certainly as respectable an undertaking as any of the crusades of modern times,—as that of the Spaniards in America, the English in India, or the United States in Mexico,—with this exception, that it was not so profitable. I am afraid that some of our modern satirists are lacking in the spirit of their profession, and allow themselves to be made the mouthpieces of that worldly wisdom which it is their office to rebuke. I can see nothing to sneer at in the crusader exiling himself from his native land, and forfeiting his life in the defence of the Holy Sepulchre; indeed, I am inclined to respect a man who makes such a sacrifice to a conscientious conviction: it is a noble conquest of the visible temporal by the unseen eternal. I can well understand how such efforts for the protection of a mere empty tomb would seem worthy of laughter and ridicule to those who can find no food for satire in the *auri sacra fames* which has been the motive of modern foreign expeditions. It would be well for the world could we bring back something of that age of chivalry which Edmund Burke regretted so eloquently. We need it sorely; for we are every day sliding farther down from its high standard of honour and of unselfish devotion to principle.

There is a little fishing village about a mile and a half from Boulogne, on the sea coast towards Calais, which is celebrated in history as having been the scene of the landing of Prince Louis Napoleon and his companions in their unsuccessful attempt to overthrow the government of Louis Philippe. Napoleon

III. has not distinguished the spot by any memorial; but he has erected a colossal statue of Napoleon I. on the spot where that insatiable conqueror, with his mighty army around him, looked longingly at the coast of England. There is something of a contrast between the day thus commemorated and that on which the "nephew of his uncle" received Queen Victoria at Boulogne, when she visited France. It must have been a great satisfaction to Louis Napoleon, after his life of exile, and particularly after the studied neglect which he experienced from the English nobility, to have welcomed the British Queen to his realm with that kiss which is the token of equality among sovereigns. Waterloo must have been blotted out when he saw the Queen—in whose realm he had served the cause of good order in the rank of special constable—bending down at his knee to confer upon him the order of the garter.

In spite of its geographical situation, Boulogne can hardly be considered a French town. The police department and the custom house are in the hands of the French, to be sure; but in the course of a walk through its streets, you hear much more of the English than of the French language. You meet those brown shooting jackets, and checked trousers, and thick shoes and gaiters that are at home every where in the "inviolate island of the sage and free." You cannot turn a corner without coming upon some of those beefy and beery countenances which symbolize so perfectly the genius of British civilization, and hearing the letter H exasperated to a wonderful degree. Every where you see bevies of young ladies wearing those peculiar brown straw hats, edged with black lace, with a brown feather put in horizontally on one side of the crown, a style of head dress to which the French and Italians have given the name of *"Ingleesh spoken here."* There is a large class among the English population of Boulogne upon which the disinterested spectator will look with interest and with pity. I mean those unfortunate persons who have been obliged by "force of circumstances" and the importunity of creditors to exile themselves for a time from their native land. You see them on every side; and all ranks in society are represented among them, from the distinguished-looking man, with the tortoise-shell spectacles, who ran through his wife's property at the club, to the pale, unhappy-looking fellow in the loose thread gloves and sleepless coat. You can distinguish them at a glance from their fellow-countrymen who have gone over for purposes of recreation, the poor devils walk about with such an evident wish to appear to be doing something or going somewhere. The condition of the prisoners, or rather the "collegians," in the old Marshalsea prison, must have been an enviable one, compared to these unfortunates, condemned to gaze at the cliffs of Old England from a distance, and wait vainly for something to turn up.

The arrival and departure of the English steamers is the only source of excitement that the quiet city of Boulogne possesses. I was astonished to find, after being there a day or two, what an interest I took in those occurrences. I found myself on the quay with the rest of the foreign population of the town, an hour before the departure of the boat, to make sure, like every body else there, that not a traveller for England should escape my notice. Besides the pleasure of inspecting the motley crowd of spectators, I was gratified one day to see the big, manly form and good-natured ugly face of Thackeray, following a leathern portmanteau on its path from the omnibus to the boat. The great satirist took an observation of the crowd through his spectacles as if he were making a mental note, to be overhauled in due season, and then hurried on board, as if he longed to get back to London among his books. He had been spending the warm season at the baths of Hombourg. But the great excitement of the day is the arrival of the afternoon boat from Folkestone. It is better as an amusement than many plays that I have seen, and it has this advantage, (an indispensable one to a large part of the English population of Boulogne,) that it costs nothing. During the days when I was there, the equinoctial gale was in full blow, and, of course, there was a greater rush than usual to the quay. It was necessary to go very early to secure a good place. From the steamer to the passport office, a distance of two or three hundred feet, ropes were stretched to keep back the spectators, forming an avenue some thirty feet wide. Through this the wretched victims of the "chop sea" of the Channel were obliged to pass, and listen to the remarks or laughter which their pitiable condition excited among the crowd of their disinterested countrymen. Any person who has ever been seasick can imagine what it would be to go on shore from a boat that has just been pitching and rolling about in the most absurd manner, and try to walk like a Christian, with the eyes of several hundred amusement-

[189]

seeking people fixed upon him. Sympathy is entirely out of the question. The pallid countenance and uncertain step, as if the walker were waiting for the pavement to rise to meet his foot, excite nothing but mirth in the spectators. The whole scene, including the lookers-on, was one of the funniest things I ever saw. The observations of the crowd, too, were well calculated to heighten the effect. "Ease her when she pitches," cried out a youngster at my side, as an old lady, who was supported by a gentleman and a maid servant, seemed to be trying to accommodate herself to the motion of the street, and testify her love for *terra firma* by lying down. "Hard a' starboard," shouted another, as a gentleman, with a felt hat close reefed to his head with a white handkerchief, sidled along up the leeward side of the passage way. "That 'ere must 'a been a sewere case of sickness," said a little old man, in an advanced state of seediness, as a tall man, looking defiance at the crowd, walked ashore with a carpet-bag in his hand, and an expression on his face very like that of Mr. Warren, in the farce, when he says, "Shall I slay him at once, or shall I wait till the cool of the evening?" "Don't go yet, Mary," said a young gentleman in a jacket and precocious hat, to his sister, who seemed to fear that it was about to begin to rain again,— "don't go yet; the best of all is to come; there 's a fat lady on board who has been *so* sick—we must wait to see her!" And so they went on, carrying out in the most exemplary manner that golden rule which, applied to the period of seasickness, enjoins upon us that we shall do unto others just as others would do to us.

PARIS TO BOULOGNE

It is no joke to most people to cross the Channel at any time, but to cross it on the tail-end of the equinoctial storm is far from being a humorous matter. I had crossed from almost all the ports between Havre and Rotterdam in former years; so I resolved to try a new route in spite of the weather, and booked myself for a passage in the boat from Boulogne to London, direct. The steamer was called the Seine; and when we had once got into the open sea, a large part of the passengers seemed to think that they were *insane* to have come in her. She was a very good sea-boat, but I could not help contrasting her with our Sound and Hudson River steamers at home. If the "General Steam Navigation Company" were to import a steamer from America like the Metropolis or the Isaac Newton, there would be a revolution in the travelling world of England. The people here would no longer put up with steamers without an awning or any shelter from sun or rain. After they had enjoyed the accommodations of one of our great floating hotels, they would not think of shutting themselves up in the miserable cabins which people pay so dearly for here. But to proceed: when we got fairly out upon the *n*asty deep, I ventured to gratify my curiosity, as a connoisseur in seasickness, by a visit to the cabin. If I were in the habit of writing for the newspapers, I suppose I should say that the scene "baffled description." It certainly was one that I shall not soon forget. The most rabid republican would have been satisfied with the equality that prevailed there. The squalls that assailed us on deck were nothing compared to the demonstrations of a whole regiment of infantry below, who were illustrating, in a manner worthy of Retsch, one of the first lines in Shakespeare's Seven Ages. Ladies of all ages were keeled up on every side in various postures of picturesque negligence, and with a forgetfulness of the conventionalities of society quite charming to look upon. The floor, where it was unoccupied by prostrate humanity, was nearly covered with hatboxes, and bonnets, and bowls, and anonymous articles of crockery ware, which were performing a lively quadrille, being assisted therein by the motion of the ship. But a little of such sights, and sounds, and smells as these goes a great way with me, and I was glad to return to the wet deck. They had managed to rig a tarpaulin between the paddle-boxes, and there I took refuge until the rain ceased. It was comparatively pleasant weather when we sailed past Walmer Castle, where that old hero died on whom all the world has conferred the title of "The Duke"; and of course there was no rough sea as soon as we got into the Downs. Black-eyed Susan might have gone on board of any of the fleet of vessels that were lying there without discolouring her ribbons by a single dash of spray. Ramsgate and Margate (the Newport and Cape May of England) looked full of company as we sailed by them, and crowds of bathers were battling with the surf. The heavy black yards of the ships of war loomed up at Sheerness in the distance, and suggested thoughts of Nelson, and Dibdin, and Ben Bowlin. Now and then we passed by some splendid American clipper ship towing up or down the river, and I felt proud of my nationality as I contrasted her graceful lines and majestic proportions with the tub-like models of British origin that

every where met my eye. The dock-yards of Woolwich seemed like a vast ant-hill for numbers and
busy life. Greenwich, with its fine architecture and
fresh foliage in the distance, was most grateful to
my eyes; and it was pleasing to reflect, as I passed the
observatory, that I could begin to reckon my longi-
tude to the westward, for it made me feel nearer
home.

LONDON

NO man can really appreciate the grandeur of
London until he has approached it from the
sea. The sail up the river from Gravesend to London Bridge is a succession of wonders, each one
more overwhelming than that which preceded it.
There is no display of fortifications; but here and
there you see some storm-tossed old hulk, which, having finished its active career, has been safely anchored
in that repose which powder magazines always enjoy. As the river grows narrower, the number of
ships, steamers, coal barges, wherries, and boats of
every description, seems to increase; and as you sail
on, the grand panorama of the world-wide commerce of this great metropolis unfolds before you,
and you are lost, not so much in admiration as in
astonishment. Woolwich, Greenwich, Rotherhithe,
Bermondsey, Blackwall, Millwall, Wapping, &c.,
follow rapidly in the vision, like the phantom kings
before the eyes of the unfortunate Scotch usurper,
until one is tempted to inquire with him, whether the
"line will stretch out to the crack of doom." The
buildings grow thicker and more unsightly as you
advance; the black sides of the enormous warehouses
seem to be bulging out over the edge of the wharves
on which they stand; far off, beyond the reach of the
tides, you see the forests of masts that indicate the
site of the docks. The bright green water of the

Channel has been exchanged for the filthy, drain-like
current of the Thames. Hundreds of monstrous
chimneys belch forth the smoke that constitutes the
legitimate atmosphere of London. Every thing
seems to be dressed in the deepest mourning for the
cruel fate of nature, and you look at the distant hills
and bright lawns, over in the direction of Sydenham,
with very much of the feeling that Dives must have
had, when he gazed on the happiness of Lazarus
from his place of torment. Every thing presents a
most striking contrast to the clean, fair cities of the
continent. Paris, with its cream-coloured palaces
adorning the banks of the Seine, seems more beautiful than ever as you recall it while surrounded by
such sights, and sounds, and smells, as offend your
senses here. The winding Arno, and the towers, and
domes, and bridges, of Florence and Pisa, seem to
belong to a celestial vision rather than to an earthly
reality, as you contrast them with the monuments of
England's commercial greatness. At last, you come
in sight of London Bridge, with its never-ceasing
current of vehicles and human beings crossing it; and
your amazement is crowned by realizing that, notwithstanding the wonders you have seen, you have
just reached the edge of the city, and that you can
ride for miles and miles through a closely-built laby-
rinth of bricks and mortar, hidden under the veil of
smoke before you.

And what a change it is—from Paris to London!
To a Frenchman it must be productive of a suicidal
feeling. The scene has shifted from the sunny
Boulevards to the blackened bricks and mortar,
which neither great Neptune's ocean, nor Lord Pal-

merston's anti-smoke enactment can wash clean. In
the place of the smiling, good-humoured Frenchman,
you have the serious, stately Englishman. One
misses the winning courtesy of which a Frenchman's
hat is the instrument, and the ready *pardon* or *merci*
is heard no more. The beggary, the drunkenness,
and the depravity, so apparent on every side, appall
one. Paris *may* be the most immoral city in the
world; but there, vice must be sought for in its own
haunts. Here in London, it prowls up and down in
the streets, seeking for its victims. Put all the other
European capitals together, and I do not believe that
you could meet with so much to pain and disgust you
as you would in one hour in the streets of London.
And yet, with all this staring people in the face here,
how do they go to work to remedy it? They pass
laws enforcing the suspension of business on Sundays, and when they succeed in keeping all the shutters closed, by fear of the law, they fold their arms,
and say, "See what a godly nation is this!" If this
is not "making clean the outside of the cup and plat-
ter," what is it? For my part, I much prefer that
perfect religious liberty which allows each man to
keep Sunday as he pleases; and the recent improvement in the observance of the day in France is all the
more gratifying, because it does not spring from any
compulsory motive. Let the Jews keep the *Sabbath*
as they are commanded to in the Old Testament; but
Sunday is the Christian's day, and Sunday is a day of
festivity and rejoicing, and not of fasting and peni-
tential sadness.

Despite the smoke, and the lack of continental
courtesy which is felt on arriving from France, de-

spite the din and hurry, I cannot help loving London. The very names of the streets have been made classical by writers whose works are a part of our own intellectual being. The illustrious and venerable names of Barclay and Perkins, of Truman, Hanbury, and Buxton, that meet our eyes at every corner, are the synonymes of English hospitality and cheer. It is a pleasure, too, to hear one's native language spoken on all sides, after so many months of French twang. The hissing and sputtering English seems under such circumstances to be more musical than the most elegant phrases of the Tuscan in the mouth of a dignified Roman. Even the omnibus conductors' talk about the "Habbey," the "Benk," 'Igh 'Olborn, &c., does not offend the ear, so delightful does it seem to be able to say beefsteak instead of *biftek*. The odour of brown stout that prevails every where is as fragrant as the first sniff of the land breeze after a long voyage. Temple Bar is eloquent of the genius of Hogarth, whose deathless drawings first made its ugly form familiar to your youthful eyes in other lands. The very stones of Fleet Street prate of Dr. Johnson and Goldsmith. You walk into Bolt Court, and if you feel as I do the associations of the place, you eat a chop in the tavern that stands where stood the house of Dr. Johnson. Then you cross over the way to Inner Temple Lane, and mourn over the march of improvement when you see that its sacrilegious hand is sweeping away a row of four brick houses, which, dilapidated and unsightly as they may appear, are dear to every lover of English literature. In No. 1, formerly dwelt Dr. Johnson; in No. 4, Charles Lamb. You walk into the Temple

Church, and muse over the effigies of the knights who repose there in marble or bronze, or go into the quiet Temple Gardens, and meditate on the wars of the red and white roses that were plucked there centuries ago, before the iron fences were built. It would be as difficult to pluck any roses there now as the most zealous member of the Peace Society could wish. You climb up Ludgate Hill, getting finely spattered by the cabs and omnibuses, and find yourself at St. Paul's. You smile when you think that that black pile of architecture, with its twopenny fee of admission, was intended to rival St. Peter's, and your smile becomes audible when you enter it, and see that while the images of the Saviour and the Saints may not be "had and retained," the statues of admirals and generals are considered perfectly in place there. You walk out with the conviction that consistency is a jewel, and tread a pavement that is classical to every lover of books. Paternoster Row receives you, and you slowly saunter through it. Nobody walks rapidly through Paternoster Row. Situated midway between the bustle and turmoil of Ludgate Hill and Cheapside, it is a kind of resting-place for pedestrians. They breathe the more quiet air of bookland there, and the windows are a temptation which few loiterers can withstand.

The old church of St. Mary le Bow reminds you that you are at the very centre of Cockneydom, as you walk on towards the Bank and the Exchange. Crossing the street at the risk of your life through a maze of snorting horses and rattling wheels, you get into Cornhill. Here the faces that you see are a proof that the anxious, money-getting look is not confined to the worshippers of the almighty dollar. You push on until you reach Eastcheap. How great is your disappointment! The very name has called up all your recollections of the wild young prince and his fat friend—but nothing that you see there serves to heighten your Shakespearean enthusiasm. Coal-heavers and draymen make the air vocal with their oaths and 'slang, which once resounded with the laughter of Jack Falstaff and his jolly companions. No Mistress Quickly stands in the doorway of any of the numerous taverns. The whole scene is a great falling-off from what you had imagined of East-cheap. The sanded floors, the snowy window cur-tains, the bright pewter pots, have given way to dirt and general frowsiness. You read on a card in a window that within you can obtain "a go of brandy for sixpence, and a go of gin for fourpence," and that settles all your Falstaffian associations. You stop to look at an old brick house which is being pulled down, for you think that perhaps its heavy timbered ceilings, and low windows, and Guy Fawkesy entries date back to Shakespeare's times; but you are too much incommoded by the dust from its crumbling walls to stop long, and you leave the place carrying with you the only reminder of Falstaff you have seen there—you leave with *lime in your sack!*

I know of nothing better calculated to take down a man's self-esteem than a walk through the streets of London. To a man who has always lived in a small town, where every second person he meets is an acquaintance, a walk from Hyde Park corner to London Bridge must be a crusher. If that does not

convince him that he is really of very little importance in the world, he is past cure. The whirl of
vehicles, the throngs upon the sidewalks, seem to
overwhelm and blot out our own individuality.
Xerxes cried when he gazed upon his assembled
forces, and reflected that out of all that vast multitude not one person would be alive in a hundred
years. Xerxes ought to have ridden through Oxford
Street or the Strand on the top of an omnibus.
Spitalfields and Bandanna (two places concerning
the geography of which I am rather in the dark)
could not have furnished him with handkerchiefs to
dry his eyes.

I was never so struck with the lack of architectural beauty in London as I have been during this
visit. There are, it is true, a few fine buildings—
Westminster Abbey, St. Paul's, Somerset House,
&c.; but they are all as black as my hat, with this
soot in which all London is clothed; so there is really
very little beauty about them. The new Houses of
Parliament are a fine pile of buildings, certainly, and
the lately finished towers are a pleasing feature in
the view from the bridges; but they are altogether
too gingerbready to wear well. They lack boldness
of light and shade; and this lack is making itself
more apparent every day as the smoke of the city is
enveloping them in its everlasting shade. Buckingham Palace looks like a second rate American hotel,
and as to St. James, the barracks at West Point are
far more palatial than that. It is not architecture,
however, that we look for in London. It has a
charm in spite of all its deformities,—in spite of its
climate, which is such an encouragement to the um-

brella makers—in spite of its smoky atmosphere, through which the sun looks like a great copper ball —in spite of its mud, which the water-carts insure when the dark skies fail in the discharge of their daily dues to the metropolis. London, with all thy fogs, I love thee still! It is this great agglomeration of towns which we, call London—this great human family of more than two millions and a half of beings that awakens our sympathy. It is the fact that through England we Americans trace our relationship to the ages that are past. It is the fact that we are here surrounded by the honoured tombs of heroes and wise men, whose very names have become, as it were, a part of our own being. These are the things that bind us to London, and which make the aureola of light that hangs over it at night time seem a crown of glory.

But we must not forget that there is a dark side to the picture. There is a serious drawback to all our enthusiasm. Poverty and vice beset us at every step. Beggary more abject than all the world besides can show appeals to us at every crossing. The pale hollow cheek and sunken eye tell such a story of want as no language can express. The mother, standing in a doorway with her two hungry-looking children, and imploring the passers-by to purchase some of the netting work her hands have executed, is a sight that touches your heart. But walk into some of those lanes and alleys which abound almost under the shadow of the Houses of Parliament and the royal residence,—slums "whose atmosphere is typhus, and whose ventilation is cholera,"—and the sentiment of pity is lost in one of fear. There you see on every side that despair and recklessness which spring from want and neglect. Walk through Regent Street, and the Haymarket, and the Strand in the evening, and you shall be astonished at the gay dresses and painted cheeks that surround you. The rummy atmosphere reëchoes with profanity from female lips. From time to time you are obliged to shake off the vice and crinoline that seek to be companions of your walk.

There is a distinguished prize-fighter here—one Benjamin Caunt. He keeps a gin shop in St. Martin's Lane, and rejoices in a profitable business and the title of the "Champion of England." He transacted a little business in the prize-fighting line over on the Surrey side of the river a few days ago, and is to sustain the honour of England against another antagonist to-morrow. During the entire week his gin shop has been surrounded by admiring crowds, anxious to catch a glimpse of the hero. And such crowds! It would be wronging the lowest of the race of quadrupeds to call those people beastly and brutal wretches. Most Americans think that the Bowery and Five Points can rival almost any thing in the world for displays of all that is disgusting in society; but London leaves us far behind. I stopped several times to note the character of Mr. Caunt's constituents. There were men there with flashy cravats around necks that reminded me of Mr. Buckminster's Devon cattle—their hair cropped close for obvious reasons—moving about among the crowd, filling the air with damns and brandy fumes. There were others in a more advanced stage of "fancy" existence —men with all the humanity blotted out of them, not a spark of intellect left in their beery countenances.

There were women drabbled with dirt, soggy with liquor, with eyes artificially black. There were children pale and stunted from the use of gin, or bloated with beer, assuming the swagger of the blackguards around them, and looking as old and depraved as any of them. It seemed as if hell were empty and all the devils were there. The police—those guardians of the public weal, who are so efficient when a poor woman is trying to earn her bread by selling a few apples—so prompt to make the well-intentioned "move on"—did not appear to interfere. They evidently considered the street to be blockaded for a just cause, and looked as if, in aiding people to get a look at the Champion of England, they were sustaining the honour of England herself.

And this is the same England that assumes to teach other nations the science of benevolence. This is the same England that laments over the tyranny of continental governments, and boasts of how many millions of Bibles it has sent to people who could not read them if they would, and would not if they could. This is the same England that turns up the whites of its eyes at American slavery, and wishes to teach the King of Naples how to govern. Why, you can spend months in going about the worst quarters of the continental cities, and not see so much of vice and poverty as you can in the great thoroughfares of London in a single day. There is vice enough in every large city, as we all know; but in most of them it has to be sought for by its votaries— in London it goes about seeking whom it may devour. The press of England may try to advance the interests of a prime minister anxious to get possession of

Sicily by slandering Ferdinand of Naples; but every body knows, who has visited that fair kingdom, that there are few monarchs more public spirited and popular with all classes of their subjects than he. Every body knows that there is no class in that community corresponding to the prize-fighting class in London—that the horrors of the mining districts are unknown there, and that an English workhouse would make even an Englishman blush when compared with those magnificent institutions that relieve the poor of Italy. I had rather be sold at auction in Alabama any day than to take my chance as a denizen of the slums of London, or as a worker in the coal mines. I have no patience with this telescopic philanthropy of the English, while there are abuses all around them so much greater than those that disgrace any other civilized country. What can be more disgusting than this pharisaical cant—this thanking God that they are not as others are—extortioners and slaveholders—when you look at the real condition of things? Englishmen always boast that their country has escaped the revolutionary storm which has so many times swept over Europe during this century, and would try to persuade people that there is little or no discontent here. The fact is, the lower classes in this country have been so ground down by the money power and the force of the government, and are so ignorant and vicious, that they cannot be organized into a revolutionary force. Walk through Whitechapel, and observe the people there—contrast them with the *blouses* in the Faubourg St. Antoine—and you will acknowledge the truth of this. The people in the manufacturing districts in France are, indeed, far from being models of morality or of intellectual culture; but they have retained enough of the powers of humanity to make them very dangerous, when collected under the leadership of demagogues of the school of Ledru Rollin. But the farming districts of France have remained comparatively free from the infection of socialism and infidelity. The late Henry Colman, in his agricultural tour, found villages where almost the entire population went to mass every morning, before commencing the labour of the day. But the degradation of the labouring classes of England is not confined to the manufacturing towns; the peasantry is in a most demoralized condition: the Chartist leaders found nearly as great a proportion of adherents among the farm labourers as among the distressed operatives of Birmingham and Sheffield; and Mormonism counts its victims among both of those neglected classes by thousands. It is, perhaps, all very well for ambitious orators to make the House of Commons or Exeter Hall resound with their denunciations of French usurpations, Austrian tyranny, Neapolitan dungeons, Russian serfdom, and American slavery; but thinking men, when they note these enthusiastic demonstrations of philanthropy, cannot help thinking of England's workhouses, the brutalized workers in her coal mines and factories, and her oppressive and cruel rule in Ireland and in India; and it strikes them as strange that a country, whose eyesight is obstructed by a beam of such extraordinary magnitude, should be so exceedingly solicitous about the motes that dance in the vision of its neighbours.

ESSAYS

STREET LIFE

THOMAS CARLYLE introduces his philosophical friend, Herr Teufelsdröckh, to his readers, seated in his watch-tower, which overlooks the city in which he dwells; and from which he can look down into that bee-hive of human kind, and see every thing "from the palace esplanade where music plays, while His Serene Highness is pleased to eat his victuals, down to the low lane where in her doorsill the aged widow, knitting for a thin livelihood, sits to feel the afternoon sun." He draws an animated picture of that busy panorama which is ever unrolling before Teufelsdröckh's eyes, and moralizes upon the scene in the spirit of a true poet who has struck upon a theme worthy of his lyre. And, most assuredly, Thomas is right. The daisies and buttercups are all very well in their way; but, as raw material for poetry, what are they to the deep-furrowed pavement and the blackened chimney-pots of a city! In spite of all our pantheistic rhapsodies, man is the noblest of natural productions, and the worthiest subject for the highest and holiest of poetic raptures. My old friend, the late Mr. Wordsworth, delighted to anathematize the railway companies, and raved finely about Nature never betraying the heart that loves her: he said that

"—— the sounding cataract
Haunted him like a passion: the tall rock,

[209]

> The mountain and the deep and gloomy wood,
> Their colours and their forms, were then to him
> An appetite;—"

and confessed that to him

> "—— the meanest flower that blows could give
> Thoughts that too often lie too deep for tears."

Yet notwithstanding all this, he was constrained to acknowledge when he stood upon Westminster Bridge, and saw the vast, dingy metropolis of Britain wearing like a garment the beauty of the morning, that

> "Earth has not anything to show more fair,—
> Dull would he be of soul who could pass by
> A sight so touching in its majesty."

When I was a young man, it was my delight to brush with early steps the dew away, and meet the sun upon the upland lawn. There was a romantic feeling about it that I liked, and I did not object to wet feet. But I have long since put away that depraved taste, although the recent application of India rubber to shoeing purposes has obviated the inconvenience of its gratification. Now, I am contented if I can find a level pavement and a clean crossing, and will gladly give up the woods and verdant fields to less prosaic and more youthful people. Your gout is a sad interferer with early poetical prejudices—but in my own case it has shown me that all such things, like most of our youthful notions, are mere fallacies. It has convinced me that the poetical abounds rather in the smoky, narrow streets of cities, than in the green lanes, the breezy hills, and the broad fields of the country. Like the toad, ugly and venomous, that fell disease is not without its jewel. It has reconciled me to life in town, and has shown me all its advantages and beauties.

If it be true that "the proper study of mankind is man," then are the crowded streets of the city more improving and elevating to us (if rightly meditated upon) than the academic groves. If you desire society,—in a city you may find it to your taste, however fastidious you may be. If you are a lover of solitude, where can you be more solitary than in the very whirl of a multitude of people intent upon their own pursuits, and all unknown to you! That honey-tongued doctor, St. Bernard, said that he was never less alone than when alone—a sentiment which, in its reversed form, might be uttered by any denizen of a metropolis. I always loved solitude: the old monastic inscription was always a favourite motto of mine:—

"O beata solitudo!
O sola beatitudo!"

But I have never found any solitude like the streets of a large city. I have walked in the cool, quiet cloister of *Santa Maria degli Angeli*, built amid the ruins of the baths of Diocletian, and—though my footfall was the only sound save the rustling of the foliage, and the song of the birds, and the bubbling of a fountain which seemed tired with its centuries of service, and which seemed to make the stillness and repose of that spacious quadrangle more profound— I could not feel so perfectly alone there as I have often felt in the thronged Boulevards or the busy

Strand. Place a mere worldling in those holy precincts, and he would summon mentally around him
the companions of his past pleasures, and his worldliness would be increased by his thus being driven to
his only resources for overcoming the ungrateful
quiet of the place. Introduce a religious man to
those consecrated shades, and his devotion would be
quickened; he would soon forget the world which he
had not loved and which had not loved him, and his
face would soon be as unwrinkled, his eye as serene,
as those of the monks who dwell there. But place
either of them in the most crowded thoroughfare of
the city, and the worldling would be made for a time
as meditative as the other. When I was a child, I
delighted to watch the busy inhabitants of an ant-
hill, pursuing their various enterprises with an in-
tentness almost human; and I should be tempted to
continue my observations of them, were it not that
the streets of my native city offer me a similar, but a
more interesting study. Xerxes, we are told, shed
tears when he saw his army drawn up before him,
and reflected that not one of all that mighty host
would be alive a century after. Who could ride from
Paddington to London Bridge, through the current
of human life that flows ceaselessly through the
streets of that great city, without sharing somewhat
in the feelings of that tender-hearted monarch?

What are all the sermons that ever were preached
from a pulpit, compared to those which may be
found in the stones of a city? When we visit Pom-
peii and Herculaneum, we are thrilled to notice the
ruts made by the wheels of chariots centuries ago.
The original pavement of the Appian Way, now for

some distance visible, carries us back more than almost any of the other antiquities of Rome, to the time when it was trodden by captive kings, and re-echoed with the triumphal march of returning conquerors. I pity him in whom these things awaken no new train of thought. The works of man have outlived their builders by centuries, and still remain a solemn testimony to the power and the nothingness which originated them. Nineveh, Thebes, Troy, Carthage, Tyre, Athens, Rome, London, Paris, have won the crown in their turn, and have passed or will pass away. The dilapidated sculptures of the former have been taken to adorn the museums of the latter, and crowds have gazed and are gazing on them with curious eyes, unmindful of their great lesson of the transitoriness of the glory of the world. These are, indeed, "sermons in stones"; but, like most other sermons, we look rather at their style of finish, than at the deep meaning with which they are so pregnant.

But I did not take up my pen to write about dead cities; I have somewhat to say about the life that now renders the streets of our own towns so pleasant, and makes us so forgetful of their inevitable fate. I am not going to claim for the street life of our new world the charms which abound in the ancient cities of Europe. We are too much troubled about many things, and too utilitarian to give thought to those lesser graces which delight us abroad, and which we hardly remember until we come home and miss them. Our street architecture, improved though it may have been within a few years, is yet far behind the grace and massive symmetry of European towns. Our builders and real estate owners need to be reminded that it costs no more to build in good taste than in bad; that brick work can be made as architectural as stone; and that architecture is a great public instructor, whose works are constantly open to the public eye, and from which we are learning lessons, good or bad, whether we will or not. I think it is Goethe who calls architecture frozen music. I am glad to see these tall piles rearing their ornamented fronts on every side of us, even though they are intended for purposes of trade; for every one of them is a reproach to the untasteful structures around it, and an example which future builders must copy, if they do not surpass. The quaint beauty which charms us in Rouen, and in the old towns of Belgium,—the high pitched gables leaning over, as if yearning to get across the narrow street,—these all belong to another age, and we may not possess them; but the architecture which, in its simplicity or its magnificence, speaks its adaptedness to our climate and our social wants, is within our reach, and is capable of making our cities equal to any in the world.

I have a great liking for streets. In the freshness of morning, the glare of noonday, and the coolness of evening, they have an equal charm for me. I like that market-carty period of the day, before Labour has taken up his shovel and his hoe, before the sun has tipped the chimneys with gold, and reinspired the dolorous symphony of human toil, just as his earliest beams were wont to draw supernal melodies from old Memnon's statue. There is a holy quiet in that hour, which, could we preserve it in our minds, would keep us clear from many a wrong and meanness, into which the bustle and the heat of passion betray us, and would sanctify our day. In that time, the city seems wrapped in a silent ecstasy of adoration. The incense of its worship curls up from innumerous chimneys, and hangs over it like the fragrant cloud which hovers over the altars where saints have prayed, and religion's most august rites have been celebrated for centuries. In the continental cities, large numbers of people may be seen at that early hour repairing to the churches. They are drawn together by no spasmodic, spiritual stimulation; they do not assemble to hear their fellow-sinners tell with nasal twang how bad they were once, and how good they are now, nor to implore the curse of Heaven upon those who differ from them in their belief or disbelief. They kneel beneath those consecrated arches, joining in a worship in which scarce an audible word is uttered, and drawing from it new strength to tread the thorns of life. In our own cities, too, people—generally of the poorer classes— may be seen wending their way in the early morning to churches and chapels, humbler than the marble and mosaic sanctuaries of Europe, but one with them in that faith and worship which radiates from the majestic Lateran basilica, (*omnium urbis et orbis ecclesiarum mater et caput,*) and encircles the world with its anthems and supplications.

A little later in the morning, and the silence is broken by the clattering carts of the dispensers of that fluid without which custards would be impossible. The washing of doorsteps and sidewalks, too, begins to interfere with your perambulations, and to dim the lustre which No. 97, High Holborn, has imparted to your shoes. Bridget leans upon her wet broom, and talks with Anne, who leaves her water-pail for a little conference, in which the affairs of the two neighbouring families of Smith and Jenkins receive, you may be sure, due attention. Men smoking short and odorous pipes, and carrying small, mysterious-looking tin pails, begin to awaken the echoes with their brogans, and to prove him a slanderer who should say they have no music in their soles. Newspaper carriers, bearing the damp chronicles of the world's latest history bestrapped to their sides, hurry along, dispensing their favours into areas and doorways, seasoning my friend Thompson's breakfast with the reports of the councils of kings, or with the readable inventions of "our own correspondent," and delighting the gentle Mrs. Thompson with a full list of deaths and marriages, or another fatal railway accident. Then the omnibuses begin to rattle and jolt along the streets, carrying such masculine loads that they deserve for the time to be called mail coaches. Later, an odour as of broiled mackerel salutes the sense; school children, with their shining morning faces, begin to obstruct your way, and the penny postman, with his burden of joy and sorrow, hastens along and rings peremptorily at door after door. Then the streets assume by degrees a new character. Toil is engaged in its workshops and in by-places, and staid respectability, in its broadcloth and its glossy beaver, wends its deliberate way to its office or its counting-house, unhindered by aught that can disturb its equanimity, unless, perchance, it meets with a gang of street-sweepers in the full exercise of their dusty avocation.

STREET LIFE

Who can adequately describe that most inalienable of woman's rights—that favourite employment of the sex—which is generally termed *shopping?* Who can describe the curiosity which overhauls a wilderness of dress patterns, and the uncomplaining patience of the shopman who endeavours to suit the lady so hard to be suited,—his well-disguised disappointment when she does not purchase, and her husband's exasperation when she does? Not I, most certainly, for I detest shops, have little respect for fashions, lament the necessity of buying clothes, and wish most heartily that we could return to the primeval fig-leaves.

I love the by-streets of a city—the streets whose echoes are never disturbed by the heavy-laden wagons which bespeak the greatness of our manufacturing interests. Formerly the houses in such streets wore an air of sobriety and respectability, and the good housewifery which reigned within was symbolized by the bright polish of the brass door-plate, or bell-pull, or knocker. Now they are grown more pretentious, and the brass has given place to an outward and visible sign of silver. But the streets retain their old characteristics, and are strangers to any sound more inharmonious than the shouts of sportive children, or the tones of a hand-organ. I do not profess to be a musical critic, but I have been gifted by nature with a tolerable idea of time and tune; yet I am not ashamed to say that I do not despise hand-organs. They have given me "Sweet Home" in the cities of Italy, Yankee Doodle in the Faubourg St. Germain; and the best melodies of Europe's composers are daily ground out under my windows. I have no patience with these canting people who talk about productive labour, and who see in the organ-grinder who limps around, looking up expectantly for the remunerating copper, only a vagabond whom it is expedient for the police to counsel to "move on." These peripatetic dispensers of harmony are full as useful members of society as the majority of our legislators, and have a far more practical talent for organization. Douglas Jerrold once said that he never saw an Italian image merchant, with his Graces, and Venuses, and Apollos at sixpence a head, that he did not spiritually touch his hat to him: "It is he who has carried refinement into the poor man's house; it is he who has accustomed the eyes of the multitude to the harmonious forms of beauty." Let me apply these kindly expressions of the dead dramatist and wit to the organ-grinders. They have carried music into lanes and slums, which, without them, would never have known any thing more melodious than a watchman's rattle, and have made the poorest of our people familiar with harmonies that might "create a soul under the ribs of death." Occasionally their music may be instrumental in producing a feeling of impatience, so that I wish that their "Mary Ann" were married off, and that Norma would "hear," and make an end of it; but my better feelings triumph in the end, and I would not interfere with the poor man's and the children's concert to hear a strain from St. Cecilia's viol. Let the grinders be encouraged! May the evil days foretold in ancient prophecy never come among us, when the grinders shall cease because they are few!

STREET LIFE

It is at evening that the poetic element is found most abundant in the streets of cities. There is to me something of the sublime in the long lines of glittering shop-windows that skirt Regent Street and the Boulevards. Dr. Johnson exhorted the people who attended the sale of his friend Thrale's brewery, to remember that it was not the mere collection of boilers, and tubs, and vats which they saw around them, for which they were about to bargain, but "the potentiality of growing rich beyond the dreams of avarice"; and, in a similar spirit, I see in the shop windows not merely the silks and laces, and the other countless luxuries and wonders which delight the eye of taste and form the source of wealth to multitudes, but a vast exposition of the results of that industry, which, next to religion and obedience to law, is the surest foundation of national greatness, and which shows us, behind the frowning Providence that laid on man the curse of labour, the smiling face of divine beneficence. There, in one great collection, may be seen the fruits of the toil of millions. To produce that gorgeous display, artists have cudgelled their weary brains; operatives have suffered; ship-masters have strained their eyes over their charts and daily observations, and borne patiently with the provoking vagaries of the "lee main brace"; sailors have climbed the icy rigging and furled the tattered topsails with hands cracked and bleeding; for that, long trains of camels freighted with the rich products of the golden East, "from silken Samarcand to cedared Lebanon," have toiled with their white-turbaned drivers across the parching desert; thousands of busy hands have plied the swift shuttle in the looms of

Brussels, and Tournai, and Lyons; and thousands in deep and almost unfathomable mines have suffered a living death. Manchester and Birmingham have been content to wear their suit of mourning that those windows may be radiant and gay. The tears, and sweat, and blood of myriads have been poured out behind those shining panes transmuted into shapes that fill the beholder with wonder and delight. "In our admiration of the plumage we forget the dying bird." Nevertheless, above the roar and bustle of those whirling thoroughfares, above the endless groan and "infinite fierce chorus" of manhood ground down, and starving in bondage more cruel because it does not bear the name of slavery, I hear the carol of virtuous and well-rewarded labour, and the cheerful song of the white-capped lace-makers of Belgium and the vine-dressers of Italy reminds me that powerful wrong does not have every thing its own way even in this world.

I did intend to have gone farther in my evening walk; but time and space alike forbid it. I wished to leave the loud roaring avenues for those more quiet streets, where every sight and sound speak of domestic comfort, or humble fidelity, or patient effort; where the brilliancy of splendid mansions is but imperfectly veiled by rich and heavy draperies; where high up gleams the lamp of the patient student, happy in his present obscurity because he dreams of coming fame; and where the tan on the pavement and the mitigated light from the windows are eloquent of suffering and the sleepless affection that ministers to its unspoken wants. But I must stop. If, however, I have shown one of my readers, who regrets that he is obliged to dwell in a city, that there is much that is beautiful in paved streets and smoke-stained walls, and that, if we only open our eyes to see them, even though the fresh fields and waving woods may be miles away, the beauties of nature daily fold us in their bosom,—I shall feel that I have not tasked my tired brain and gouty right hand entirely in vain.

HARD UP IN PARIS

MONEY, whatever those who affect misanthropy or a sublime superiority to all temporal things may say to the contrary, is a very
desirable thing. We all enjoy the visit of the great
Alexander to the contented inhabitant of the imper-
ishable tub, who was alike independent of the good
will and displeasure of that mighty monarch; we
sympathize with all the bitter things that Timon says
when he is reduced from wealth to beggary; and we
are never tired of lamenting, with Virgil, that the
human heart should be such an abject prey to this
accursed hunger for gold. I am not sure that Horace
would not be dearer to us, if he had lived in a "three-
pair-back" in some obscure street, and his deathless
odes had been inspired by fear of a shrewish landlady or an inexorable sheriff, instead of being an
honoured guest at the imperial court, and a recipient
of the splendid patronage of a Mæcenas and an
Augustus. Poetical justice seems to require a setting
of the most cheerless poverty for the full development of the lustre of genius. At least, we think so,
at times;—though, under it all, admire as we may the
successful struggles of the want-stricken bard,—we
do not envy him his penury. We should shrink from
his gifts and his fame, if they were offered to us with
his sufferings. For underneath our abstract magnanimity lurks the conviction that money is by no

means a bad thing, after all. Our enthusiasm is awakened by contemplating the self-forgetful career of Francis of Assisi, who chose Poverty for his bride, and whose name is in benediction among men, even six centuries after he entered into possession of that kingdom which was promised to the poor in spirit; and, if we should chance to see a more modern bearer of that Christian name, who worshipped the wealth which the ancient saint despised; who trampled down honest poverty in his unswerving march towards opulence; who looked unmoved upon the tears of the widow and the orphan; who exercised his sordid apostolate even to the last gasp of his miserable life; and whose name (unblessed by the poor, and unhonoured by canonization) became, in the brief period that it outlived him, a byword and a synonyme of avarice,—we should not fail to visit his memory with a cordial malediction. But, in spite of all our veneration for Francis, the apostle of holy poverty, and of loathing for his namesake, the apostle of unholy wealth, we cannot help wishing that we had a little more of that which the Saint cast away, and the miser took in exchange for his soul.

A little more—that is the phrase—and there is no human being, rich or poor, who does not think that "a little more" is all that is needed to fill up the measure of his earthly happiness. It is for this that the gambler risks his winnings, and the merchant perils the gains of many toilsome years. For this, some men labour until they lose the faculty of enjoying the fruit of their exertions; and this is the *ignis fatuus* that goes dancing on before others, leading them at last into that bog of bankruptcy from which they never wholly extricate themselves. Enough is a word unknown in the lexicon of those who have once tasted the joy of having money at interest, and there are very few men who practically appreciate the wisdom of the ancient dramatist who tells us that

"He is most rich who stops at competence,—
Not labours on till the worn heart grows sere,—
Who, wealth attained, upon some loftier aim
Fixes his gaze, and never turns it backward."

"Give me neither poverty nor riches," has been my prayer through life, as it was that of the ancient sage; and it has always been my opinion that a man who owns even a single acre of land within a convenient distance of State Street or of the Astor House, is just as well off as if he were rich. My petition has been answered: but it must be confessed that when I mouse in the book shops, or turn over the rich portfolios of the print dealers, I feel that I am poor indeed. I do not envy him who can adorn the walls of his dwelling with the masterpieces of ancient or modern art on their original canvas; but I do crave those faithful reproductions which we owe to the engraver's skill, and which come so near my grasp as to aggravate my covetousness, and make me speak most disrespectfully of my unelastic purse.

Few people have spent any considerable time abroad without being for a season in straitened circumstances. A mistake may have been made in reckoning up one's cash, or a bill may be longer than was expected, or one's banker may temporarily suspend payment; and suddenly he who never knew a moment's anxiety about his pecuniary affairs finds himself wondering how he can pay for his lodgings, and where his next day's beefsteak is coming from. It was my good fortune once to undergo such a trial in Paris. I say good fortune—for, unpleasant as it was at the time, it was one of the most precious experiences of my life. I do not think that a true, manly character can be formed without placing the subject in the position of a ship's helm, when she is in danger of getting aback; to speak less technically, he must (once in his life, at least) be *hard up*.

I was younger in those days than I am now, and was living for a time in the gay capital of France. My lodgings were in one of those quiet streets that lead to the *Place Ventadour,* in which the Italian Opera House stands. My room was about twelve feet square, was handsomely furnished, and decorated with a large mirror, and a polished oaken floor that rivalled the mirror in brilliancy. Its window commanded an unobstructed view of a court-yard about the size of the room itself; but, as I was pretty high up (on the second floor coming down) my light was good, and I could not complain. As I write, it seems as if I could hear the old *concierge* blacking boots and shoes away down at the bottom of that well of a court-yard, enlivening his toil with an occasional snatch from some old song, and now and then calling out to his young wife within the house, with a clear voice, "Marie!"—the accent of the final syllable being prolonged in a preternatural manner. And then out of the same depths came a melodious response from Marie's blithesome voice, that made me stop shaving to enjoy it—a voice that seemed in perfect harmony with the cool breath and bright sky of that sunny spring morning. Marie was a representative woman of her class. I do not believe that she could have been placed in any honest position, however high, that she would not have adorned. Her simplicity and good nature conciliated the good will of every one who addressed her, and I have known her quiet, lady-like dignity to inspire even some loud and boastful Americans, who called on me, with a momentary sentiment of respect. They appeared almost like gentlemen for two or three minutes after speaking with her. Upon my honour, sir, it was worth considerably more than I paid for my room to have the privilege of living under the same roof with such a cheery sunbeam—to see her seated daily at the window of the *conciergerie* with a snow-white cap on her head and a pleasant smile on her face; to interrupt her sewing, with an inquiry whether any letters had come for me, and be charmed with her alacrity in handing me the expected note, and the key of *numero dix-huit.* Her nightly *Bon soir, M'sieur,* was like a benediction from a guardian angel; her vivacious *Bon jour* was an augury of an untroubled day; it would have made the darkest, foggiest November afternoon seem as bright, and fresh, and exhilarating as a morning in June. These are trifles, I know, but it is of trifles such as these that the true happiness of life is made up. Great joys, like great griefs, do not possess the soul so completely as we think, as Wellington victorious, or Napoleon defeated, at Waterloo, would have discovered, if, in that great hour, they had been visited with a twinge of neuralgia in the head, or a gnawing dyspepsia.

The influenza, or *grippe,* as the French call it, is

not a pleasant thing under any circumstances; but I think of a four days' attack, during which Marie attended to my wants, as a period of unmixed pleasure. She seemed to hover about my sick bed, she moved so gently, and her voice (to use the words of my former cherished friend, S. T. Coleridge,) was like

> "—— a hidden brook
> In the leafy month of June,
> That to the sleeping woods all night
> Singeth a quiet tune."

"Was it that Monsieur would be able to drink a little tea, or would it please him to taste some cool lemonade?" *Hélas!* Monsieur was too *malade* for that; but the kind attentions of that estimable little woman were more refreshing than a Baltic Sea of the beverage that cheers but does not inebriate, or all the aid that the lemon groves of Italy could afford. Marie's politeness was the genuine article, and came right from her pure, kind heart. It was as far removed from that despicable obsequiousness which passes current with so many for politeness, as old-fashioned Christian charity is from modern philanthropy.

But—pardon my garrulity—I am forgetting my story. In a moment of kindly forgetfulness I lent a considerable portion of my available funds to a friend who was short, and who was obliged to return to America, *via* England. I was in weekly expectation of a draft from home that would place me once more upon my financial legs. One, two, three weeks passed away, and the letters from America were distributed every Tuesday morning, but there was none for me. It gave me a kind of faint sensation when the clerk at the banker's gave me the disappointing answer, and I went into the reading-room of the establishment to read the new American papers, and to speculate upon the cause of the unremitting neglect of my friends at home. I shall never forget my feelings when, in the third week of my impecuniosity, I found my exchequer reduced to the small sum of eight francs. I saw the truth of Shakespeare's words describing the "consumption of the purse" as an incurable disease. I had many acquaintances and a few friends in Paris, but I determined not to borrow if it could possibly be avoided. Five days would elapse before another American mail arrived, and I resolved that my remaining eight francs should carry me through to the eventful Tuesday, which I felt sure would bring the longed-for succor. I found a little dingy shop, in a narrow street behind the Church of St. Roch, where I could get a breakfast, consisting of a bowl of very good coffee and piece of bread (I asked for the end of the loaf) for six sous. My dinners I managed to bring down to the sum of twelve sous, by choosing obscure localities for the obtaining of that repast, and confining myself to those simple and nutritious viands which possessed the merit attributed to the veal pie by Samuel Weller, being "werry fillin' at the price." Sometimes I went to bed early, to avoid the inconveniences of a light dinner. One day I dined with a friend at his lodgings, but I did not enjoy his hospitality; I felt guilty, as if I had sacrificed friendship to save my dwindling purse. The coarsest bread and the most suspicious beef of the Latin Quarter would have been more delicious to me under such circumstances than the best ragout of the Boulevards or the Palais Royal.

Of course, this state of things weighed heavily upon my spirits. I heard Marie tell her husband that Monsieur l'Anglais was *bien triste*. I avoided the friends with whom I had been used to meet, and (remembering what a sublime thing it is to suffer and be strong) sternly resolved not to borrow till I found myself completely gravelled. It grieved me to be obliged to pass the old blind man who played the flageolet on the *Pont des Arts* without dropping a copper into his tin box; but the severest blow was the being compelled to put off my obliging washerwoman and her reasonable bill. The time passed away quickly, however. The *Louvre*, with its treasures of art, was a blessed asylum for me. It cost me nothing, and I was there free from the importunities of distress which I could not relieve. In the halls of the great public library—now the *Bibliothèque Impériale*—I found myself at home. Among the studious throng that occupied its vast reading rooms, I was as independent as if my name had been Rothschild, or the treasures of the Bank of France had been at my command. The master spirits with whom I there communed do not ask what their votaries carry in their pockets. There is no property-test for admission to the privileges of their companionship. I felt the equality which prevails in the republic of letters. I knew that my left hand neighbour was not, in that quiet place, superior to me on account of his glossy coat and golden-headed cane, and that I was no better than the reader at my right hand because he wore a blouse. I jingled my two or three remaining francs in my pocket, and thought how useless money was, when the lack of it was no bar to entrance into the hallowed presence of

"Those dead but sceptred sovereigns who still rule
Our spirits from their urns."

I shall not soon forget the intense satisfaction with which I read in the regulations of the library a strict prohibition against offering any fees or gratuities whatever to its blue-coated officials.

At last the expected Tuesday morning came. My funds had received an unlooked-for diminution by receiving a letter from my friend whose wants had led me into difficulty. He was just embarking at Liverpool—hoped that my remittance had arrived in due season—promised to send me a draft as soon as he reached New York—envied my happiness at remaining in Paris—and left me to pay the postage on his valediction. It would be difficult for any disinterested person to conceive how dear the thoughtless writer of that letter was to me in that unfortunate hour. Then, too, I was obliged to lay out six of those cherished copper coins for a ride in an omnibus, as I was caught in a shower over in the vicinity of St. Sulpice, and could not afford to take the risk of a rheumatic attack by getting wet. I well remember the cool, business-like air with which that relentless *conducteur* pocketed those specimens of the French currency that were so precious in my sight. Yet, in spite of these serious and unexpected drains upon my finances, I had four sous left after paying for my breakfast on that memorable morning. I felt uncommonly cheerful at the prospect of being relieved from my troubles, and stopped several minutes after finishing my coffee, and conversed with the tidy shop-woman with a fluency that astonished both of us. I really regretted for the moment that I was so soon to be placed in funds, and should no longer enjoy her kindly services. I chuckled audibly to myself as I pursued my way to the banker's, to think what an immense joke it would be for some skilful Charley Bates or Artful Dodger to try to pick my pocket just then. An ancient heathen expecting an answer from the oracle of Delphos, a modern candidate for office awaiting the count of the vote, never felt more op-pressed with the importance of the result than I did when I entered the banking-house. My delight at having a letter from America put into my hands could only be equalled by my dismay when I opened it, and found, instead of the draft, a request from a casual acquaintance who had heard that I might possibly return home through England, and who, if I did, would be under great obligations if I would take the trouble to procure and carry home for him an English magpie and a genuine King Charles spaniel!

I did not stop to read the papers that morning. As I was leaving the establishment, I met its chief partner, to whom I could not help expressing my disappointment. He was one of your hard-faced, high-cheek-boned Yankees, with a great deal of speculation in his eyes. I should as soon have thought of attempting the cultivation of figs and dates at Franconia as of trying to get a small loan from *him*. So I pushed on into those busy streets whose liveliness seemed to mock my pitiable condition. I had come to it at last. I had got to borrow. A physician, who now stands high among the faculty in Boston, was then residing in Paris, and, as I had been on familiar terms with him, I determined to have recourse to him. He occupied two rooms in the fifth story of a house in the Rue St. Honoré. His apartments were more remarkable for their snugness than for the extent of accommodation they afforded. A snuff-taking friend once offered to present the doctor with one of his silk handkerchiefs to carpet that parlour with. But the doctor's heart was not to be measured by the size of his rooms, and I knew that he would be a friend in need. The *concierge* told me that the doctor had not gone out, and, in obedience to the instructions of that functionary, I mounted the long staircase and *frapped* at the door of that estimable disciple of Galen. It was not my usual thrice-repeated stroke upon the door; it was a timid and uncertain knock—the knock of a borrower. The doctor said that he had been rather short himself for a week or two, but that he should undoubtedly find a letter in the General Post that morning that would place him in a condition to give me a lift. This was said in a manner that put me entirely at my ease, and made me feel that by accepting his loan I should be conferring an inestimable favour upon him. As we walked towards the Rue Jean Jacques Rousseau, I amused him with the story of the preceding week's adventures. He laughed heartily, and after a few minutes I joined with him, though I must say that the events, as they occurred, did not particularly impress me as subjects for very hilarious mirth. The doctor inquired at the *poste restante* in vain. His friends had been as remiss as mine, and we had both got to wait another week. The doctor was not an habitually profane man, but as we came through the court-yard of the post office, he expressed his anxiety as to what the devil we should do. He examined his purse, and found that his available assets amounted to a trifle more than nineteen francs. He looked as troubled as he had before looked gay. I generously offered him my four remaining coppers, and told him that I would stand by him as long as he had a centime in his pocket. Such an exhibition of magnanimity could not be made in vain. We stopped in front of the church of Our Lady of Victories, and took the heroic resolve to club our funds and go through the week of expectation together. And we did it. I wish that space would allow of my describing the achievements of that week. Medical books were cast aside for the study of domestic economy. I do not believe that a similar sum of money ever went so far before, even in Paris. We found a place in a narrow street, near the Odeon, where fried potatoes were sold very cheap; we bought our bread by the loaf, as it was cheaper—the loaves being so long that the doctor said that he understood, when he first saw them, why bread was called the staff of life. We resorted to all sorts of expedients to make a franc buy as much as possible of the necessaries of life. We frequented with great assiduity all places of public amusement where there was no fee for admission. The public galleries, the libraries, the puppet shows in the Champs Elysées, were often honoured with our presence. We made a joke of our necessities, and carried it through to the end. The next Tuesday morning found us, after breakfasting, on our way to the post office, with a franc left in our united treasury. I had begun to give up all hopes of our ever getting a letter from home, and insisted upon the doctor's trying his luck first. He was successful, but the severest part of the joke came when he found that his letter (contrary to all precedent) was not postpaid. The polite official at the window must have thirty-two sous for it, and we had but twenty. Our laughter showed him the whole state of the case, and we left him greatly amused at our promises to return soon, and get the desirable prize. My application at the banker's was successful, too, and before noon we were both prepared to laugh a siege to scorn. I paid the rosy-cheeked washerwoman, bought Marie a neat crucifix to hang up in the place of a very rude one in her *conciergerie*, out of sheer good humour; and that evening the doctor and I laughed over the recollections of the week and a good dinner in a quiet restaurant in the Palais Royal.

THE OLD CORNER

THE human heart loves corners. The very word "corner" is suggestive of snugness and cosy comfort, and he who has no liking for them is something more or less than mortal. I have seen people whose ideas of comfort were singularly crude and imperfect; who thought that it consisted in keeping a habitation painfully clean, and in having every book or paper that might give token of the place being the dwelling of a human being, carefully out of sight. We have great cause for thankfulness that such people are not common, (for a little wholesome negligence is by no means an unpleasant thing,) so that we can say that mankind generally likes to snuggify itself, and is therefore fond of a corner. This natural fondness is manifested by the child with his playthings and infantile sports, in one of which, at least, the attractions of corners for the feline race are brought strongly before his inquisitive mind. And how is this liking strengthened and built up as the child increases in secular knowledge, and learns in the course of his poetical and historical researches all about the personal history of Master John Horner, whose sedentary habits and manducation of festive pastry are famous wherever the language of Shakespeare and Milton is spoken!

This love of nooks and corners is especially observable in those who are obliged to live in style and splendour. Many a noble English family has been glad to escape from the bondage of its rank, and has found more real comfort in the confinement of a Parisian *entresol* than amid the gloomy grandeur of its London home. Those who are condemned to dwell in palaces bear witness to this natural love of snugness, by choosing some quiet sunny corner in their marble halls, and making it as comfortable as if it were a cosy cottage. Napoleon and Eugenie delight to escape from the magnificence of the Tuileries to that quiet and homelike refuge for people who are burdened with imperial dignity, amid the thick foliage and green alleys of St. Cloud. Even in that mighty maze, the Vatican, the rooms inhabited by the Sovereign Pontiff are remarkably comfortable and unpalatial, and prove the advantages of smallness and simplicity over gilding and grandeur, for the ordinary purposes of life. An American gentleman once called on the great and good Cardinal Cheverus, and while talking with him of his old friends in America, said that the contrast between the Cardinal's position in the episcopal palace of Bordeaux and in his former humble residence when he was Bishop of Boston, was a very striking one. The humble and pious prelate smiled, and taking his visitor by the arm, led him from the stately hall in which they were conversing, into a narrow room furnished in a style of austere simplicity: "The palace," said he, "which you have seen and admired is the residence of the Cardinal Archbishop of Bordeaux; but this little chamber is where John Cheverus *lives*."

Literary men and statesmen have always coveted

the repose of a corner where they might be undisturbed by the wranglings of the world. Twickenham, and Lausanne, and Ferney, and Rydal Mount have become as shrines to which the lover of books would fain make pilgrimages. Have we not a Sunnyside and an Idlewild even in this new land of ours! Cicero, in spite of his high opinion of Marcus Tullius, and his thirst for popular applause, often grew tired of urban life, and was glad to forsake the *Senatus populusque Romanus* for the quiet of his snug villa in a corner of the hill country overlooking Frascati. And did not our own Tully love to fling aside the burden of his power, and find his Tusculum on the old South Shore? In the Senate Chamber or the Department of State you might see the Defender of the Constitution, but it was at Marshfield that Webster really lived. Horace loved good company and the entertainment of his wealthy patrons and friends, but he loved snugness and quiet even more. In one of his odes he apostrophizes his friend Septimius, and describes to him the delight he takes in the repose of his Tiburtine retreat from the bustle of the metropolis, saying that of all places in the world that corner is the most smiling and grateful to him:—

> Ille terrarum mihi præter omnes
> Angulus ridet.

If we look into our hearts, I think we shall most of us find that we have a clinging attachment to some favourite corner, as well as Mr. Horatius Flaccus. There is at least one corner in the city of Boston, which has many pleasant associations for the lover of literature. Allusion was made a few days since, in an evening paper, to the well-known fact that the old building at the corner of Washington and School Streets was built in 1713, and is therefore older by seventeen years than the Old South Church. That little paragraph reminded me of some passages in the history of that ancient edifice related to me by an ancestor of mine, for whom the place had an almost romantic charm.

The old building (my grandfather used to tell me) was originally a dwelling-house. It had the high wainscots, the broad staircases, the carved cornices, and all the other blessed old peculiarities of the age in which it was built, which we irreverently have improved away. One hundred years ago the old corner was considered rather an aristocratic place of residence. It was slightly suburban in its position, for the town of Boston had an affection for Copp's Hill, and the inhabitants clustered about that sacred eminence as if the southern parts of their territory were a quicksand. Trees were not uncommon in the vicinity of the foot of School Street in those days, and no innovating Hathorne had disturbed the quiet of the place with countless omnibuses. The old corner was then occupied by an English gentleman named Barmesyde, who gave good dinners, and was on intimate terms with the colonial governor. My venerated relative, to whom I have already alluded, enjoyed his friendship, and in his latter days delighted to talk of him, and tell his story to those who had heard it so often, that Hugh Greville Barmesyde, Esquire, seemed like a companion of their own young days.

THE OLD CORNER

Old Barmesyde sprang from an ancient Somerset-shire family, from which he inherited a considerable property, and a remarkable energy of character. He increased his wealth during a residence of many years in Antigua, at the close of which he relinquished his business, and returned to England to marry a beautiful English lady to whom he had engaged himself in the West Indies. He arrived in England the day after the funeral of his betrothed, who had fallen a victim to intermittent fever. Many of his relations had died in his absence, and he found himself like a stranger in the very place where he had hoped to taste again the joys of home. The death of the lady he loved so dearly, and the changes in his circle of friends, were so depressing to him, that he resolved to return to the West Indies. He thought it would be easier for him to continue in the associations he had formed there than to recover from the shock his visit to England had given him. So he took passage in a brig from Bristol to Antigua, and said farewell forever, as he supposed, to his native land. Before half the voyage was accomplished, the vessel was disabled: as Mr. Choate would express it, a north-west gale inflicted upon her a serious, an immedicable injury; and she floated a wreck upon the foamy and uneven surface of the Atlantic. She was fallen in with by another British vessel, bound for Boston, which took off her company, and with the renewal of the storm she foundered before the eyes of those who had so lately risked their lives upon her seaworthiness. When Mr. Barmesyde arrived in Boston, he found an old friend in the governor of the Province of Massachusetts Bay. Governor

Pownall had but lately received his appointment from the Crown, and being a comparative stranger in Boston, he was as glad to see Mr. Barmesyde as the latter was to see him. It was several months before an opportunity to reach the West Indies offered itself, and when one did occur, Mr. Barmesyde only used it to communicate with his agent at Antigua. He had given up all ideas of returning thither, and had settled down, with his negro servant Cato, to housekeeping at the corner of School Street, within a few doors of his gubernatorial friend.

Governor Pownall's term of office was not a long one, but even when he was removed, Mr. Barmesyde stuck faithfully to the old corner. He had found many warm friends here, and could no longer consider himself alone in the world. He was a man of good natural powers, and of thorough education. He was one of those who seem never to lose any thing that they have once acquired. In person he was tall and comely, and my grandfather said that he somewhat resembled General Washington as he appeared twenty-five years later, excepting that Mr. Barmesyde's countenance was more jolly and port-winy. From all I can learn, his face, surmounted by that carefully-powdered head of hair, must have resembled a red brick house after a heavy fall of snow. If Hugh Barmesyde had a fault, I am afraid it was a fondness for good living. He attended to his marketing in person, assisted by his faithful Cato, who was as good a judge in such matters as his master, and who used to vindicate the excellence of his master's fare by eating until he was black in the face. For years there were few vessels arrived from England without bringing choice wines to moisten the alimentary canal of Mr. Barmesyde. The Windward Isles contributed bountifully to keep alight the festive flame that blazed in his cheery countenance, and to make his flip and punch the very best that the province could produce. Every Sunday morning Mr. Barmesyde's best buckles sparkled in the sunbeams as he walked up School Street to the King's Chapel. Not that he was an eminently religious man, but he regarded religion as an institution that deserved encouragement for the sake of maintaining a proper balance in society. The quiet order and dignity of public worship pleased him, the liturgy gratified his taste, and so Sunday after Sunday his big manly voice headed the responses, and told that its possessor had done many things that he ought not to have done, and had left undone a great many that he ought to have done.

Mr. Barmesyde was not a mere feeder on good things, however; he had a cultivated taste for literature, and his invoices of wine were frequently accompanied by parcels of new books. The old gentleman took a great delight in the English literature of that day. Fielding and Smollett were writing then, and no one took a keener pleasure in their novels than he. He imported, as he used to boast, the first copy of Dr. Johnson's Dictionary that ever came to America, and was never tired of reading that stately and pathetic preface, or of searching for the touches of satire and individual prejudice that abound in that entertaining work. His well-worn copy of the Spectator, in eight duodecimo volumes, presented by him to my grandfather, now graces one of my book shelves. His books were always at the service of his friends, who availed themselves of the old gentleman's kindness to such an extent that his collection might have been called a circulating library. But it was not merely for the frequent "feast of reason and flow of soul" that his friends were indebted to him. He was the very incarnation of hospitality. I am afraid that my excellent grandparent had an uncommon admiration for this trait in the old fellow's character, for a frequent burning twinge in one of the toes of my right foot, and occasionally in the knuckles of my left hand, reminds me of his fondness for keeping his legs under Mr. Barmesyde's festive mahogany. A few years ago, when a new floor was laid in the cellar at the old corner, a large number of empty bottles was discovered, whose appearance bore witness to the previous good character of the place as a cellar. Some labels were also found bearing dates like 1697, 1708, 1721, &c. To this day the occupants of the premises take pleasure in showing the dark wine stains on the old stairs leading to the cellar.

But Mr. Barmesyde's happiness, like the *gioia de profani*, which we have all heard the chorus in the last scene of Lucrezia Borgia discordantly allude to, was but transient. The dispute which had been brewing for years between the colonies and the mother country, began to grow unpleasantly warm. Mr. B. was a stanch loyalist. He allowed that injustice had been done to the colonies, but still he could not throw off his allegiance to his most religious and gracious king, George III., Defender of the Faith. He was ready to do and to suffer as much for his principles as the most ardent of the revolutionists. And he was not alone in his loyalty. There were many old-fashioned conservative people in this revolutionary and ismatic city in those days as well as now. The publication in this city of a translation of De Maistre's great defence of the monarchical principle of government, (the Essay on the Generative Principle of Political Constitutions,) and of the late Mr. Oliver's "Puritan Commonwealth," proves that the surrender of Cornwallis and the formation of the Federal Constitution did not destroy the confidence of a good many persons in the truth of the principles on which the loyalists took their stand. The unfortunate occurrence in State Street, March 5, 1770, gave Mr. B. great pain. He regretted the bloodshed, but he regretted more deeply to see many persons so blinded by their hatred of the king's most excellent majesty, as to defend and praise the action of a lawless mob just punished for their riotous conduct. The throwing overboard of the tea excited his indignation. He stigmatized it (and not without some reason on his side) as a wanton and cowardly act,—a destruction of the property of parties against whom the town of Boston had no cause of complaint,—a deed which proved how little real regard for justice and honour there might be among those who were the loudest in their shrieks for freedom. Of course he could not give utterance to these sentiments without exciting the ire of many people; and feeling that he could no longer safely remain in this country, he concluded to return to England. In the spring of 1774, Hugh Greville Barmesyde gave his last dinner to a few of the faithful at the old corner, and sailed the next day with a sorrowing heart and his trusty Cato for the land of his birth. He spent the remainder of his days in London, where he died in 1795. He was interred in the vault belonging to his family, in the north transept of the Parish Church of Shepton Mallet, in Somersetshire, where there is still a handsome tablet commemorating his many virtues and the inconsolable grief of the nephews and nieces whom his decease enriched.

Some of the less orderly "liberty boys" bore witness to the imperfect sympathy that existed between them and the late occupant of the old corner, by breaking sundry panes of glass in the parlour windows the night after his departure. The old house, during the revolutionary struggle, followed the common prosaic course of ordinary occupancy. There was "marrying and giving in marriage" under that steep and ancient roof in those days, and troops of clamorous children used to play upon the broad stone steps, and tarnish the brasses that Cato was wont to keep so clean and bright. In the latter part of the last century the old house underwent a painful transformation. An enterprising apothecary perverted it to the uses of trade, and decorated its new windows with the legitimate jars of various coloured fluids. It is now nearly half a century since it became a bookstore. Far be it from me to offer any disturbance to the modesty of my excellent friends, Messrs. Ticknor and Fields, by enlarging upon the old corner in its present estate. It were useless to write about any thing so familiar. They are young men yet, and must pardon me if I have used the prerogative of age and spoken too freely about their old establishment and its reminiscences. I love the old corner, and should not hesitate to apply to it the words of Horace which I have quoted above. I love its freedom from pretence and ostentation. New books seem more grateful to me there than elsewhere; for the dinginess of Paternoster Row harmonizes better with literature than the plate glass and gairish glitter of Piccadilly or Regent Street.

The large looking-glass which stands near the Washington Street entrance to the old corner used to adorn the dining-room where Mr. Barmesyde gave so many feasts. It is the only relic of that worthy gentleman now remaining under that roof. If that glass could only publish its reflexions during the past century, what an entertaining work on the curiosities of literature and of life it might make! It is no ordinary place that may boast of having been the familiar resort of people like Judge Story, Mr. Otis, Channing, Kirkland, Webster, Choate, Everett, Charles Kemble and the elder Vandenhoff with their gifted daughters, Ellen Tree, the Woods, Finn, Dickens, Thackeray, James, Bancroft, Prescott, Emerson, Brownson, Dana, Halleck, Bryant, Hawthorne, Longfellow, Holmes, Lowell, Willis, Bayard Taylor, Whipple, Parkman, Hilliard, Sumner, Parsons, Sprague, and so many others whose names will live in literature and history. It is a very pleasant thing to see literary men at their ease, as they always are around those old counters. It is a relief to find that they can throw off at times the dignity and restraint of authorship. It is pleasant to see the lecturer and the divine put away their tiresome earnestness and severe morality, and come down to the jest of the day. It refreshes one to know that Mr. Emerson is not always orphic, and that the severely scholastic Everett can forget his elegant and harmonious sentences, and descend to common prose. For we can no more bear to think of an orator living unceasingly in oratory than we could of Signorina Zanfretta being obliged to remain constantly poised on the *corde tendue*.

The bust of Sir Walter Scott has filled the space above the mirror I have spoken of, for many years. It is a fine work of Chantrey's, and a good likeness of that head of Sir Walter's, so many *stories* high that one can never wonder where all his novels came from. Except this specimen of the plastic art, and one of Professor Agassiz, there is little that is ornamental in the ancient haunt. The green curtain that decorates the western corner of the establishment is a comparatively modern institution. It was found necessary to fence off that portion of the shop for strict business purposes. The profane converse of the world cannot penetrate those folds. Into that *sanctissimum sanctissimorum* no joke, however good, may enter. What a strange dispensation of Providence is it, that a man should have been for years enjoying the good society that abounds at that corner, and yet should seem to have so little liking for a quiet jest as the estimable person who conceals his seriousness behind that green curtain!

But every thing must yield to the law of nature, and the old corner must share the common lot. Some inauspicious night, the fire-alarm will sound for District III.; hoarse voices will echo at the foot of

School Street, calling earnestly on No. 3 to "hold on," and No. 9 to "play away"; where erst good liquor was wont to abound water will more abound, and when the day dawns Mr. Barmesyde's old house will be an unsightly ruin,—there will be mourning and desolation among the lovers of literature, and wailing in the insurance offices in State Street. When the blackened ruins are cleared away, boys will pick up scraps of scorched manuscripts, and sell them piecemeal as parts of the original copy of Hiawatha, or Evangeline, or the Scarlet Letter. In the fulness of time, a tall, handsome stone or iron building will rise on that revered site, and we lovers of the past shall try to invest it with something of the unpre· tending dignity and genial associations of the present venerable pile, which will then be cherished among our most precious memories.

SACRED TO THE MEMORY
OF THEATRE ALLEY

WE are all associationists. There is no man
who does not believe in association in some
degree. For myself, I am firm in the faith. Let me
not be misunderstood, however; I do not mean that
principle of association which the late Mr. Fourier
advocated in France, and Mr. Brisbane in America.
I do not believe in the utopian schemes which have
been ground out of the brains of philosophers who
mistake vagueness and impracticability for sublimity, and which they have misnamed association.
The principle of association to which I pay homage
is one which finds a home in every human heart. It
is that principle of our nature which, when the bereaved Queen Constance was mourning for her
absent child, "stuffed out his vacant garments with
his form." It is that principle which makes a man
love the scenes of his boyhood, and which brings
tears to the eyes of the traveller in a foreign land,
when he hears a familiar strain from a hand organ,
however harsh and out of tune. Even the brute
creation seems to share in it; the cat is sure to be
found in her favourite place at the fireside, while the
tea kettle makes music on the hob; the dog, too, (let
Hercules himself do what he may,) will not only
have his day, but will have his chosen corner for repose, and will stick to it, however tempting you may

make other places by a superabundance of door mats and other canine furniture. And the tired cart horse, when his day's labour is over, and he finds himself once more in the familiar stall, with his provender before him—do you not suppose that the associations of equine comfort by which he is surrounded are dearer to him than any hopes of the luxury and splendour of Her Britannic Majesty's stables at Windsor could be? Ask him if he would leave his present peck of oats for the chances of royal service, and a red-waistcoated, white-top-booted groom to wait upon him, and I will warrant you that he will answer *nay!*

There is no nation nor people that is free from this bondage of association. We treasure General Jackson's garments with respectful care in a glass case in the Patent Office at Washington; in the Louvre, you shall find preserved the crown of Charlemagne and the old gray coat of the first Napoleon; and at Westminster Abbey, (if you have the money to pay your admission fee,) you may see the plain old oaken chair in which the crowned monarchs of a thousand years have sat. Go to Rome, and stand "at the base of Pompey's statua," and association shall carry you back in imagination to the time when the mighty Julius fell. Stand upon the grassy mounds of Tusculum, and you will find yourself glowing with enthusiasm for Cicero, and wonder how you could have grown so sleepy over *Quousque tandem,* &c., in your school-boy days. Climb up the Trasteverine steep to where the convent of San Onofrio suns itself in the bright blue air of Rome, and while the monks are singing the divine office where the bones of Tasso repose, you may fill your mind with memories of the bard of the crusades, in the chamber where his weary soul found the release it craved. Go to that fair capital which seems to have hidden itself among the fertile hills of Tuscany; walk through its pleasant old streets, and you shall find yourself the slave of many pleasing associations. The very place where Dante was wont to stand and gaze at that wondrous dome which Michel Angelo said he was unwilling to copy and unable to excel, is marked by an inscription in the pavement. Every street has its associations that appeal to your love of the beautiful or the heroic. Walk out into the lively streets of that city which stands at the head of the world's civilization, and you are overwhelmed with historic associations. You seem to hear the clatter of armed heels in some of those queer old alleys, and the vision of Godfrey or St. Louis, armed for the holy war, would not astonish you. The dim and stately halls of the palaces are eloquent of power, and you almost expect to see the thin, pale, thoughtful face of the great Richelieu at every corner. Over whole districts, rebellion, and anarchy, and infidelity, once wrote the history of their sway in blood, and even now, the names of the streets, as you read them, seem to fill you with terrible mementoes.

But to us, Americans, connected as we are with England in our civilization and our literature, how full of thrilling associations is London! From Whitehall, where Puritanism damned itself by the murder of a king, to Eastcheap, where Mistress Quickly served Sir John with his sherris-sack; from St. Saviour's Church, where Massinger and Fletcher

lie in one grave, to Milton's tomb in St. Giles's, Crip-
plegate, there is hardly a street, or court, or lane, or
alley, which does not appeal by some association to
the student of English history or literature. He
perambulates the Temple Gardens with Chaucer; he
hears the partisans of the houses of York and Lan-
caster, as they profane the silence of that scholastic
spot; he walks Fleet Street, and disputes in Bolt
Court with Dr. Johnson; he smokes in the coffee-
houses of Covent Garden with Dryden and Pope,
and the wits of their day; he makes morning calls in
Leicester Square and its neighbourhood, on Sir Philip
Sidney, Hogarth, Reynolds, and Newton; he buys
gloves and stockings at Defoe's shop in Cornhill;
and makes excursions with Dicky Steele out to Ken-
sington, to see Mr. Addison. Drury Lane, despite
its gin, and vice, and squalour, has its associations.
The old theatre is filled with them. They show you,
in the smoky green-room, the chairs which once were
occupied by Siddons and Kemble; the seat of Byron
by the fireside in the days of his trusteeship; the mirrors in which so many dramatic worthies viewed
themselves, before they were called to achieve their
greatest triumphs.

Every where you find men acknowledging in their
actions their allegiance to this great natural law.
Our own city, too, has its associations. Who can
pass by that venerable building in Union Street,
which, like a deaf and dumb beggar, wears a tablet
of its age upon its unsightly front, without recalling
some of the events that have taken place, some of the
scenes which that venerable edifice has looked down
upon, since its solid timbers were jointed in the year

[251]

of salvation 1685? Who can enter Faneuil Hall without a quickening of his pulse? Who can walk by the old Hancock House, and not look up at it as if he expected to see old John (the best writer on the subject of American independence) standing at the door in his shad-bellied coat, knee-breeches, and powdered wig? Who can look at the Old South Church without thinking of the part it played in the revolution, and of the time when it was obliged to yield its unwilling horsepitality to the British cavalry? Boston is by no means deficient in associations. Go to Brattle Street, to Copp's Hill, to Mount Washington, to Deer Island,—though it must be acknowledged, the only association connected with the last-named place is the Provident Association.

If there be a fault in the Yankee character, I fear it is a lack of sufficient respect for the memory of the past. Nature will have her way with us, however we may try to resist her and trample old recollections under foot. We worship prosperity too much; and the wide, straight streets of western cities, with the telegraph posts standing like sentinels on the edge of the sidewalks, and a general odour of pork-packing and new houses pervading the atmosphere, seem to our acquisitive sense more beautiful than the sculptured arch, the moss-grown tower, the quaint gable, and all the summer fragrance of the gardens of the Tuileries or the *Unterdenlinden*. I am afraid that we almost deserve to be classed with those who (as Mr. Thackeray says) "have no reverence except for prosperity, and no eye for any thing but success."

Many are kindled into enthusiasm by meditating upon the future of this our country,—"the newest born of nations, the latest hope of mankind,"—but for myself I love better to dwell on the sure and unalterable past, than to speculate upon the glories of the coming years. While I was young, I liked, when at sea, to stand on the top-gallant forecastle, and see the proud ship cut her way through the waves that playfully covered me with spray; but of late years my pleasure has been to lean over the taffrail and muse upon the subsiding foam of the vessel's wake. The recollection even of storms and dangers is to me more grateful than the most joyful anticipation of a fair wind and the expected port. With these feelings, I cannot help being moved when I see so many who try to deaden their natural sensibility to old associations. When the old Province House passed into the hands of the estimable Mr. Ordway, I congratulated him on his success, but I mourned over the dark fate of that ancient mansion. I respected it even in its fallen state as an inn,—for it retained much of its old dignity, and the ghosts of Andros and his predecessors seemed to brush by you in its high wainscoted passages and on its broad staircases; but it did seem the very ecstasy of sacrilege to transform it into a concert-room. I rejoiced, however, a few years since, when the birthplace of B. Franklin, in Milk Street, was distinguished by an inscription to that effect in letters of enduring stone. That was a concession to the historic associations of that locality which the most sanguine could hardly have expected from the satinetters of Milk Street.

But I am forgetting my subject, and using up my time and ink in the prolegomena. My philosophy of association received a severe blow last week. It was

a pleasant day, and I hobbled out on my gouty timbers for a walk. I wandered into Franklin Place,
but it was not the Franklin Place of my youth. The
rude hand of public improvement had not been kept
even from that row of houses which, when I was a
boy, was thought an ornament to our city, and was
dignified with the name of the Tontine Buildings.
Franklin Place looked as if two or three of its front
teeth had been knocked out. I walked on, and my
sorrow and dismay were increased to find that the
last vestige of Theatre Alley had disappeared. It
was bad enough when the old theatre and the residence of the Catholic bishops of Boston were swept
away: I still clung to the old alley, and hoped that it
would not pass away in my time—that before the old
locality should be improved into what the profane
vulgar call sightliness and respectability, I should (to
use the common expressions of one of our greatest
orators, who, in almost every speech and oration
that he has made for some years past, has given a
sort of obituary notice of himself before closing)
have been "resting in peace beneath the green sods
of Mount Auburn," or should have "gone down to
the silent tomb."

Do not laugh, beloved reader, at the tenderness of
my affection for that old place. There is a great
deal of romance of a quiet and genial kind about
Theatre Alley. As I first remember it, commerce
had not encroached upon its precincts; no tall warehouses shut out the light from its narrow footway,
and its planks were unencumbered by any intrusive
bales or boxes. Old Dearborn's scale factory was
the only thing to remind one of traffic in that neigh-

bourhood, which struck a balance with fate by becoming more scaley than before, when Dearborn and
his factory passed away. The stage door of the theatre was in the alley, and the walk from thence,
through Devonshire Street, to the Exchange Coffee
House, which was the great hotel of Boston at that
time, was once well known to many whose names are
now part of the history of the drama. How often
was I repaid for walking through the alley by the
satisfaction of meeting George Frederick Cooke, the
elder Kean, Finn, Macready, Booth, Cooper, Incle-
don, old Mathews, or the tall, dignified Conway—
or some of that goodly company that made Old
Drury classical to the play-goers of forty years
ago.

The twò posts which used to adorn and obstruct
the entrance to the alley from Franklin Street, when
they were first placed there, were an occasion of indignation to a portion of the public, and of anxiety
and vexation to Mr. Powell, the old manager. That
estimable gentleman had often been a witness to the
terror of the children and of those of the weaker sex
(I hope that I shall be forgiven by the "Rev. Antoinette Brown" for using such an adjective) who
sometimes met a stray horse or cow in the alley; so
he placed two wooden posts just beyond the theatre,
to shut out the dreaded bovine intruders. But the
devout Hibernians who used to worship at the
church in Franklin Street could not brook the placing
of any such obstacles in their way to the performance
of their religious duties; and they used to cut the
posts down as often as Mr. Powell set them up,
until he took refuge in the resources of science, and

covered and bound them with the iron bands which imprisoned them up to a very recent period.

Old Mr. Stoughton, the Spanish consul, used to occupy the first house in Franklin Street above the alley, behind which his garden ran back for some distance. How little that worthy gentleman thought that his tulip beds and rose bushes would one day give place to a dry goods shop! Señor Stoughton was one of the urbanest men that ever touched a hat. If he met you in the morning, the memory of his bland and gracious salutation never departed from you during the day, and seemed to render your sleep sweeter at night. He always treated you as if you were a prince in disguise, and he were the only person in the secret of your incognito. He enjoyed the intimate friendship of that great and good man, Dr. Cheverus, the first Bishop of Boston, who was afterwards transferred to the archiepiscopal see of Bordeaux, and decorated with the dignity of a Prince of the Church. He, too, often walked through the old alley. The children always welcomed his approach. They respected Don Stoughton; Bishop Cheverus they loved. His very look was a benediction, and the mere glance of his eye was a *Sursum corda*. That calm, wise, benignant face always had a smile for the little ones who loved the neighbourhood of that humble Cathedral, and the pockets of that benevolent prelate never knew a dearth of sugar plums. Years after that happy time, a worthy Protestant minister of this vicinity—who was blessed with few or none of those prejudices against "Romanism" which are nowadays considered a necessary part of a minister's education,—visited Cardinal Cheverus in his palace at Bordeaux, and found him keenly alive to every thing that concerned his old associations and friends in Boston. He declared, with tears in his eyes, and with that air of sincerity that marked every word he spoke, that he would gladly lay down the burden of the honour and power that then weighed upon him, to return to the care of his little New England flock. Now, Cardinal Cheverus was a man of taste and of kind feelings, and I will warrant you that when he thought of Boston, Theatre Alley was included among his associations, and enjoyed a share in his affectionate regrets.

Mrs. Grace Dunlap's little shop was an institution which many considered to be coexistent with the alley itself. It was just one of those places that seem in perfect harmony with Theatre Alley as it was twenty-five years ago. It was one of those shops that always seem to shun the madding crowd's ignoble strife, and seek a refuge in some cool sequestered way. The snuff and tobacco which Mrs. Dunlap used to dispense were of the best quality, and she numbered many distinguished persons among her customers. The author of the History of Ferdinand and Isabella was often seen there replenishing his box, and exchanging kind courtesies with the fair-spoken dealer in that fragrant article which is productive of so many bad voices and so much real politeness in European society. Mrs. Dunlap herself was a study for an artist. Her pleasant face, her fair complexion, her quiet manner, her white cap, with its gay ribbons, rivalling her eyes in brightness, were all in perfect keeping with the scrupulous neatness and air of repose that always reigned in her shop. Her parlour was as comfortable a place as you would wish to see on a summer or a winter day. It had a cheerful English look that I always loved. The plants in the windows, the bird cage, the white curtains, the plain furniture, that looked as if you might use it without spoiling it, the shining andirons, and the blazing wood fire, are all treasured in my memory of Theatre Alley as it used to be. Mrs. Dunlap's customers and friends (and who could help being her friend?) were always welcome in her parlour, and there were few who did not enjoy her simple hospitality more than that pretentious kind which sought to lure them with the pomp and vanity of mirrors and gilding. Her punch was a work of art. But I will refrain from pursuing this subject further. It is no pleasure to me to harrow up the feelings of my readers by dwelling upon the joys of their *præteritos annos*.

When Mrs. Dunlap moved out of the alley, its glory began to decline. From that day its *prestige* seemed to have gone. Even before that time an attempt had been made to rob it of its honoured name. Signs were put up at each end of it bearing the inscription, "Odeon Avenue"; but the attempt was vain, whether it proceeded from motives of godliness or of respectability; nobody ever called it any thing but Theatre Alley. At about that time nearly all the buildings left in it were devoted to the philanthropic object of the quenching of human thirst. We read that St. Paul took courage when he saw *three* taverns. Who can estimate the height of daring to which the Apostle of the Gentiles might have risen had it been vouchsafed to him to walk through Theatre Alley. One of the most frequented resorts there rejoiced in the name of "The Rainbow"—an auspicious title, certainly, and one which would attract those who were averse to the cold water principle. Some of the places were below the level of the alley, and verified, in a striking manner, the truth of Virgil's words, *Facilis descensus taverni*. Among certain low persons, not appreciative of its poetic associations, the alley at that time was nicknamed "Rum Row"; and he was considered a hero who could make all the ports in the passage through, and carry his topsails when he reached Franklin Street. Various efforts were made at that period to bring the alley into disrepute. Among others, a sign was put up announcing that it was *dangerous passing* through there; I fear that Father Mathew would have thought a declaration that it was dangerous *stopping*, to have been nearer the truth. But the daily deputations from the Old Colony and Worcester Railways could not be kept back by any signs, and the alley echoed to their multitudinous tramp every morning. Mr. Choate, too, was faithful to the alley through good and evil report, and while there was a plank left, it was daily pressed by his India rubbers. To such a lover of nature as he, what shall take the place of a morning walk through Theatre Alley!

But *venit summa dies et ineluctabile tempus*, and the old alley has been swept away. During the past century how many thousands have passed through it! how many anxious minds, engrossed with schemes of commercial enterprises, how many hearts weary with defeat, how many kind, and generous, and great, and good men, who have passed away from earthly existence, like the alley through which they walked! But while I mourn over the loss, I would not restore it if I could. When so many of its old associations had been blotted out; when low dram-drinking dens had taken the place of the ancient, quiet dispensatories of good cheer; when grim and gloomy warehouses, with their unsocial, distrustful iron shutters, had made the warm sunlight a stranger to it,—it was time for it to go. It was better that it should cease to exist, than continue in its humiliation, a reproach to the neighbourhood, and a libel upon its ancient and honourable fame.

THE OLD CATHEDRAL

IN many people who have been abroad, the mere mention of the old city of Rouen is enough to kindle an enthusiasm. If you would know why this is,—why those who are familiar with the cathedrals of Cologne, Milan, Florence, and the basilicas of Rome, have yet so deep a feeling about the old capital of Normandy,—the true answer is, that Rouen, with its Gothic glories and the thrilling history of the middle ages written on its every stone, was the first ancient city that they saw, and made the deepest impression on their minds. They had left the stiff and unsympathetic respectability of Boston, the tiresome cleanliness of Philadelphia, or the ineffable filth of New York behind them; or perchance they had been emancipated from some dreary western town, whose wide, straight, unpaved streets seemed to have no beginning and to end nowhere; whose atmosphere was pervaded with an odour of fresh paint and new shingles, and whose inhabitants would regard fifty years as a highly respectable antiquity,— and had come steaming across the unquiet Atlantic to Havre, eager to see an old city. A short railway ride carried them to one in which they could not turn a corner without seeing something to remind them of what they had seen in pictures or read in books about the middle ages. The richly-carved window frames, the grotesque faces, the fanciful devices, the profusion of ornament, the shrines and statues of the saints at the corners of the streets, and all the other picturesque peculiarities of that queer old city, filled them with wonder and delight. Those fantastic gables that seemed to be leaning over to look at them, inspired them with a respect which all the architectural wonders and artistic trophies of the continent are powerless to disturb.

It was not my fortune thus to make acquaintance with Rouen. I had several times tasted the pleasure of a continental sojourn. The streets of several of the great European capitals were as familiar to me as those of my native city. Yet Rouen captivated me with a charm peculiarly its own. I shall not easily forget the delicious summer day in which I left Paris for a short visit to Rouen. That four hours' ride over the Western Railway of France was full of solid enjoyment for every sense. The high cultivation of that fertile and unfenced country—the farmers at work in the sunny broad-stretched fields—the hay-makers piling up their fragrant loads—the château-like farm houses, looking as stately as if they had strayed out of the city, and, getting lost, had thought it beneath their dignity to inquire the way back—and those old compactly built towns, in each of which the houses seem to have nestled together around a moss-grown church tower, like children at the knees of a fond mother,—made up a scene which harmonized admirably with my feelings and with the day, "so calm, so cool, so bright, the bridal of the earth and sky." My fellow-passengers shared in the general joy which the blithesomeness of nature inspired. We all chatted merrily together, and a

German, who looked about as lively as Scott's Commentaries bound in dark sheep-skin, tried to make a joke. So irresistible was the contagion of cheerfulness, that an Englishman, who sat opposite me, so far forgot his native dignity, as to volunteer the remark that it was a "nice day."

At last we began to consult our watches and time tables, and, after a shrill whistle and a ride through a long tunnel, I found myself, with a punctuality by which you might set your Frodsham, in the station at Rouen. I obeyed the instructions of the conductor to *Messieurs les voyageurs pour Rouen* to *descendez*, and was, in a very few minutes, walking leisurely through narrow and winding streets, which I used to think existed only in the imaginations of novelists and scene-painters. I say walking, but the fact is, I did not know what means of locomotion I employed in my progress through the town. My eyes and mind were too busy to take cognizance of any inferior matters. My astonishment and delight at all that met my sight was not so great as my astonishment and delight to find myself astonished and delighted. I had seen so many old cities that I had no thought of getting enthusiastic about Rouen, until I found myself suddenly in a state of mental exaltation. I had visited Rouen as many people visit churches and galleries of art in Italy—because I had an opportunity, and feared that in after years I might be asked if I had ever been there. But, if a dislike to acknowledge my ignorance led me to Rouen, it was a very different sentiment that took possession of me as soon as I caught the spirit of the place. The genius of the past seemed to inhabit every street and alley of that strange city. I half expected, whenever I heard the hoofs of horses, to find myself encompassed by mailed knights; and if Joan of Arc, with her sweet maidenly face beaming with the inspiration of religious patriotism, had galloped by, it would not have surprised me so much as it did to realize that I—a Yankee, clad in a gray travelling suit, with an umbrella in my hand, and drafts to a limited amount on Baring Brothers in my pocket— was moving about in the midst of such scenes, and was not arrested and hustled out of the way as a profane intruder.

Wandering through the mouldy streets without any definite idea whither they led, and so charmed by all I saw, that I did not care, I suddenly turned a corner and suddenly found myself in a market-place well filled with figures, which would have graced a similar scene in any opera-house, and facing that stupendous cathedral which is one of the glories of France. I do not know how to talk learnedly about architecture; so I can spare you, dear reader, any criticism on the details of that great church. I have no doubt that it is full of faults, but my unskilful eyes rested only on its beauties. I would not have had it one stroke of the chisel less ornate, nor one shade less dingy. I could not, indeed, help thinking what it must have been centuries ago, when it was in all the glory of its fresh beauty; but still I rejoiced that it was reserved for me to behold it in the perfected loveliness and richer glory of its decay. Never until then did I fully appreciate the truth of Mr. Ruskin's declaration, that the greatest glory of a building is not in its sculptures or in its gold, but in its age,—nor did I ever before perfectly comprehend his eloquent words touching that mysterious sympathy which we feel in "walls that have long been washed by the passing waves of humanity."

After lingering for a while before the sacred edifice, I entered, and stood within its northern aisle. Arches above arches, supported by a forest of massive columns, seemed to be climbing up as if they aspired to reach the throne of Him whose worship was daily celebrated there. The sun was obscured by a passing cloud as I entered, and that made the ancient arches seem doubly solemn. The stillness that reigned there was rendered more profound by the occasional twitter of a swallow from some "jutty frieze," or "coigne of vantage," high up above my head. I walked half way up the aisle, and stopped on hearing voices at a distance. As I stood listening, the sun uncovered his radiant face, and poured his golden glory through the great western windows of the church, bathing the whole interior with a prismatic brilliancy which made me wonder at my presumption in being there. At the same moment a clear tenor voice rang out from the choir as if the sunbeams had called it into being, giving a wonderful expression to the words of the Psalmist, *Dominus illuminatio mea et salus mea; quem timebo.* Then came a full burst of music as the choir took up the old Gregorian Chant—the universal language of prayer and praise. As the mute groves of the Academy reëcho still the wisdom of the sages, so did that ancient church people my mind with forms and scenes of an age long passed away. "I was all ear," and those solemn strains seemed to be endowed with the accumulated melody of the *Misereres* and *Glorias* of a thousand years.

I have an especial affection for an old church, and I pity with all my heart the man whom the-silent eloquence of that vast cathedral does not move. The very birds that build their nests in its mouldering towers have more soul than he. Its every stone is a sermon on the transitoriness of human enterprise and the vanity of worldly hopes. Beneath its pavement lie buried hopes and ambitions which have left no memorial but in the unread pages of forgotten historians. Richard, the lion-hearted, who made two continents ring with the fame of his valour, and yearned for new conquests, was obliged at last to content himself with the dusty dignity and obscurity of a vault beneath those lofty arches which stand unmoved amid the contentions of rival dynasties and the insane violence of republican anarchy.

But it was not merely to write of the glories of Rouen and its churches, that I took up my neglected pen. The old cathedral of which I have now a few kind words to say, does not, like that of Rouen, date back sixteen centuries to its foundation; neither is it one of those marvels of architecture in which the conscious stone seems to have grown naturally into forms of enduring beauty. No great synods or councils have been held within its walls; nor have its humble aisles resounded daily with the divine office chanted by a chapter of learned and pious canons. Indeed it bears little in its external appearance that would raise a suspicion of its being a cathedral at all. Yet its plain interior, its simple altars, and its unpretentious episcopal throne, bear witness to the abiding-place of that power which is radiated from the shrine of the Prince of the Apostles—as unmistakably as if it were encrusted with mosaics, and the genius of generations of great masters had been taxed in its adornment.

The Cathedral of Boston is the last relic of Franklin Street as I delight to remember it. One by one, the theatre, the residence of the Catholic bishops, and the old mansions that bore such a Berkeley Square-y look of respectability have passed away; and the old church alone remains. Tall warehouses look down upon it, as if it were an intruder there, and the triumphal car of traffic makes its old walls tremble and disturbs the devotion of its worshippers. An irreverent punster ventured a few months since to suggest that, out of regard to its new associations, it ought to be rededicated under the invocation of St. Casimir, and to be enlarged by the addition of a chapel built in honor of St. Pantaleone.

> Quid non mortalia pectora cogis,
> Joci sacra fames!

But it is well that it should follow the buildings with which it held companionship through so many quiet years. The charm of the old street has been destroyed, and the sooner the last monument of its former state is removed the better it will be. The land on which it stands formerly belonged to the Boston Theatre corporation. It was transferred to its present proprietorship in the last week of the last century, and the first Catholic church in New England was erected upon it. That church (enlarged considerably by the late Bishop Fenwick) is the one which still stands, and towards which I feel a veneration similar in kind to that inspired by the cathedrals of the old world. Even now I remember with pleasure how I used to enjoy an occasional visit to that strange place in my boyhood. "Logic made easy" and "Geometry for Infant Schools" were things unknown in my young days. I was weaned from the Primer and Spelling-book with the Arabian Nights' Entertainments, and the works of Defoe, Goldsmith, Addison, and Shakespeare. Therefore the romantic instinct was not entirely crushed out of my youthful heart, and it would be difficult, dear reader, for you to conceive how much I found to feed it on, within those plain brick walls.

The lamp which used to burn constantly before the altar, until an anxiety for "improvement" removed it out of sight behind the pulpit, filled me with an indescribable awe. I was ignorant of its meaning, and for years was unaware that my childish reverence for its mild flicker was a blind homage to one of the profoundest mysteries of the Catholic faith. I remember to this day the satisfaction I took in the lighting of those tall candles, and what a halo of mysterious dignity surrounded even the surpliced boys grouped around that altar. That strange ceremonial surpassed my comprehension. The Latin, as I heard it sung there, was pronounced so differently from what I had been taught at school, that it was all Greek to me. Yet, when I saw the devotion of that congregation, and the pious zeal of the devoted clergymen who built that church, I could not call their worship "mummery," nor join in the irreverent laughter of my comrades at those ancient rites.

There was something about them that seemed to fill up my ideal of worship—a soothing and consoling influence which I found nowhere else.

I never entertained the vulgar notion of a Catholic priest. Of course my education led me to regard the dogmas of the Roman Church with any thing but a friendly eye; but my ideas of the clergy of that Church were not influenced by popular prejudice. I was always willing to believe that Vincent de Paul, and Charles Borromeo, and Fénelon were what they were, *in consequence* of their religion, rather than *in spite* of it, as some people, who make pretensions to liberality, would fain persuade us. When I recall the self-denying lives of the two founders of the Catholic Church in Boston,—Matignon and Cheverus,—I wonder that the influence of their virtues has not extended even to the present day, to soften prejudice and do away with *ir*religious animosity. They were regarded with distrust, if not with hatred, when they first came among us to take charge of that humble flock; but their devotedness, joined with great acquirements and rare personal worth, overcame even the force of the great Protestant tradition of enmity towards their office. Protestant admiration kept pace with Catholic love and veneration in their regard, and when they built the church which is now so near the term of its existence, there were few wealthy Protestants in Boston who did not esteem it a privilege to aid them with liberal contributions. The first subscription paper for its erection was headed by the illustrious and venerable name of John Adams, the successor of Washington in the presidency of the United States.

The memory of the first Bishop of Boston, Dr. Cheverus, is (for most Bostonians of my age) the most precious association connected with the Cathedral. He was endeared to the people of this city by ten years of unselfish exertion in the duties of a missionary priest, before he was elevated to the dignity of the episcopate. His unwillingness to receive the proffered mitre was as characteristic of his modest and humble spirit, as the meekness with which he bore his faculties when the burden of that responsibility was forced upon him. His "episcopal palace," as he used facetiously to term his small and scantily-furnished dwelling, which was contiguous to the rear of the church, was the resort of all classes of the community. His simplicity of manner and ingenuous affability won all hearts. The needy and opulent, the learned and illiterate, the prosperous merchant and the Indians in the unknown wilds of Maine, found in him a father and a friend. Children used to run after him as he walked down Franklin Place, delighted to receive a smile and a kind word from one whose personal presence was like a benediction.

His face was the index of a pure heart and a great mind. It was impossible to look at him without recalling that fine stanza of the old poet.—

> "A sweete attractive kind of grace,
> A full assurance given by lookes,
> Continuall comfort in a face,
> The lineaments of Gospel bookes;—
> I trow that countenance cannot lie
> Whose thoughts are legible in the eye."

THE OLD CATHEDRAL

One of the ancient Hebrew prophets, in describing the glories of the millennial period, tells us that upon the bells of the horses shall be the words, *Holiness unto the Lord*—a prophecy which always reminded me of Cheverus; for that divine inscription seemed to have been written all over his benign countenance as with the luminous pen of the rapt evangelist in Patmos.

But Bishop Cheverus was not merely a good man —he was a great man. He did not court the society of the learned, for his line of duty lay among the poor; but, even in that humble sphere, his talents shone out brightly, and won the respect even of those who had the least sympathy with the Church to which his every energy was devoted. Boston valued him highly; but few of her citizens thought, as they saw him bound on some errand of mercy through her streets, that France envied them the possession of such a prelate, that the peerage of the old monarchy was thought to need his virtuous presence, and that the scarlet dignity of a Prince of the Church was in reserve for that meek and self-sacrificing servant of the poor. Had he been gifted with prophetic vision, his humility would have had much to suffer, and his life would have been made unhappy, by the thought of coming power and honour. He had given the best part of his life to Boston, and here he wished to die. He had buried his friend and fellow-labourer, Dr. Matignon, in the Church of St. Augustine at South Boston, and when he placed the mural tablet over the tomb of that venerable priest, he left a space for his own name, and expressed the hope that, as they had lived together harmoniously for so many years, they might not in death be separated. It was a strange sight to see more than two hundred Protestants remonstrating against the translation of a Catholic bishop from their city, and speaking of him in such terms as these: "We hold him to be a blessing and a treasure in our social community, which we cannot part with, and which, without injustice to any man, we may affirm, if withdrawn from us, can never be replaced." And when he distributed all that he possessed among his clergy, his personal friends and the poor, and left Boston as poor as he had entered it, with the single trunk that contained his clothes when he arrived, twenty-seven years before,—public admiration outran the power of language. Doctrinal differences were forgotten. Three hundred carriages and other vehicles escorted him several miles on the road to New York, where he was to embark.

Of his life as Bishop of Montauban, Archbishop of Bordeaux, a Peer of France, and a Cardinal, there is not space for me to speak. Suffice it to say, that amid all the dignities to which he was successively promoted, he lived as simply and unostentatiously as when he dwelt in Franklin Street; and that in time of pestilence and public distress he showed the same unbounded charity which caused his departure from Boston to be considered a public calamity. To the last day of his life he maintained his interest in his American home, and would gladly have relinquished all his dignities to return and minister at the altar of the church he here erected. Throughout France he was honoured and beloved, even as he had been in the metropolis of New England, and a nation sorrowed at his death. Full as his life was of good works, it was not in his eloquence, nor his learning, nor in the pious and charitable enterprises which he originated, that the glory of Cardinal Cheverus consisted; it was in the simplicity of his character and the daily beauty of his life:—

> "His thoughts were as a pyramid up-piled,
> On whose far top an angel stood and smiled,
> Yet in his heart he was a little child."

The gentle and benevolent spirit of that illustrious prelate has never departed from the church he built. When Channing died, and was buried from the church which his eloquence had made famous, the successor of Cheverus caused the bell of the neighbouring Cathedral to be tolled, that it might not seem as if the Catholics had forgotten the friendly relations which had existed between the great Unitarian preacher and their first bishop. And when the good Bishop Fenwick was borne from the old Cathedral, with all the pomp of pontifical obsequies, his courtesy and regard for Dr. Channing's memory was not forgotten, and the bell which was so lately removed from the tower, where it had swung for half a century, joined with that of the Cathedral in giving expression to the general sorrow, and proved that no dogmatic differences had disturbed the kindly spirit which Channing inculcated and had exemplified in his blameless life.

Of the later history of the Cathedral of the Holy Cross I may not speak. My youthful respect for it has in no degree diminished, and I shall always consider it a substantial refutation of the old apothegm,

"Familiarity breeds contempt." There are, I doubt not, those who regard that old edifice with deeper feelings than mine. Who can estimate the affection and veneration in which it is held by those who may there have found an asylum from harassing doubts, who have received from that font the joy of a renovated heart, and from that altar the divine gift which is at the same time a consolation for past sorrows and a renewal of strength to tread the rough path of life!

I am told that it will not probably be long before the glittering cross which the pure-hearted Cheverus placed upon the old church will be removed, and the demolition of his only monument in Boston will be effected. Permit me to conclude these reminiscences with the expression of the hope that the new Cathedral of Boston will be an edifice worthy of this wealthy city, and that it may contain some fitting memorial of the remarkable man who exercised his beneficent apostolate among us during more than a quarter of a century. The virtues which merited the gratitude of the poor and the highest honours which pontiffs and kings can bestow, ought not to go uncommemorated in the city which witnessed their development, and never hesitated to give expression to its love and veneration for their possessor. But whatever the new Cathedral may be,—however glorious the skill of the architect, the sculptor, and the painter may render it,—there are those in whose affections it will never be able to replace the little unpretending church which Cheverus built, and which the remembrance of his saintly life has embalmed in all their hearts.

THE PHILOSOPHY OF
SUFFERING

> I am old,
> And my infirmities have chained me here
> To suffer and to vex my weary soul
> With the vain hope of cure.* * *
> Yet my captivity is not so joyless
> As you would think, my masters. Here I sit
> And look upon this eager, anxious world,—
> Not with the eyes of sour misanthropy,
> Nor envious of its pleasures,—but content,—
> Yea, blessedly content, 'mid all my pains,
> That I no more may mingle with its brawlings.

HUMAN suffering is an old and favourite theme. From the time when the woes of Job assumed an epic grandeur of form, and the adventures and pains of Philoctetes inspired the tragic muse of Sophocles, down to the publication of the last number of the *London Lancet,* there would seem to have been no subject so attractive as the sufferings of poor humanity. Literature is filled with their recital, and, if books were gifted with a vocal power, every library would resound with wailings. Ask your neighbour Jenkins, who overtakes you on your way to your office, how he is, and it is ten chances to one that he will entertain you with an account of his influenza or his rheumatism. It is a subject, too, which age cannot wither nor custom stale. It knows none of the changes which will at times dwarf or keep out of sight all other themes. The weather, which forms the raw material of so much conversation, is nothing compared to it. There is nothing which men find so much pleasure in talking about as their own ailments. The late Mr. Webster, of Marshfield, was once stopping for a single day in a western city, where he had never been before, and where there was a natural curiosity among many of the inhabitants to see the Defender of the Constitution. He therefore set apart two hours before the time of his departure for the reception of such persons as might seek the honour of a shake of his hand. The reception took place in one of the parlours of a hotel, the crowd filing in at one door, being introduced by the mayor, and making their exit by another. In the course of the proceedings, a little man, with a lustrous beaver in one hand and a gold-headed cane in the other, and whose personal apparel appeared to have been got up (as old Pelby would have said) without the slightest regard to expense, and on a scale of unparalleled splendour, walked forward, and was presented by the mayor as "Mr. Smith, one of our most eminent steamboat builders and leading citizens." Mr. Webster's large, thoughtful, serene eyes seemed to be completely filled by the result of the combined efforts of the linen-draper, the tailor, and the jeweller, that confronted him, and his deep voice made answer—"Mr. Smith, I am happy to see you. I hope you are well, sir." "Thank you, thir," said the leading citizen, "I am not very well. I wath tho unfortunate ath to take cold yethterday by thitting in a draught. Very unpleathant, Mr. Webthter, to have a cold! But

THE PHILOSOPHY OF SUFFERING

Mrs. Smith thays that the thinks that if I put my feet in thome warm water to-night, and take thomething warm to drink on going to bed, that I may get over it. I thertainly hope tho, for it really givth me the headache, and I can't thmell at all." Mr. Webster expressed a warm interest in Mr. Smith's case, and a hope that Mrs. Smith's simple medical treatment would result beneficially, and then turned with undisturbed gravity to the next citizen, who, with some six hundred others, was anxiously waiting his turn. We are all like Mr. Smith. We laugh, it is true, at his affectations, but we are as likely to force our petty ailments upon a mind burdened with the welfare of a nation; and we never tire of hearing ourselves talk about our varying symptoms. Politeness may hold us back from importuning our friends with the diagnosis of our case, but our self-centred hearts are all alike, and a cold in the head will awaken more feelings in its victim than the recital of all the horrors of the hospital of Scutari. Nothing can equal the heroic fortitude with which we bear the sufferings of our fellows, or the saintliness of our pious resignation and acquiescence in the wisdom of the divine decrees when our friends are bending under their afflictive stroke.

I wish to say a few words about suffering. Do not be afraid, beloved reader, that I am going to carry you into rooms from which the light is excluded, and which are strangers to any sound above a whisper, or the casual movement of some of the phials on the mantel-piece. I am going to speak of suffering in its strict sense of pain,—bodily pain,—and sickness is not necessarily accompanied with pain. I cannot re-

[277]

gard your sick man as a real sufferer. His fever rages, and he tosses from side to side as if he were suffering punishment with Dives; but from the incoherent phrases which escape from his parched lips, you learn that his other self is rapt in the blissfulness that enfolds Lazarus. He prattles childishly of other lands and scenes—he thinks himself surrounded by friends whose faces once were grateful to his sight, but who long since fell before the power with which he is struggling—or he fancies himself metamorphosed into a favourite character in some pleasant book which he has lately read. After a time he wakes forth from his delirium, but he cannot even then be called a sufferer. On the contrary, his situation, even while he is so entirely dependent upon those around him, is really the most independent one in the world. His lightest wish is cared for as if his life were the price of its non-accomplishment. All his friends and kinsmen, and neighbours whom he hardly knows by sight, vie with each other in trying to keep pace with his returning appetite. He is the absolute monarch of all he surveys. There is no one to dispute his reign. The crown of convalescence is the only one which does not make the head that wears it uneasy. He has nothing to do but to satisfy his longings for niceties, to listen to kind words from dear friends, to sleep when he feels like it, and to get better. I am afraid that we are all so selfish and so enslaved by our appetites, that the period of convalescence is the pleasantest part of life to most of us.

Therefore I shut out common sickness, fevers, and the like, from any share in my observations on suffer-

ing. If you ask me what I should be willing to consider real bodily pain,—since I am unwilling to allow
that ordinary sick men participate in it,—I should
say that you can find it in a good, old-fashioned attack of rheumatism or gout. I think it was Horace
Walpole who said that these two complaints were
very much alike, the difference between them being
this: that rheumatism was like putting your hand or
foot into a vice, and screwing it up as tight as you
possibly can, and gout was the same thing, only you
give the screw one more turn. It is no flattery to
speak of the victim to either of these disorders as a
sufferer. The rheumatic gout is a complaint which
possesses all the advantages and peculiarities which
its compound title denotes. It unites in itself all the
potentiality of gout and all the ubiquity of rheumatism. Its characteristics have been impressed
upon me in a manner that sets at defiance that weakness of memory which generally accompanies old
age. Sharp experience, increasing in sharpness as
my years pile up, makes that complaint a specialty
among my acquirements. These stinging, burning,
cutting pains deserve the superlative case, if any
thing does. Language (that habitual bankrupt) is
reduced to a most abject state when called upon to
describe rheumatic gout. The disease does not seem
to feel satisfied with poisoning your blood by its
aciduousness, it makes your flesh tingle and burn,
and, like the late Duke of Wellington, does not rest
until it has conquered the bony part. The very bone
seems to be crumbling wherever the demon of gout
pinches. There are moments in the life of every
gouty man when it seems as if nothing would be so re-

freshing as to indulge for a while in the use of that energetic diction, savouring more of strength than of righteousness, which is common among cavalry troops and gentlemen of the seafaring profession, but which, in society, is considered to be a little in advance of the prejudices of the age. No higher encomium could be passed upon a gouty man than to say that, with all his torments, he never swore, and was seldom petulant. But there are very few whose merits deserve this canonization.

But gout, with all its pains, has yet its redeeming characteristics. That great law of compensation which reduces the inequalities of our lot, and makes Brown, Jones, and Robinson come out about even in the long run, is not inoperative here. The gout is painful, but its respectability is unquestionable. It is the disease of a gentleman. It is a certificate of good birth more satisfactory than any which the Heralds' College or the Genealogical Association can furnish. It is but right, too, that the man who can date back his family history to Plymouth or Jamestown in this country, and to Runnymede on the other side of the Atlantic, should pay something for such a privilege. A man may never have indulged in "the sweet poison of the Tuscan grape" himself, but can he reasonably complain of an incontrovertible testimony to the fact that his ancestors lived well! *Chacun à son goût:* for myself, I should much prefer my honoured family name, with all its associations with the brave knight who made it famous, accompanied by the only possession which I have received by hereditary right, to the most unequivocal state of health burdened with such a name as Jinkins.

THE PHILOSOPHY OF SUFFERING

Mentally and spiritually, the gout is far from being a useless institution. It ripens a man's judgment, and prunes away the radical tendencies of his nature. It will convert the wildest of revolutionists into the stiffest of conservatives. It teaches a man to look at things as they really are, and not as enthusiasm would have them represented. No gouty man would ever look to the New York Tribune as the exponent of his religious or political creed. His complaint has a positive character, and it makes him earnest to find something positive in religion and politics. The negativeness of radicalism tires him. He deprecates every thing like change. He thinks that religion, and society, and government were established for some better end than to afford a perpetual employment to the destructive powers of visionary reformers and professional philanthropists. He longs to find constancy and stability in something besides his inexorable disorder.

There is another disorder which people generally seem to consider a very trifling affair, but which any one who knows it will allow to be productive of the most unmistakable pain. I refer to neuralgia. Who pities a neuralgic person? Any healthy man, when asked about it, will answer in his ignorance that it is "only a headache." But ask the school teacher, whose throbbing head seems to be beating time to the ceaseless muttering and whispering of her scholars as they bend over their tasks—ask the student, whose thoughts, like undisciplined soldiers, will not fall into the ranks, and whose head seems to be occupied by a steam engine of enormous power, running at the highest rate of pressure, with the driver

sitting on the safety-valve—ask them whether neuralgia is "only a headache"! Who can tell the
cause of the prevalence of this scourge? whether it
proceeds from our houses overheated with intolerable furnaces and anthracite coal, or from our treach-
erous and unconstant climate so forcibly described by
Choate: "Cold to-day; hot to-morrow; mercury at
eighty degrees in the morning, with wind at south-
west; and in three hours more a sea turn, with wind
at east, a thick fog from the very bottom of the
ocean, and a fall of forty degrees of Fahrenheit."
The uncertainty which seems to attend all human
science, and the science of medicine in particular, en-
velops this mysterious disease, and thousands of us
are left to suffer and wonder what the matter is.

But all of these pains, gouty, neuralgic, and
otherwise, have yet their sweet uses, and like the vile
reptile Shakespeare tells us of, are adorned with a
precious jewel. The old Roman emperors in the
hour of triumph used to have a slave stand behind
them to whisper in their ear, from time to time, the
unwelcome but salutary truth that they were but
mortal men. Even now, on the occasion of the en-
thronement of a Pope, a lighted candle is applied to
a bunch of flax fixed upon a staff, and as the smoke
dissipates itself into thin air before the newly-
crowned Pontiff, surrounded as he is by all the em-
blems of religion and all the insignia and pomp of
worldly power, the same great truth of the perish-
ableness of all mortal things is impressed upon his
mind by the chanting of the simple but eloquent
phrase, *Sic transit gloria mundi.* But we neuralgic
and gouty wretches need no whispering slave nor

smoking flax to remind us of our frailty and the transientness of our happiness and glory. We carry with us a monitor who checks our swelling pride, and teaches us effectually the brevity of human joys. We are very apt, in our impatience and short-sightedness, to think that if we had the management of the world and the dispensation of pleasure and suffering, every thing could be conducted in a much more satisfactory manner. If it were so, we should undoubtedly carry things on in the style of a French restaurant, so that we could have *pain à discretion*. But on the whole, I am inclined to think that we had better leave these matters to the management of that infinite Power which gives us day by day our daily pain, and from which we receive in the long run about what is meet for us. I hope that I shall not be thought ill-bred or profane in using such expressions as these. At my time of life it is too late to begin to murmur. A few twinges more or less are nothing when the hair grows gray and the eye is dimmed with the mists of age. The man who knows nothing of the novitiate of patience—who has passed through life without the chastening discipline of bodily pain—has missed one of the best parts of existence. To suffer is one of the noblest prerogatives of human nature. Without suffering, life would be robbed of half its zest, and the thought of death would drive us to despair.

When I was a young man, and gave little thought to the gout and the other ills that vex me at present, I saw a wonderful exhibition of patience, which I now daily recall to mind, and wish I could imitate. I was sojourning in Florence, that lovely city, whose every association is one of calm and satisfactory

pleasure undisturbed by any thing like bodily suffering. I enjoyed the friendship of a young American
amateur artist of unquestioned talent, but whose
artistic efforts were interfered with by the frequent
attacks of a serious and excruciating disorder. It
was considerable time after I made his acquaintance
before I knew that he was an invalid. I noticed his
lameness, but whenever we met he wore a smiling
face, and had a cheerful word for every body. One
evening I called in at his quiet lodgings near the
Lung' Arno, and found a party of some six or eight
Americans talking over their recollections of home.
He was entertaining them with the explanation of an
imaginary panorama of New England, and a musical
friend threw in illustrative passages from the piano
in the intervals. The parlour resounded with our
laughter at his irresistible fun; but in the midst of it
all, he asked us to excuse him for a moment, and
went into his bed-room. After a little while, another
engagement calling me away, I went into his chamber
to speak with him before leaving. I found him lying
upon his bed, writhing like Laocoön, while great
drops stood upon his brow and agony was depicted
on his patient face. He resisted all my attempts to
do any thing for him; the attack had lasted all day,
but was at some times severer than at others; he
should feel better soon, and would go back to his
friends; I had better not stop with him, as it might
attract their attention in the parlour, &c. So I took
my leave. The next morning I met one of his
friends, who told me that he returned to his company a few minutes after my departure, and entertained them for an hour or more with an exhibition

of his powers of wit and humour, which eclipsed all his previous efforts. Poor S. C.! His weary but uncomplaining spirit laid down that crippled body, which never gave aught but pain to its possessor, three or four years ago, and passed, let us hope, into a happier state of existence, which flesh and blood, with their countless maladies and dolours, may not inherit.

The traveller in the south of Europe frequently encounters, in his perambulations through the streets and squares of cities, a group of people gathered around a monk, who is discoursing to them of those sublime truths which men are prone to lose sight of in their walks abroad. The style of the sermon is not, it is true, what we should look for from Newman, or Ravignan, or Ventura, but it has in it those fundamental principles of true eloquence, simplicity and earnestness; and the coarse brown habit, the knotted cord, and the pale, serene, devout face of the preacher, harmonize wondrously with the self-denying doctrine he teaches, and give a double force to all his words. His instructions frequently concern the simple moral duties of life and the exercise of the cardinal virtues, which he enforces by illustrations drawn from the lives of canonized saints, who won their heavenly crown and their earthly fame of blessedness by the practice of those virtues. Allow me to close my sermon on suffering in the manner of the preaching friars, though I may not draw my illustrations from the ancient martyrologies; for I apprehend that it will be more in keeping with the serious character of this essay to take them from another source. We have all laughed at Dickens's characters of Mark Tapley and Mr. Toots. The former was celebrated for "keeping jolly under disadvantageous circumstances," and seemed to mourn over those dispensations of good fortune which detracted from his credit in being jolly. The latter was never known to indulge in any complaint, but met every mishap and disappointment with a manly resignation and the simple remark, "It's of no consequence." Even when he was completely ingulfed in misfortunes, when Pelion seemed to have been heaped upon Ossa, and both upon him, he did not give way to despair. He only gave utterance more fervently to his favourite maxim, "It's of no consequence. Nothing is of any consequence whatever!" Now, laugh at it as we may, this is a great truth. It is the foundation of all true philosophy—of all practical religion. A few years more, and what will it avail us to have bargained successfully, to have lived in splendour, to have left in history a name that shall be the synonyme of power! A few years, and what shall we care for all our present sufferings and the light afflictions which are but for a moment! May we not say with Solomon, that "All is vanity," and with poor Toots, that "Nothing is of any consequence whatever"? Now, if there are any people who are likely to arrive at this satisfactory conclusion, and who need the consolation imparted by the reception and full appreciation of the deep truth it contains, it is the gouty, and rheumatic, and neuralgic wretches whom I have had in mind while writing this paper. Let me, in conclusion, as one who has had some experience, and is not merely theorizing, exhort all such persons to meditate upon the lives of the two great patterns of patience whom I have brought forward as examples; and to bear in mind that it is only through the resignation of Toots, that they can attain to the jollity of Tapley. Likewise let me counsel those who may be passing through life unharmed by serious misfortune and untrammelled by bodily pain, never to lose sight of that striking admonition of old Sir Thomas Browne's, "Measure not thyself by thy morning shadow, but by the extent of thy grave; and reckon thyself above the earth, by the line thou must be contented with under it."

BOYHOOD AND BOYS

HUMAN nature is a very telescopic "institution." It delights to dwell on whatever is
most distant. Lord Rosse's famous instrument
dwindles down to a mere opera glass if you compare
it with the mental vision of a restless boy, looking
forward to the time when he shall don a tail-coat and
a beaver hat. How his young heart swells with
pride as he anticipates the day when he shall be his
own master, as the phrase is—when he shall be able
to stay out after nine o'clock in the evening, and to
go home without being subjected to the ignominy of
being escorted by a chambermaid! If he be of a
particularly sanguine temperament, his wild imagination is rapt in the contemplation of the possibility of
one day having his name in the newspapers as secre-
tary of some public meeting, or as having made a
vigorous speech at a political caucus where liberty of
speech runs out into slander, and sedition is mistaken
for patriotism,—or perhaps even of being one day a
Common Councilman, or a member of the Great and
General Court. A popular poet of the present day
has expressed the same idea in a less prosaic manner:—

> "Not rainbow pinions coloured like yon cloud,
> The sun's broad banner o'er his western tent,
> Can match the bright imaginings of a child
> Upon the glories of his coming years:"—

and another bard avers that human blessings are always governing the future, and never the present tense,—or something to that effect. The truth of this nobody will deny who has passed from the boxes of childhood upon the stage of manhood which so charmed his youthful fancy, and finds that the heroes who dazzled him once by their splendid achievements are mere ordinary mortals like himself, whom the blindness or caprice of their fellows has allowed to be dressed in a little brief authority; that the cloud-capped towers and gorgeous palaces he used to gaze on from afar, prove, on a closer inspection, to be mere deceptions of paint and canvas, and that he has only to look behind them to see the rough bricks and mortar of every-day life.

The voyager who sails from the dark waters of the restless Atlantic into the deep blue Mediterranean, notices at sunset a rich purple haze which rises apparently from the surface of that fair inland sea, and drapes the hills and vales along the beautiful shore with a glory that fills the heart of the beholder with unutterable gladness. The distant, snow-covered peaks of old Granada, clad in the same bright robe, seem by their regal presence to impose silence on those whom their majestic beauty has blessed with a momentary poetic inspiration which defies all power of tongue or pen. It touches nothing which it does not adorn, and the commonest objects are transmuted by its magic into fairy shapes which abide ever after in the memory. Under its softening influence, the dingy sail of a fisherman's boat becomes almost as beautiful an object to the sight as the ruins of the temple which crowns the height of Cape Colonna.

But when you approach nearer to that which had seemed so charming in its twilight robes, your poetic sense is somewhat interfered with. You find the fishing boat as unattractive as any that anchor on the Banks from which we obtain such frequent discounts of nasty weather, and the shore, though it may still be very beautiful, lacks the supernal glory imparted to it by distance. It is very much after this fashion with manhood, when we compare its reality with our childish expectations. We find that we have been deceived by a mere atmospheric phenomenon. But the destruction of the charm which age had for our eyes as children, is compensated for by the creation of a new glory which lights up our young days, as we look back upon them with the regret of manhood, and realize that their joys can never be lived over again.

Pardon me, gentle reader, for all this prosing. I have been reading that pleasant, hearty book, "Tom Brown's School Days at Rugby," during the past week, and it has set me a-thinking about my own boyhood; for, strange as it may seem, there was a time when this troublesome foot was more familiar with the football and the skate than with gout and flannel, —and Tom Brown's genial reminiscences have revived the memory of that time most wonderfully. There was considerable fun in Boston in my childhood, even though most of the faces which one met in Marlboro' Street and Cornhill were such as might have appropriately surrounded Cromwell at Naseby or Marston Moor. There were many people, even then, who did not regard religion as an affair of spasmodic emotions, and long, bilious-looking faces, and psalm-singing, and neck-ties. They thought that, so long as they were honest in their dealings, and did not swear to false invoices at the custom-house, and did as they would be done by, and lived virtuously, that He to whom they had been taught by parental lips to pray, would overlook the smaller ·offences—such as an occasional laugh or a pleasant jest—into which weak nature would now and then betray them. I cannot help thinking that they were about right, though I fear that I shall be set down as little better than one of the wicked by Stiggins, Chad-band, Sleek & Co.

Yes, there was a good deal of fun among the boys in those old days. Boys will be boys, however serious the family may be; and if you take away their mar-bles, some other "vanity" will be sure to take their place. What jolly times we used to have Artillery Election! How good the egg-pop used to taste, in spite of the dust of Park Street, which mingled itself liberally with the nutmeg! How we used to save up our money for those festive days! How hard the arithmetic lessons seemed, particularly in the days immediately preceding vacation! How dreary were those long winters; and yet how short and pleasant they seemed to us! for we loved the runners, and skates, and jingling bells, and, as Pescatore, the Nea-politan poet, sings, "though bleak our lot, our hearts were warm."

Newspapers were not a common luxury in those times, and I suppose that I took as little notice of passing events as most children; yet I well remember the effect produced upon my mind one dark, threaten-ing afternoon, near the close of the last century, by the announcement of the death of General Washington. I had been accustomed to hear him talked about as the Father of his Country; I had studied the lineaments of his calm countenance, as they were set forth for the edification of my patriotism on some coarse handkerchiefs presented to me by a public-spirited aunt, until I began to look upon him as almost a supernatural being. If I had been told that the Old South had been removed to Dorchester Heights, or that the solar system was irreparably disarranged, I should not have been more completely taken aback than I was by that melancholy intelligence. I need not say that afterwards, when I grew up and found that Washington was not only a mortal like the rest of us, but that he sometimes spelt incorrectly enough to have suited Noah Webster, (the inventor of the American language,) my supernatural view of that estimable general and patriot was very materially modified. I remember, too, how much I used to hear said about an extraordinary man who had risen up in France, and who seemed to be bending all Europe to his will. I never shall forget my astonishment on finding that Marengo was not a man, but a place. The discovery shamed me somewhat, and afterwards I always read whatever newspapers came in my way. When some slow tub of a packet had come across the ocean, battling with the nor'-westers, and was announced to have made a "quick passage of forty-eight days," how eagerly I followed the rapid fortunes of the first Napoleon! His successes, as they intoxicated him, dazzled and bewildered my boyish imagination. I understood the matter imperfectly, but I loved Napoleon, and delighted to repeat to myself those stirring names, Austerlitz, Jena, Wagram, &c. How I hated Russia after the disastrous campaign of 1812! (By the way, the exhibition of the Conflagration of Moscow, which used to have its intermittent terms of exhibition here some years since, always brought back all my youthful feelings about the old Napoleon; the march of the artillery across the bridge, in the foreground of the scene, the rattling of the gun carriages, —that most warlike of all warlike sounds,—the burning city, the destruction of the Kremlin, all united in my mind to form a sentiment of admiration and sympathy for the baffled conqueror. If that admirable show were to be revived once more, I should be tempted to take a season ticket to it, for I have no doubt that it would thrill me just as it did before my head could boast of a single gray hair.) Nor was my admiration for Napoleon's old marshals much below that which I entertained for the mighty genius who knew so well how to avail himself of their surpassing bravery and skill. I felt as if the unconquerable Murat, Lannes, Macdonald, Davoust, were my dearest and most intimate friends. The impetuous Ney, "the bravest of the brave," as his soldiers called him; and the inflexible Masséna, "the favourite child of victory," figured in all my dreams, heading gallant charges, and withstanding deadly assaults, and occupied the best part of my waking thoughts. I do not doubt that there is many a school-boy nowadays who has dwelt with equal delight on the achievements of Scott and Taylor, of Canrobert, Bosquet and Pélissier, of Fenwick Williams and Havelock, and poor old Raglan, (that brave man

upon whom the Circumlocution Office tried to fasten
the blame of its own inefficiency, and who died
broken-hearted, a melancholy illustration of the
truth of Shakespeare's lines,—

"The painful warrior, famouséd for fight,
After a thousand victories once foiled,
Is from the book of honour razéd quite,
And all the rest forgot for which he toiled,")

and who cherishes them as I did the heroes of half a
century ago.

But, as I was saying, Tom Brown's happy reminiscences of Rugby have awakened once more all my
boyish feelings; for New England has its Rugby, and
many of the readers of the old Rugby boy's pleasant
pages will grow enthusiastic with the recollection of
their schoolboy days at Exeter,—their snowballings,
their manly sports, their mighty contests with the
boys of the town,—and, though they may not claim
the genius of the former head-master of Rugby for
the guardian of their youthful sports and studies,
will apply all of the old boy's praises of Dr. Arnold
to the wise, judicious, and lovable Dr. Abbot.

I always cherished an unbounded esteem for boys.
The boy—the genuine human boy—may, I think,
safely be set down as the noblest work of God. Pope
claims that proud distinction for the honest man, but
at the present time, the nearest we can come to such
a mythological personage as an honest man, (even
though we add Argand burners, expensive Carcels,
Davy safeties, and the Drummond light to the offi-
cially recognized lantern of Diogenes,) is a real
human boy, without a thought beyond his next holi-

day, with his heart overflowing with happiness, and his pockets chock full of marbles. Young girls cannot help betraying something of the in-dwelling vanity so natural to the sex; you can discern a self-consciousness in their every action which you shall look for in vain in the boy. Bless your heart!—you may dress a real boy up with superhuman care, and try to impress on his young mind that he is the pride of his parents, and one of the most remarkable beings that ever visited this mundane sphere, and he will listen to you with becoming reverence and docility; but his pure and honest nature will give the lie to all your flattery as soon as your back is turned, and in ten minutes you will find him kicking out the toes of his new boots, or rumpling his clean collar by "playing horse," or using the top of his new cap for a drinking vessel, and mixing in with the Smiths, and Browns, and Jinkinses, on terms of the most unquestioned equality. The author of Tom Brown says that "boys follow one another in herds like sheep, for good or evil; they hate thinking, and have rarely any settled principles." This is undoubtedly true; but still there is a generous instinct in boys which is far more trustworthy than those sliding, and unreliable, and deceptive ideas which we call settled principles. The boy's thinking powers may be fallible, but his instinct is, in the main, sure. There is no aristocracy of feeling among boys. Linsey-woolsey and broadcloth find equal favour in their eyes. What they seek is just as likely to be found under coarse raiment as under purple and fine linen. If their companion is a real good feller, even though he be a son of a rich merchant or banker, he is esteemed as

highly as if his father were an editor of a newspa·
per.

The nature of the boy is full of the very essence of
generosity. The boys who hide away their gingerbread, and eat it by themselves,—who lay up their
Fourth of July five-cent pieces, for deposit in that
excellent savings institution in School Street, instead
of spending them for the legitimate India crackers of
the "Sabbath Day of Freedom,"—are exceptions
which only put the general rule beyond the pale of
controversy. The real boy carries his apple in one
of his pockets until it is comfortably warm, and he
has found some companion to whom he may offer a
festive bite; for he feels, with Goethe, that

> "It were the greatest misery known
> To be in paradise alone;"

and if, occasionally, when he sees his friend gratifying his palate with a fair round specimen of the same
delicious fruit, he asks for a return of his kindness,
with a beckoning gesture, and a free and easy—"I
say, you know me, Bill!"—he is moved thereto by no
mere selfish liking for apples, but by a natural sense
of friendship, and of the excellence of the apostolic
principle of community of goods. This spirit of
generosity may be seen in the friendships of boys,
which are more entire and unselfish than those by
which men seek to mitigate the irksomeness of life.
There are more Oresteses and Pyladeses, more Da-
mons and Pythiases, at twelve years of age than at
any later period of life. The devotedness of boyish
friendship is peculiar from the fact that it is generally reciprocal. In this it is superior to what we

[296]

call love, which, if we may believe the French satirist, in most instances consists of one party who loves, and another who allows himself or herself to be loved. This phenomenon has not escaped the notice of that great observer of human nature, Thackeray.

"What generous boy," he asks, "in his time has not worshipped somebody? Before the female enslaver makes her appearance, every lad has a friend of friends, a crony of cronies, to whom he writes immense letters in vacation; whom he cherishes in his heart of hearts; whose sister he proposes to marry in after life; whose purse he shares; for whom he will take a thrashing if need be; who is his hero."

The generosity, and all the priceless charms of boyhood, rarely outlive its careless years of happiness. They are generally severely shaken, if not wholly destroyed, when the youth enters upon that crepuscular period of manhood in which his jacket is lengthened into a sack, and he begins to take his share in the conceit, and ambition, and selfishness of full-grown humanity. It is sad to think that a human boy, like the morning star, full of life and joy, may be stricken down by death, and all his hilarity stifled in the grave; but to my mind it is even more melancholy to think that he may live to grow up, and be hard, and worldly, and ungenerous as any of the rest of us. For this latter fate is accompanied by no consolations such as naturally assuage our sorrow when an innocent child is snatched from among his playthings,—when "death has set the seal of eternity upon his brow, and the beautiful hath been made permanent." I have seen few men who would be willing to live over again their years of manhood, however prosperous and comparatively free from trouble they may have been; but fewer still are those whom I have met, in whose memory the records of boyhood are not written as with a sunbeam. No, talk as we may about the happiness of manhood, the satisfaction of success in life, of gratified ambition, of the possession of the Mary or Lizzie of one's choice,—what is it all compared to the unadulterate joy of that time when we built our card houses, and made our dirt pies, or drove our hoops, unvexed by the thoughts that Jinkins's house was larger than ours, or by any anxiety concerning the possibility of obtaining our next day's mutton-chop and potatoes? Except the momentary pain occasioned by the exercise of a magisterial rattan upon our persons, or an occasional stern reproof from a hair-brush or the thin sole of a maternal shoe, that halcyon period is imperturbed, and may safely be called the happiest part of life.

My venerated friend, Baron Nabem, who has been through all these "experiences," and therefore ought to know, insists upon it that no man really knows any thing until he is forty years old. For when he is eighteen or twenty years of age, he esteems himself to be a sort of combination of the seven wise men of Greece in one person, with Humboldt, Mezzofanti, and Macaulay thrown in to make out the weight; at twenty-five, his confidence in his own infallibility begins to grow somewhat shaky; at thirty, he begins to wish that he might really know a tenth part as much as he thought he did ten years before; at thirty-five, he thinks that if he were added up, there would be very little to carry; and at forty the great truth bursts upon him in all its effulgence that he is an ass. There are some who reach this desirable state of self-knowledge before they attain the age specified by the Baron; other some there are who never reach it at all,—as we all see numerous instances around us,—but these are mere exceptions strengthening rather than invalidating the common rule. It is a humiliating acknowledgment, but if we consider the uncertainty of all earthly things, if we try the depth of the sea of human science, and find how easy it is to touch bottom any where therein, if we convince ourselves of the impenetrability of the veil which bounds our mental vision,—I think that we shall be obliged to allow that the recognition of our own nothingness and asininity is the sum and perfection of human knowledge. Now, Solomon tells us that he who increases knowledge increases sorrow; and it naturally follows that when a man has reached the knowledge which generally comes with his fortieth year, he is less happy than he was when he wrapped himself in the measureless content of his twentieth year's self-deception. And it follows, too, most incontrovertibly, that he is happier when unpossessed by that exaggerated self-esteem which rendered the discovery of his fortieth year necessary to him; and when is that time, if not during the careless, happy years of boyhood?

The period of boyhood has been shortened very considerably within a few years; and real boys are becoming scarce. They are no sooner emancipated from the bright buttons which unite the two principal articles of puerile apparel, than they begin to pant for virile habiliments. Their choler is roused if they are denied a stand-up dickey. They sport canes. They delight to display themselves at lectures and concerts. Their young lips are not innocent of damns and short-sixes; and they imitate the vulgarity and conceit of the young men of the present day so successfully that you find it hard to believe that they are mere children. Since this period of dearth in the boy market set in, of course the genuine, marketable article has become more precious to me. I remember seeing an old physician in Paris, who was as true a boy as any beloved twelve-year-old that ever snapped a marble or stuck his forefinger into a preserve jar on an upper shelf in a china closet. A charming old fellow he was, too. He used to stop to see the boys play in the gardens of the Tuileries, and I knew him once to spend a whole afternoon in the avenue of the Champs Elysées looking at the puppet shows and other sights with the rest of the youngsters. He told me afterwards that that was one of the happiest days of his life; for he had felt as if he were back again in the pleasant time before he knew any thing of that most uncertain of all uncertain things—the science of medicine; and he doubted whether any boy there had enjoyed the cheap amusement more than himself. I envied him, for I knew that he who retained so much of the happy spirit of boyhood could not have outlived all of its generosity and simplicity. "Once a man and twice a child," says the old proverb; and I cannot help thinking that if at the last we could only recall something of the sincerity, and innocence, and unselfishness of our early life, second childhood would indeed be a blessed thing.

JOSEPHINE

GIRLHOOD AND GIRLS

A BRIGHT-EYED, fair, young maiden, whose satchel I should insist upon carrying to school for her every morning if I were half a century younger, came to me a day or two after the publication of my last essay, and, placing her white, taper fingers in my rough, Esau-like hand, said, "I liked your piece about the boys very much; and now I hope that you'll write something about girls." "My dear Nellie," replied I, "if I should do that I should lose all my female acquaintances. I have a weakness for telling the truth, and there are some subjects concerning which it is very dangerous to speak out 'the whole truth and nothing but the truth.'" The gentle damsel smiled, and looked

> "Modest as justice, and did seem a palace
> For the crown'd truth to dwell in,"

as she still urged me on, and refused to see any danger in my giving out the plainest truth about girlhood. *She* had no fear, though all the truth were told; and I suppose that if we had some of Nellie's purity and gentleness remaining in our sere and selfish hearts, we should be much better and happier men and women, and should dread the truth as little as she does. But I must not begin my truth-telling by seeming to praise too highly, though it must be confessed, even at my time of life, if I were to describe the charming young person I have referred to, with the merciless fidelity of a daguerreotype and an absence of hyperbole worthy of the late Dr. Bowditch's work on Navigation, I should seem to the unfortunate "general reader" who does not know Nell, to be indulging in the grossest flattery, and panting poesy would toil after me in vain. So I will put aside all temptations of that kind, and come down to the plain prose of my subject.

There is, in fact, very little that can be said about girlhood. Those calm years that come between the commencement of the bondage of the pantalettes and emancipation from the tasks of school, present few salient points upon which the essayist (observe he never so closely) may turn a neat paragraph. They offer little that is startling or attractive either to writer or reader,—

> "As times of quiet and unbroken peace,
> Though for a nation times of blessedness,
> Give back faint echoes from the historian's page."

The rough sports of boyhood, the out-door life which boys always take to so naturally, and all their habits of activity, give a strength of light and shade to their early years which is not to be found in girlhood. It is not enough to say that there is no difference in kind, but simply one in degree,—that the years of boyhood are calm and happy, and that those of girlhood are so likewise,—that the former resemble the garish sunshine, and the latter the mitigated splendour of the moon; for the characters of boys seem to be struck in a sharper die than those of girls, which gives them an absoluteness quite distinct from the feminine grace we naturally look for in the latter. The free-hearted boy, plunging into all sorts of fun without a thought of his next day's arithmetic lesson, and with a charming disregard of the expense of jackets and trousers, and the gentle girl, who clings to her mother's side, like an attendant angel, and contents herself with teaching long lessons to docile paper pupils in a quiet corner by the fireside, are representatives of two distinct classes in the order of nature, and (untheologically, of course, I might add) of grace. There is not a greater difference between a hockey and a crochet needle than there is between them.

I have, as a general thing, a greater liking for boys than for girls; for the vanity so common to all mankind is not developed in them at so early an age as in the latter. Still I must acknowledge that I have seen some splendid exceptions, the mere recollection of which almost tempts me to draw my pen through that last sentence. Can I ever forget—I can never forget—one into whose years of girlhood the beauty and grace of a long, pure life seemed to have been compressed? It was many years ago, and I was younger than I am now—so pardon me if I should seem to catch a little enthusiasm of spirit from the remembrance of those days. Like the ancient Queen of Carthage, *Agnosco veteris vestigia flammæ.* I was living in London at that time, or rather at Hampstead, which had not then become a mere suburb of the great metropolis, but was a quiet town, whose bright doorplates, and well-scoured doorsteps, and clean window curtains contrasted finely with the dingy brick walls of its houses, and impressed the visitor with the general prosperity and quiet respectability of its inhabitants. In my daily walks to and from the city, I frequently met a gentleman whose gray hairs and simple dignity of manners always attracted me towards him, and exacted from me an involuntary tribute of respectful recognition. One day he overtook me in a shower, and gave me the benefit of his umbrella and his friendship—for an intimacy which ended only with his death commenced between us from that hour. He was a gentleman of good family and education, who had seen thirty years of responsible service in the employ of the Honourable East India Company, had attained a competency, and had forsworn Leadenhall Street for a pension and a quiet retreat on the heights of Hampstead. His wife was a lady of cultivated tastes, whose sober wishes never learned to stray from the path of simple domestic duty, and the presence of the books in which she found her daily pleasures.

> "Type of the wise, who soar, but never roam;
> True to the kindred points of Heaven and Home."

Their only child, "one fair daughter, and no more," was a gentle and merry-hearted creature, who, in the short and murky days of November, filled that cottage with a more than June-like sunshine. Her parents always had a deep sympathy with that unfortunate Empress of France whose dismission from the throne was the commencement of the downward career of the first Napoleon, and bore witness to it by giving her name to their only child. They lived only three or four doors from my lodgings, and there were few days passed after the episode of the umbrella in which I did not find a welcome in their quiet home. Their daughter was their only idol, and I soon found myself a convert to their innocent system of paganism. We all three agreed that Josey was the incarnation of all known perfections, and the lapse of forty years has not sufficed to weaken that conviction in my mind. She had risen just above the horizon of girlhood, and the natural beauty of her character made the beholder content to forget even the promise of her riper years. I do not think she was what the world calls handsome. I sometimes distrust my judgment in the matter of female beauty; indeed, some of my candid friends have told me that I had no judgment in such things. Well, as I was saying, Josey was not remarkable for personal beauty—in fact, I think I remember some persons of her own sex who thought her "very plain"—"positively homely"—and wondered what there was attractive about her. There are circumstances under which I should not have hesitated to attribute such remarks to motives of envy and jealousy; but as they came from girls whose attractions of every kind were far below those of the gentle creature whom they delighted to criticise, how can I account for them? Josey's complexion was dark—her forehead, like those of the best models of female comeliness among the ancients, low. Her teeth were pearly and uniform, and her clear, dark eyes seemed to reflect the happiness and hope which were the companions of her youth. Her beauty was not of that kind which consists in mere regularity of features; it was far superior to that. You could discern under those traits, none of which were conspicuous, a combination of mental and social qualities which were far above the fleeting charms that delight so many, and which age, instead of destroying, would increase and perfect. She was quiet and gentle, without being dull or moody; light-hearted and cheery, without being frivolous; and witty, without being pert or conceited. Her unaffected goodness of heart found many an opportunity of exercise. I often heard of her among the poor, and among those who needed words of consolation even more than the necessaries of life. It was her delight to intercede with the magistrate who had inflicted a punishment on some disorderly brother of one of her poor clients, and to obtain his pardon by promising to watch over him and insure his future good behaviour; and there were very few, among the most reckless, who were not restrained by the thought that their offences would give pain to the kind-hearted girl who had so willingly become their protector.

During the months that I lived at Hampstead my intercourse with that excellent family was as familiar as if I had been one of their own kindred. A little attack of rheumatism, which confined me to my lodging for a fortnight or three weeks, proved the constancy of their friendship. The old gentleman came daily to see me—told me all the news from the city, and read to me; the mother sent me some of her favourite books; and Josey came to get assistance in her Latin and French, and brought me sundry little pots of grape jelly and other preserves, which tasted all the sweeter for being the work of her fair hands.

It was a sad parting when I was called away to America—sad for me; for I told them that I hoped that my absence from England would be but temporary, when I felt inwardly that it might extend to several years.

Two or three months after my arrival at home, I received a letter from the old gentleman, written in his deliberate, round, clerk-like style, informing me of his wife's death. A note was enclosed from Josey, in which she described with her pencil the spot where her mother was buried in the old churchyard, and told me of her progress in her studies. More than a year passed by without my hearing from them at all, two or three of my letters to them having miscarried. Nearly seven years elapsed before I visited England again. Two years before that, I had read the decease of the old gentleman, in a stray London newspaper. I had written to Josey, sympathizing with her in her desolation, but had received no answer. So, the day after my arrival in London, I determined to make a search for the beloved Josey. I went to Hampstead, and my heart beat quicker as I approached the cottage where I had spent so many happy hours. My throat felt a little choky, as I recognized the neat bit of hedge before the door, the graceful vine which overhung it, and the familiar arrangement of the flower pots in the frames outside the windows; but my hopes received a momentary check when I found a strange name on the plate above the knocker. I knocked, and inquired concerning the former occupants of the house. After a severe effort to overcome the Bœotian stupidity of the housemaid, she ushered me into the little break-

fast room, and said she would "call her missus."
Almost before I had time to look about me, Josey
entered the room. The little girl whose Latin exercises I had corrected, and who had always lived in
my memory as she appeared in those days, suddenly
came before me

> "A perfect woman, nobly planned,
> To warn, to comfort, and command;
> And yet a spirit still and bright
> With something of an angel light."

Yet she was hardly changed at all. She had lost
none of those charming qualities which had made the
thought of her precious to me during long years of
absence. She had gained the maturity and dignity
of womanhood without losing any of the simplicity
and light-heartedness of girlhood. She was married. Her husband was a literary man of considerable reputation. Though only in middle age, he was
a great sufferer with the gout. He was, generally
speaking, a patient man; but I found, after I became
intimate with him, that his pains sometimes made
him express himself with a force of diction somewhat in advance of the religious prejudices of his
gentle Josey, who tended him and ministered to his
wants like an angel, as she was. But excuse me for
wandering so far from my theme. To make a long
story short, Josey went to Italy with her husband,
who had been ordered thither by his physicians, and
I never saw her afterwards. She deposited her husband's remains in the cemetery where those of Shelley and Keats repose, and found for two or three
years a consolation for her bereaved spirit in resi-

dence in that city which more than all others pro-
claims to our unwilling hearts the vanity and
transitoriness of this world's hopes, and the glory of
the unseen eternal. Years after, I met one of her
husband's friends in Paris, who told me that some
four years after his death, she had entered a convent
of a religious order devoted to the reclaiming of the
degraded of her sex, in Brussels. There she had
found a fitting occupation for the natural benevolence
of her heart, and the peace which the world could
not give. She had concealed the glory of her good
works under her vow of obedience—her personality
was hidden under the common habit of her Order—
the very name which was so dear to me had been
exchanged for another on the day that saw her covered with the white veil of the novice. I was about
returning to England from the continent when I
heard this, and I resolved to take Belgium's fair
capital in my route. I found the convent readily
enough, and waited in its uncarpeted but scrupulously
clean parlour some time for the Lady Superior. She
was a lady of dignified mien, with the clear complexion, the serene brow, and the dovelike eyes so
common among nuns, and her face lighted up, as she
spoke, with a gentle smile, which seemed almost like
a presage of immortality. I explained my errand,
and she told me that the good English sister had
been dead more than a year. The intelligence pained
me, and it gave me a feeling of self-reproach to
notice that the nun, who had been with her in her last
hour, spoke of her as if she had merely passed into
another part of the convent we were in. The Superior, perceiving my emotion, conducted me through

the garden of the convent to a shady corner of the grounds, where there were several graves She stopped before a mound, over which a rose bush bent affectionately, as if its white blossoms craved something of the purity which was enshrined beneath it. At its head was a simple wooden cross, on which was inscribed the name of "Sister Helen Agnes," the date of her death, and the common supplication that she might rest in peace; and that was the only memorial of Josey that remained to me.

I have not forgotten, dear reader, that I am writing about girls; but having brought forward one who always seemed to me to be about as near perfection as it is vouchsafed to poor humanity to approach, I could not help following her to the end, and showing how she went from a beautiful girlhood to a still more beautiful womanhood, and a death which all of us might envy; and how lovely and harmonious was her whole career. For I feel that the consideration of the contrast which most of the young female readers of these pages will discover between themselves and Josey, will do them some good.

I do not know of a more quietly funny sight than a group of school-girls, all talking as fast as their tongues can wag, (forty-woman power,) and clinging inextricably together like a parcel of macaroni, à la Napolitaine. Their independence is quite refreshing. Lady Blessington in her diamonds never descended the grand staircase at Covent Garden Opera House with half the consciousness of making a sensation, that you may notice in these school-girls whenever you take your walks abroad. It is delightful to see them step off so proudly, and look you in the face so coolly, thinking all the time of just nothing at all. Their boldness is the boldness of innocence; for perfect modesty does not even know how to blush. How vain they grow as they advance in their teens! How careful they are that the crinoline "sticks out" properly before they venture on the road to school! If Mother Goose (of blessed memory) could take a look into this world now, she would wish to revise her ancient rhyme to her patrons,—

"Come with a whoop—come with a call," &c.,—

for she would find that it is now their custom to come with a *hoop* when they come for a call.

When unhappy Romeo stands in old Capulet's garden, under the pale beams of the "envious moon," and watches the unconscious Juliet upon the balcony, he utters, in the course of his incoherent soliloquial apostrophe, these remarkable words concerning that interesting young person:—

"She speaks, yet she says nothing."

I have seen many young ladies of Juliet's time of life in my day of whom the same thing might be said. They indeed speak, yet say nothing. Yet take them on such a subject as the trimming of a new bonnet for Easter Sunday, or any of those entertaining topics more or less connected with the adornment of their persons, and how voluble they are! To the stronger sex, which of course cares nothing about dress, being entirely free from vanity, the terms used in their never-ending colloquies on such themes are mere unmeaning words; but I must do the gentler side of humanity the justice to say that they are not all vanity, as their fathers and husbands find to their dismay, when the quarterly bills come in, that gimp, and flounces, and trimming generally, have a real, tangible existence.

How sentimental they are! In my young days albums were all the rage among young ladies; but now they seem to be somewhat out of date, and young ministers have taken their place. What pains will they not take to get a bow from the Rev. Mr. Simkins! They swarm around him after service, like flies around the bung of a molasses cask. Raphael never had such a face as his; Massillon never preached as he does. What a wilderness of worsted work are they not willing to travel over for his sake! How do they exhaust their inventive faculties in the search after new patterns for lamp mats, watch cases, pen wipers, and slippers to encase the feet at which they delight to sit! But when Simkins marries old Thompson's youngest daughter and a snug property, he finds a sad abatement in his popularity. The Rev. Mr. Jenkins, a young preacher with a face every whit as milk-and-watery as his own, succeeds to the throne he occupied, and reigns in his stead among the volatile devotees; and Simkins then sees that his popularity was no more an evidence of the favour his preaching of the gospel found among those thoughtless young people than was the popularity of the good-looking light comedian, after whom the girls ran as madly as they did after his own white neckerchief and nicely-brushed black frock coat.

Exaggeration is one of the great faults of girl-hood. Whatever meets their eyes is either "splen-did" or "horrid." They delight to exaggerate their likes and dislikes. Self-restraint seems to be a term not contained in their lexicon. They take a momen-tary fancy to a young man, and flatter him with their smiles until some new face takes his place in their fleeting memory. In this way many young hearts are frittered away in successive flirtations before their possessors have reached womanhood. But it would be wrong to confine action from mere blind impulse and exaggeration to young girls alone. I think it is St. Paul who gives us some good counsel about "speaking the truth in love." I fear that very few victims of the tender passion, from Pyramus and Thisbe down to Petrarch and Laura, and from the latter couple down to Mr. Smith with Miss Brown hanging on his arm,—who have not sadly needed the advice of the Apostle of the Gentiles. I have seen very few people in my day who really speak the truth in love. Therefore I will not blame girls for a fault which is common to all mankind.

Impulse is commonly supposed to be inconsistent with cunning; but in most girls I think the two things are singularly combined. I am told that there is an academy in this city, frequented by many young wo-men, known as the School of Design. The fact is a gratifying one to me; for my observation of girlish nature had led me to suppose that there were very few indeed of the young ladies of these days who required any tuition in the arts of design. I hail the fact as a good omen for the sex. Action from im-pulse carries its young victims to the extremes of good and evil. Queen Dido is a fair type of the majority of her sex. Defeated in their hopes, they are willing to make a funeral pile of all that remains to them. But there is a spirit of generosity in them which does not find a place in the hearts of men. It was the part of Eve to bring death into this world, and all our woe, by her inquisitiveness and credulity; but it was reserved for Adam to inaugurate the meanness of mankind by laying all the blame to his silly little wife. The accusation ought to have blistered Adam's cowardly tongue.

But I am making a long preachment, and yet I have said very little. I must leave my young friends, however, to draw their own lessons from the portrait I have given of one whose perfections would far outweigh the silliness and vanity of a generation of girls. Let them take the gentle Josey as the model of their youth, and they will not wish to sculpture their later career after any less perfect shape. There will then be fewer heartless flirts, fewer vain exhibitors of the works of the milliner and dressmaker parading the streets, and more true women presiding over the homes of America. The imitation of her virtues will be found a better preservative of beauty than any *eau lustrale;* for it will create a beauty which "time's effacing fingers" are powerless to destroy, and give to those who practise it a serene and lovely old age, whose recollection of the past, instead of awakening any self-reproach, shall be a source of perpetual benediction.

SHAKESPEARE AND HIS COMMENTATORS

IT was a favourite wish of the beneficent Caligula that all mankind had but one neck, that he might finish them off at a single chop. It would ill comport with my known modesty, were I to lay claim to any thing like the all-embracing humanity of the old Roman philanthropist; but I must acknowledge that I have frequently felt inclined to apply his pious aspiration to the commentators on Shakespeare. Impatience is not my prevailing weakness; but these pestilent annotators have often been instrumental in convincing me that I am no stoic. I have frequently regretted the days of my youth, when no envious commentary obscured the brilliancy of that genius which has consecrated the language through which it finds utterance, and made it venerable to the scholars of all lands and ages. My love of Shakespeare, like the gout which has been stinging my right foot all the morning, is hereditary. My revered grandmother was very fond of solid English literature. She had not had, it is true, the advantages which the young people of the present day rejoice in; she had not studied in any of those seminaries which polish off an education in a most Arabian-Nightsy style of expedition, and send a young lady home in the middle of her teens, accomplished in innumerable ologies, and knowing little or nothing that is really useful, or that will attract her to intellectual pursuits or pleasure in after life. She had acquired what is infinitely better than the superficial omniscience which is so much cultivated in these days. The more active duties of life pleased her not; and Shakespeare was the never-failing resource of her leisure hours. Mr. Addison's Spectator was for her a "treasure of contentment, a mine of delight, and, with regard to style, the best book in the world." I shall never forget that happy day (anterior even to the jacket era of my life) when she took me upon her knee, and read to me the speeches of Marullus, and Mark Antony, and Brutus. In that hour I became as sincere a devotee as ever bent down before the shrine of Shakespeare's genius. Nor has that innocent fanaticism abated any of its ardour under the weight laid upon me by increasing years. The theatre has lost many of its old charms for me. The friendships of youth—the only enduring intimacies, for our palms grow callous in the promiscuous intercourse of the world, and cannot easily receive new impressions —have either been terminated by that inexorable power whose chilling touch is merciless alike to love and enmity, or have been interfered with by the varying pursuits of life. But Shakespeare still maintains his wonted sway, and my loyalty to him has not been disturbed by any of the revolutionary movements which have made such changes in most other things. Martin Farquhar Tupper has written, but I am so old-fashioned in my prejudices that I find myself constantly turning to my Shakespeare, in preference even to that gifted and proverbially philosophic bard.

But I am wandering. From the day I have mentioned, Robinson Crusoe was obliged to abdicate, and England's "monarch bard" (as Mr. Sprague calls Anne Hathaway's husband) reigned in his stead. I first devoured the Julius Cæsar. I say "devoured," for no other word will express the eager earnestness with which I read. The last time I read that play through, it was "within a bowshot where the Cæsars dwelt," and but a few minutes' walk from the palace which now holds great Pompey's statua, at whose foot the mighty Julius fell. Increase of appetite grew rapidly by what it fed on, and I was not long in learning as much about the black-clad prince, the homeless king, the exacting usurer, the fat knight and his jolly companions, the remorseful Thane, and generous, jealous Moor, as I knew about Brutus and the other red republican assassins of imperial Rome. My love of Shakespeare was greatly edified by a friendship which I formed in my earliest foreign journeyings. It was before the days of railways,—which, convenient as they are, have robbed travelling of half its zest, by rendering it so common. I had been making a little tour through the north of France. I had admired the white caps and pious simplicity of the peasants of Normandy, and had drunk in that exaltation of soul which the lofty nave of the majestic Cathedral of Amiens always imparts, and was about returning to Paris, when a rheumatic attack arrested my progress and prolonged my stay in the pleasant city of Douai. I there met accidentally with an English monk of that grand old Benedictine order, whose history for more than twelve centuries has been the history of civilization, and literature, and religion. He was descended from one of those old families which refused to modify their creed at the demand of a divorce-seeking klng. He was a man of clear intellect and fascinating simplicity of character. He seemed to carry sunshine with him wherever he went. He occupied a professional chair in the English College attached to the Benedictine Monastery at Douai, and when his class hours were ended, he daily came to visit me. His sensible and sprightly conversation did more towards untying the rheumatic knots in my poor shoulder, than all the pills and lotions for which *M. le Médecin* charged me so roundly. When I visited him in his cell, I found that a well-worn copy of Shakespeare was the only companion of his Breviary, his Aquinas and St. Bernard on his study table. He loved Shakespeare for himself alone. He never used him as a lay figure on which he might display the drapery of a pedant. He hated commentators as heartily as a man so sincerely religious can hate any thing except sin, and was as earnest in his predilection for Shakespeare, "without note or comment," as his dissenting fellow-countrymen would have wished him to be for a similar edition of the only other inspired book in the world. He had his theories, however, concerning Shakespeare's characters, and we often talked them over together; but I must do him the justice to say that he never published any of them. I always regarded this fact as a splendid evidence of the entireness of his self-abnegation, and of his extraordinary advancement in the path of religious perfection. Many have taken the three monastic vows by which he was bound, and have lived up to them with conscientious fidelity; but few scholars have studied Shakespeare as he did, and yet resisted the temptation to tell the world all about it in a book.

Mousing the other day in the library of a venerable citizen of Boston, who is no less skilled in the gospel (let us hope) than in the law, I stumbled over a seedy-looking folio containing *A Treatise of Original Sinne,* by one Anthony Burgesse, who flourished in England something more than two centuries ago. One of the discoloured fly-leaves of this entertaining tome informed me, in a hand-writing which resembled a dilapidated rail-fence looked at from the window of an express train, that *Jacobus Keith me possedit, An. Dom.* 1655; and also bore this inscription, so pertinent to my present theme: "Expositors are wise when they are not otherwise." I feel that it is safe to leave my readers to make the application of this apothegm to the Shakespearean annotators of their acquaintance, so few of whom are wise, so many otherwise. I think it was the late Mr. Hazlitt who said (and if it was not, it ought to have been) that if you desire to know to what sublimity human genius is capable of ascending, you must read Shakespeare; but that if you seek to ascertain to what a depth of imbecility the intellect of man may be brought down, you must read his commentators.

Notwithstanding the low estimate which I am inclined to place upon the labour of the majority of the commentators on Shakespeare, still I have often felt a strong temptation to enroll myself among them. Not all their stupidity in explaining things which are clear to the meanest capacity, not all their pedantry in elucidating matters which are simply inexplicable, not all their inordinate voluminousness, could quench my ambition to fasten my roll of waste paper to the bob (already so unwieldy) of the Shakespearean kite. Others have soared into fame by such means; why should not I? We ought not to study Shakespeare so many years for nothing, and I feel that a sacred duty would be neglected if the result of my researches were withheld from my suffering fellow-students. But let me be more merciful than other commentators; let me confine my remarks to a single play. From that one you may learn the tenor of my theories concerning the others; and if you wish for another specimen, I shall consider that I have achieved an unheard-of triumph in this department of literature.

The tragedy of *Hamlet* has always been regarded as one of the most creditable of Shakespeare's performances. It needs no new commendation from me. Dramatic composition has made great progress within the two hundred and sixty years that have elapsed since Hamlet was written, yet few better things are produced nowadays. We may as well acknowledge the humiliating fact that Hamlet, with all its age, is every whit as good as if it had been written since Lady Day, and were announced on the playbills of to-morrow night, with one of Mr. Boucicault's most eloquent and elaborate prefaces. The character of Hamlet has been much discussed, but, with all due respect for the genius of those who have fatigued their reader with their treatment of the subject, I would humbly suggest that they are all wrong. Hamlet resembles a picture which has been scoured, and retouched, and varnished, and restored, until you can hardly see any thing of the original. Critics and commentators have bedaubed the original character so thoroughly, and those credulous people who rejoice that Chatham's language is their mother tongue, have heard so much of their estimate of Hamlet's character, that they receive them on faith, flattering themselves all the while that they are paying homage to the Hamlet of Shakespeare. High-flown philosophy exerts its powers upon the theme, and Goethe gives it as his opinion that the dramatist wished to portray the effects of a great action, imposed as a duty upon a mind too feeble for its accomplishment, and compares it to an oak planted in a china vase, proper to receive only the most delicate flowers, and which flies to pieces as soon as the roots begin to strike out.

Now let us drop all this metaphysical and poetical cant, and go back to the play itself. Shakespeare will prove his own best expositor, if we read him with docile minds, having previously instructed ourselves concerning the history of the time of which he wrote. There is a tradition common in the north of Ireland that Hamlet's father was a native of that country, named Howndale, and that he followed the trade of a tailor; that he was captured by the Danes, in one of their expeditions against that fair island, and carried to Jutland; that he married and set up in business again in that cold region, but that he afterwards forsook the sartorial for the regal line, by usurping the throne of Denmark. The tradition represents him to have been a man of violent character, a hard drinker, and altogether a most unprincipled and unamiable person, though an excellent tailor. Now, if we take the old chronicle of Saxo Grammaticus, (*Historia Danorum,*) from which Shakespeare drew the plot for his tragedy, we shall find there little that does not harmonize with this tradition. Saxo Grammaticus tells us that Hamlet was the son of Horwendal, who was a famous pirate of Jutland, whom the king, Huric, feared so much, that, to propitiate him, he was obliged to appoint him governor of Jutland, and afterwards to give him his daughter Gertrude in marriage. Thus he obtained the throne. The old Irish name, Howndale, might easily have been corrupted into Horwendal by the jaw-breaking Northmen, and for the rest, the Danish chronicle and the Irish tradition are perfectly consistent. That there was frequent communication at that early period between Denmark and Ireland, I surely need not take the trouble to prove. All the early chronicles of both of those countries bear witness to it. It was to the land evangelized by St. Patrick that Denmark was indebted for the blessings of education and the Christian faith. But the visits of the Danes were not dictated by any holy zeal for the salvation or mental advancement of their benefactors, if we may believe all the stories of their piratical expeditions. An Irish monk of the great monastery of Banchor, who wrote very good Latin for the age in which he lived, alludes to this period in his country's history in a poem, one line of which is sometimes quoted, even now:—

Timeo Danaos et dona ferentes.
"Time was, O Danes, we feared your gifts."

SHAKESPEARE AND HIS COMMENTATORS

The great Danish poet, Œhlenschlæger, makes frequent allusions in the course of his epic, *The Gods of the North*, to the relations that once existed between Denmark and Ireland, and to the fact that his native land received from Ireland the custom of imbibing spirituous liquors in large quantities.

Hamlet's Irish parentage would naturally be concealed as much as possible by him, as it might prejudice his claims to the throne of Denmark; therefore we can hardly expect to find the ancient legend confirmed in the play, except in a casual manner. The free, outspoken, Irish nature would make itself known occasionally. Thus we find that when Horatio tells him that "there 's no offence," he rebukes him with

"Yes, *by St. Patrick,* but there is, Horatio!"

There certainly needs no ghost come from the grave to tell us that no true-born Scandinavian would have sworn in an unguarded moment by the Apostle of Ireland. Again, when Hamlet thinks of killing his uncle, the wrongful king, he apostrophizes himself by the name which he probably bore when he assisted his father (whose death he wishes to avenge) in his shop in Jutland:—

"Now, might I do it, Pat, now he is praying."

Then, too, he speaks to Horatio of the "funeral baked meats" coldly furnishing forth the marriage table at his mother's second espousal. The custom of baking meats is as well known to be of Irish origin, as that of roasting them is to be peculiar to the northern nations of continental Europe.

The frequent allusions in the course of the play to drinking customs not only prove that Hamlet descended from that nation whose hospitality is its greatest fault, but that he and his family were far from being the refined and philosophic people some of the commentators would have us believe. Thus he promises his old companion,—

"We 'll teach you to drink deep ere you depart,"—

which the most prejudiced person will freely allow to be truly a *Cork*onian phrase. This frailty of the family may be seen throughout the play. In the last scene, it is especially apparent. All the royal family of Denmark seem to have joined an intemperance society. The queen even, in spite of her husband's remonstrances, joins in the carousal. Hamlet, too, while he is dying, starts up on hearing Horatio say, "Here's yet some liquor left," and insists upon the cup being given to him. I know that it may be urged, on the other hand, that in the scene preceding the first appearance of the ghost before Hamlet, he indulges in some remarks which would prove him to have entertained sentiments becoming his compatriot, the noble Father Mathew. Speaking of the custom of draining down such frequent draughts of Rhenish, he pronounces it to his mind

"a custom
More honoured in the breach than the observance."

It must be remembered that the occasion on which this speech was uttered was a solemn one. Under such supernatural circumstances old Silenus or the King of Prussia himself might be pardoned for growing somewhat homiletic on the subject of temperance. The conclusion of this speech has given the commentators a fine chance to exercise their ingenuity.

> "The dram of bale
> Doth all the noble substance often doubt
> To his own scandal."

They have called it the "dram of base," the "dram of eale," &c., and then have been as much in the dark as before. Some have thought that Shakespeare intended to have written it "the dram of Bale," as a sly hit at Dr. John Bale, the first Protestant Bishop of Ossory in Ireland, who was an unscrupulous dram-drinker as well as dramatist, for he wrote a play called "Kynge Johan," which was reprinted under the editorial care of my friend, Mr. J. O. Halliwell, by the Camden Society, in 1838. But this attempt to make it reflect upon the Ossory prelate is entirely uncalled for. A little research would have showed that *bale* was a liquor somewhat resembling our whiskey of the true R. G. brand, the consumption of which in the dram-shops of his country the Prince Hamlet so earnestly deplored. The great Danish philosopher, V. Scheerer Homboegger, in his autobiography, speaks of it, and says that like all the Danes he prefers it to either wine or ale, or water even: *Der er vand, her er vun og oel,—men allested* BAELE *drikker saaledes de Dansker.* (Autobiog. II. xiii. Ed. Copenhag.)

As to the proofs that Hamlet's family was closely connected with the tailoring interest, they are so thickly scattered through the entire tragedy, and are so apparent even to the casual reader, that, even if

I had room, it would only be necessary to mention a few of the principal ones. In the very first scene in which he is introduced, Hamlet talks in an experienced manner about his "inky cloak," "suits of solemn black," "forms" and "modes," and tries to defend himself from the suspicion which he feels is attached to him by many of the courtiers, by saying plainly, "I know not *seams*." This first speech of Hamlet's is a key to the wanton insincerity of his character. His mother has begged him to change his clothes,—to "cast his nighted colour off,"—and he answers her requests with, "I shall *in all my best* obey you, madam;" yet it is notorious that he heeds not this promise, but wears black to the end of his career.

He repeatedly uses the expressions which a tailor would naturally employ. His figures of speech frequently smell of the shop. As, for instance, he says to Rosencrantz and Guildenstern, "The appurtenance of welcome is fashion and ceremony. Let me comply with you in this garb;" in the scene preceding the play he declares that, though the devil himself wear black, he'll "have a suit of sables." In the interview with his mother, who may be supposed not to have forgotten the early history of the family, he uses such figures with still greater freedom:—

> "That monster *custom* who all sense doth eat·
> Of *habit's* devil, is angel yet in this;
> That to the use of actions fair and good
> He likewise gives a *frock* or *livery*,
> That aptly is put on."

In his instruction to the players he speaks of tearing "a passion to *tatters*, to very *rags*," and says of certain actors that when he saw them it seemed to him as if "some of nature's *journeymen* had made men and not made them well." In the fourth act, he calls Rosencrantz a *sponge*.

What better evidence of the skill of Hamlet and his father in their common trade can we have than that afforded by the fair Ophelia, who speaks of the Prince as "the glass of fashion and the mould of form"? In the chamber scene with his mother, Hamlet is taken entirely off his guard by the sudden appearance of his father's ghost, whom he apostrophizes, not in the set phrases which he used when Horatio and Marcellus were by, but as *"a king of shreds and patches."* Old Polonius does not wish his daughter to marry a tailor, but is too polite to tell her all of his objections to Lord Hamlet's suit; so he cloaks his reasons under these figures of speech, instead of telling her, out of whole cloth, that Hamlet is a tailor, and the match will never do:—

> "Do not believe his vows, for they are brokers,
> Not of that dye which there in vestments show,
> But implorators of unholy suits," &c.

Some late editions of the Bard make the second line of this passage read,—

> "Not of that die which their investments show,"——

which is as evident a corruption of the text as any of those detected by the indefatigable Mr. Payne Collier.

If any further proof is needed of a matter which must be clear to every reasoning mind, it may be found in that solemn scene in which the Prince, oppressed by the burden of a life embittered and defeated in its highest aims, meditates suicide. Now, if there is a time when all affectation of worldly rank would be likely to be forgotten and swallowed up in the contemplation of the terrible deed which occupies the mind, it is such a time as this. And here we find Shakespeare as true as Nature herself. The soldier, weary of life, uses the sword his enemies once feared, to end his troubles. Hamlet's mind overleaps the interval of his princely life, and the weapon which is most naturally suggested by his youthful career is *"a bare bodkin."*

Had I not already written more than I intended on this subject, I might go on with many other evidences of the truth of my view of this remarkable character. I did wish also to show that Hamlet was a most disreputable character, and by no means entitled to the sympathy or admiration of men. Suffice it to say that he was, even to his last hour, fonder of drink than became a prince (except perhaps a Prince Regent)—that he treated Ophelia improperly—that he often spoke of his step-father in profane terms— that he indulged in the use of profane language even in his soliloquies, as for example,—

> "The spirit I have seen
> May be a devil; and the devil hath power
> To assume a pleasing shape; yea, and perhaps
> Out of my weakness, and my melancholy,
> (As he is very potent with such spirits)
> Abuses me too,—damme!"

His familiarity with the players likewise is an incontrovertible proof of his depravity; for the theatrical people of Denmark in his age were not what the players of our day are. They were too often people of loose and reckless lives, careless of moral and social obligations, and whose company would by no means be acceptable to a truly philosophic prince. If this pre-Raphaelite sketch of Hamlet's character should seem unsatisfactory, it can be filled out by a perusal of the play itself, if the reader will only cast aside the trammels which the commentators have placed in his way. It may be a new view to most of my readers; but I am convinced that the theory, of which I have given an outline, is fully as tenable as many of the countless conjectural essays to which that matchless drama has given rise. If it be untrue, why, then we must conclude that all similar theories, though they may be sustained by as many passages as I have adduced in support of my Hibernico-sartorial hypothesis, are equally devoid of a foundation of common sense. If my theory stands, I have the satisfaction of having connected my name (which would else be soon forgotten) with one of Shakespeare's masterpieces; and that is all that any commentator has ever done. And if my theory proves false, it consoles me to think that the splendour of the genius which I so highly reverence is in no wise obscured thereby; for the stability and grandeur of the temple cannot be impaired by the obliteration of the ambitious scribblings and chalk-marks with which some aspiring worshippers may have defaced its portico.

MEMORIALS OF MRS. GRUNDY

O F all the studies to which I was ever impelled in
my youth, either by fear of the birch or by the
hope of the laurel or the bays, mythology was perhaps the most charming. It was refreshing, after
trying in vain to conjugate a verb, and being at last
obliged to decline it—after adding up a column of
figures several times, and getting many different results, and none of them the right one—and after
making a vain attempt to comprehend the only al-
gebraic knowledge that ever was forced into my
unmathematical brain, viz., that x equals an unknown
quantity,—it was, I say, refreshing to turn over the
leaves of my Classical Dictionary, and revel among
the gods and heroes whose wondrous careers were
embalmed in its well-thumbed pages. Lemprière
was the great magician who summoned up before
my delighted eyes the denizens of a sphere where
existence was unvexed by any pestilent arithmetics,
and where the slavery of the inky desk was unknown.
It always seemed to me as if the knowledge that I
gained out of those enchanted chronicles not only
improved my mind, but made my body more robust;
for I joined in the chase, fought desperate battles, as
the gods willed it, and breathed all the while the
pure, invigorating air of old Olympus. The con-

secrated groves were the dwelling-place of my mind, and I became for a time a sharer in the joys of beings in whom I believed with all the ardour and simplicity of childhood. I enjoyed my mythological readings all the more because they did not generally find favour with my school companions, most of whom vindicated their nationality by professing their affection for the Rule of Three. One of them, I remember, was especially severe on the uselessness of the studies in which I took pleasure. He, *parcus deorum cultor, et infrequens,* could get no satisfaction out of the books in which I revelled; if *he* had got to study or read, he could not afford to waste his brains over the foolish superstitions of three thousand years ago. He did not care how much romance and poetic beauty there might be in the ancient mythology: what did it all come to in the end? It didn't pay. It was a humbug. Our paths in life separated when we graduated from jackets and peg-tops. He remained faithful to his boyish instincts, and pursued the practical as if it were a reality. After a few years his face lost all its youthful look; an intense spirit of acquisitiveness gleamed in his calculating eye, and an interest table seemed to be written in the lines of his care-worn countenance. We seldom had any conversation in our after years, for he always seemed to be under some restraint, as if he feared that I wished to borrow a little money of him, and he did not wish to refuse for the sake of the old time when we sat at the same desk, although he knew that my note was good for nothing. His devotion to his deity, the practical, did not go unrewarded. He became like the only mythological personage whom he would have envied, had he known any thing of the science he despised. His touch seemed to transmute every thing into gold. His speculations during the war of 1812 were all successful. Eastern lands harmed him not. The financial panic of 1837 only put money in his purse. He rolled up a large fortune, and was happy. He looked anxious, but of course he was happy. What man ever devoted his life to the working out of the dreams of his youth in the acquisition of riches, and succeeded beyond his anticipations, without being very happy? But, if his gains were something practical and real, his losses were doubly so. Each one of them was as a dagger stuck into that sere heart. His only son gave him much trouble by his wild life, and, what touched him still more, wasted the money he had laboured to pile up, at the gaming tables of Baden. I saw him walking down Tremont Street the other day, looking careworn and miserable, and I longed to ask him what he thought of the real and practical after trying them. He would certainly have been willing to acknowledge that there is more reality in the romance and poetry of mythology than in the thousands which he invested in the Bay State Mills. His practical life has brought him vanity and vexation of spirit, while the old Lemprière, which he used to treat so contemptuously, flourishes in immortal youth, unhurt amid the wreck of fortunes and the depreciation of stocks.

But I am not writing an essay on mythology. I wish to treat of one who is sometimes considered a myth, but who is a living and breathing personality like all of us. This wide-spread scepticism is one of the most fatal signs of the times. Because the late Mrs. Sairey Gamp supposed herself justified in cultivating a little domestic mythology in the shade of the famous Mrs. Harris, are we to take all the personages who have illustrated history as myths and unrealities? Shade of Herodotus, forbid it! There are some unbelieving and irreverent enough to doubt whether there is really such a person as Mrs. Partington; other some there are so hardened in their incredulity as to question the existence of the individual who smote Mr. William Patterson, and even of the immortal recipient of the blow himself. Therefore we ought not to think it strange that the lady whose name adorns the title of this article should not have escaped the profane spirit of the age.

Unfortunately for us, Mrs. Grundy is no myth, but a terrible reality. She is a widow. The late Mr. Grundy bore it with heroic patience as long as he could, and then, by a divine dispensation in which he gladly acquiesced, was relieved of the burden of life. If he be not happy now, the great doctrine of compensation is nought but a delusion and a sham. If endless happiness could only be attained through such a purgatory as poor Grundy's life, few of us, I fear, would yearn to be counted among the elect. Martyrs, and confessors, and saints of every degree have won their crowns of beatitude with comparative ease; if they had been subjected to a twenty years' novitiate with Mrs. Grundy and her tireless tongue, they would have found how much more terrible that was than the laborious life or cruel death by which they passed from earth, and fewer bulls of canoniza-

tion would have received the Seal of the Fisherman.
I have heard from those who were acquainted with
that estimable and uncomplaining man that he married for love. His wife was a person of considerable
attractions, of an inquiring turn of mind, and of
uncommon energy of character. In her care of his
household there was nothing of which he might with
reason complain. She kept a sharp look-out over all
those matters in which the prudent housewife delights to show her skill; her table was worthy to receive regal legs beneath its shining mahogany and
spotless cloth, and I have even heard that her husband never had occasion to curse mentally over the
lack of a shirt-button. Yet was Giles Grundy,
Esquire, one of the most miserable of men. Of what
avail was it to him that his wife could preserve
quinces, if she could not preserve her own peace of
mind? What did it matter how well she cured hams,
if she always failed so miserably in curing her
tongue? What profit was it that her accounts with
her butcher and grocer were always correctly kept, if
her accounts of all her neighbours constantly over-
ran and kept her and her spouse in a perpetual state
of moral bankruptcy? What difference did it make
how well she took care of her own family, if they
were to be kept in an unending turmoil by her solicitude concerning that of every body else?

If you had visited Mrs. Grundy, and remarked
the brightness of the door-knocker, the stair-rods, the
andirons, and every other part of her premises that
was susceptible of polish, and the scrupulous cleanliness that held absolute sway around her, you would
have sworn that she was gifted with the hundred

arms of Briareus: if you had listened for fifteen minutes to her observations of men and things, you would have had a conviction amounting to absolute certainty that she possessed the eyes of Argus. Nobody ever doubted that she was a most religious person. She attended to all her religious duties with most edifying exactness. She was always in her seat at church, and could tell you, to a bonnet ribbon, the dress of every person who honoured the sacred edifice with his or her presence. If you would know who of the congregation were so lacking in fervour of spirit as to neglect to bow in the creed, or to commit the impropriety of nodding during the sermon, Mrs. Grundy could give you all the information you could wish. She carried out the divine precept to the letter: she watched as well as prayed. But her religion did not waste itself in mere devotional ecstasy; it took the most attractive form of religion—that of active benevolence. And her pious philanthropy was not of that exclusively telescopic character that looks out for the interests of the Cannibal Islands and the king thereof, and cannot understand that there is any spiritual destitution nearer home. She subscribed, it is true, to support the missionaries with their wives and numerous children, who were devoted to the godly work of converting the Chinese and the Juggernauts; but she did something also in the way of food and flannel for the victims of want in her own neighbourhood. She established a sewing circle in the parish where she lived, and never appeared happier than when busily engaged with her female companions in their weekly task and talk. I am afraid that there was other sowing done in that

circle besides plain sewing. The seeds of domestic
unhappiness and strife were carried from thence into
all parts of the parish. Reputations as well as garments took their turn among those benevolent ladies,
and were cut out, and fitted, and basted, and sewed
up, and overcast. The sewing circle was Mrs.
Grundy's confessional. Do not misapprehend me—
I would not asperse her character by accusing her of
what are known at the present day as "Romanizing
tendencies"; for she lived long before the "scarlet
fever" invaded the University of Oxford and carried
off its victims by hundreds; and nobody ever suspected her of any desire to tell her own offences in
the ear of any human being. No, she detested the
Roman confessional in a becoming manner; but she
upheld, by word and example, that most scriptural
institution, the sewing circle—the Protestant confessional, where each one confesses, not her own sins,
but the sins of her neighbours. Mrs. Grundy's success with her favourite institution encouraged others
to emulate her example; and now sewing circles are
common wherever the mother tongue of that benevolent lady is spoken. It must in justice be acknowledged that there are few institutions of human
invention which have departed from the spirit of
their original founder so little as the sewing circle.

Yet, in spite of all her virtues as a housekeeper, a
philanthropist, and a Christian, Mrs. Grundy had
her enemies. Some people were uncharitable enough
to say that she was the cause of more trouble than
all the rest of the female population of the town.
They accused her of setting herself up as a censor,
and giving judgments founded upon hearsay testi-

mony rather than sound legal evidence. They even said that she made her visits among the poor a cloak for the gratification of her inquisitiveness; and, if it is ever pardonable to judge of the motives of a fellow-being, I think that, in consideration of their exasperation, they must be excused for making so unkind a charge, it seemed to be so well founded. Far be it from me to say that Mrs. Grundy ever wilfully misrepresented. She would have shrunk instinctively from a falsehood. But she delighted to draw inferences; and no fact or rumour ever came to her without being classified properly in her mental history of her neighbours, and being made to shed its full influence upon her next conversation. It is astonishing how much one pair of eyes and ears will do in the collection of information when a person is devoted to it in earnest. In her younger days, Mrs. Grundy had taken pleasure in watching her neighbours and keeping up a running commentary on their movements; as she advanced in life, it became her business. Her efforts in that way were rather in the style of an amateur up to the time of her marriage; afterwards she adopted a professional air. She placed herself at her favourite window, ornamenting its seat with her spools, and though she stitched away with commendable industry, nothing escaped her that came within range of her keen powers of observation.

If Mr. Brown called on Mrs. White over the way, Mrs. Grundy set it down as a remarkable occurrence: if he repeated his visit a week later, she would not declare it positively scandalous, but it was evident that her nicer sense of propriety was deeply wounded: if he passed by the door without calling, it was clear that there had been a falling out—that Mrs. White had seen the error of her ways, or that her husband had, and had given Brown a warning. If a stranger was seen exercising Jones's bell-pull on two consecutive days, this indefatigable woman allowed not her eyes to sleep nor her eyelids to slumber until she had satisfied herself concerning his name and purpose. If Mr. Thompson waited upon pretty Miss Jenkins home in a shower, and treated her kindly and politely, (and who could do otherwise with a young angel in blue and drab, who might charm a Kaffir or a Sepoy into urbanity?) Mrs. Grundy straightway instituted inquiries among all the neighbours as to whether it was true that they were engaged. After this fashion did Mrs. Grundy live. Her words have been known to blast a reputation which under the sunshine of prosperity and the storms of misfortune had sustained itself with equal grace and honour. It was useless to bring up proofs of a life of integrity against her sentence or her knowing smile. There was no appeal from her decision. Not that she was uncharitable,—only it did seem as if she were rather more willing to believe evil of her neighbours than good; and she appeared slow to trust in the repentance of any one who had ever fallen into sin, especially if the person were of her own sex. I am not complaining of this peculiarity; we must be circumspect and strict, and mercy is a quality too rare and divine to be wasted on every trivial occasion. But I cannot help thinking that, if the penitent found it as hard to gain the absolving smile of that Power to which alone we are answerable for our misdeeds as to reinstate himself in the good graces of Mrs. Grundy, how few of us could have any hope of the beatific vision!

Mrs. Grundy had great influence; she was respected and feared. People found that she would give her opinion *ex cathedra,* and that, however unfounded that opinion might be, there were those who would reëcho it until common repetition gave it the force of truth; so they tried to conciliate her by graduating their actions according to what they supposed would be her judgment. When this was seen, she began to be envied by some who had once hated her, and her idiosyncrasies were made the study of many of her sex who longed to share her empire over the thoughts and actions of their fellow-creatures. Thus, by a sort of multiplex metempsychosis, were Mrs. Grundy's virtues perpetuated, and she was endowed with a species of omnipresence. In this country Mrs. Grundy is a power. She is the absolute sovereign of America. Her reign there is none to dispute. Our national motto ought to be, instead of *E pluribus unum,* "What will Mrs. Grundy say?" There is no class in our community over which she does not exercise more or less power. Our politicians, when they cease to regard their influence as a commodity to be sold to the highest bidder, act, not from any fixed principles, but with a single eye to the good will of Mrs. Grundy. If a man is buying a house, it is ten chances to one that Mrs. Grundy's opinion concerning gentility of situation will carry the day against cosiness and real comfort. If your wife or daughter goes to buy a dress, Mrs. Grundy's taste will be consulted in preference to the durability of the fabric or the condition of your purse. Mrs. Grundy dictates to us how we shall furnish our houses, and prescribes to us our whole rule of life. Under her stern sway, multitudes are living beyond their means, and trying to avert the bankruptcy and unhappiness that inevitably await them. It is not merely in the management of temporal affairs that Mrs. Grundy makes her power felt. Her vigilance checks many a generous impulse, stands between the resolution to do justice and its execution, and is a fruitful source of hypocrisy. She presides over the pulpit; the power of wardens and vestrymen is swallowed up by her; and the minister who can dress up his weekly dish of moral commonplaces so as not to offend her discriminating taste deserves to retain his place, and merits the unanimous admiration of the whole sewing circle. She is to be found in courts of law, animating the opposing parties, and enjoying the contest; actions of slander are an agreeable recreation to her; petitions for divorce give her unmixed joy. Like the fury, Alecto, so finely described by Virgil, Mrs. Grundy can arm brothers to deadly strife against each other, and stir up the happiest homes with infernal hatred; to her belong a thousand woful arts—*Sibi nomina mille, mille nocendi artes.* Mrs. Grundy's philanthropy confines itself to no particular class; it is universal. Nothing that relates to human kind is alien to her. There is nothing earthly so high that she does not aspire to control it, nor any thing too contemptible for her not to wish to know all about it.

Mrs. Grundy is omnipresent. Go where you will, you cannot escape from her presence. She stands guard unceasingly over your front door and back windows. Her watchful eye follows you whene'er you take your walks abroad. Your name is never mentioned that she is not by, and seriously inclined to hear aught that may increase her baleful stock of knowledge. It is all the same to her whether you have lived uprightly or viciously; beneath her Gorgon glance all human actions are petrified alike. And if she does not succeed in sowing discord around your hearthstone, and in driving you to despair and self-murder, as she did poor Henry Herbert the other day, it will be because you are not cursed with his fiery sensitiveness, and not because she lacks the will to do it.

There is but one way in which the Grundian yoke can be thrown off. We must treat her as the English wit treated an insignificant person who had insulted him; we must "let her alone severely." We pay a certain kind of allegiance to her if we take notice of her for the purpose of running counter to her notions. We must ignore her altogether. It is true, this requires a great deal of moral courage, particularly in a country where every body knows every body else's business; but it is an easier task to acquire that courage than to submit patiently to Mrs. Grundy's dictation and interference. Who shall estimate the happiness of that millennial period when we shall cease to ask ourselves before our every action, "What will Mrs. Grundy say?" and shall begin in earnest to live up to the golden rule that counsels us to mind our own business? When that day comes, what a world this will be! How will superficial morality and skin-deep propriety,

envy and uncharitableness, be diminished! How
will contentment, and mutual good will, and domestic peace be augmented! Think on these things, O
beloved reader; mind your own business, and the day
is not far distant when, for you at least, the iron
sceptre of Dame Grundy shall be powerless, and the
spell broken that held you in so humiliating a thraldom.

THE PHILOSOPHY OF LIFE

LIFE is what we make it. The same scenes wear a very different appearance to an ingenuous youth "in the bright morning of his virtues, in the full spring blossom of his hopes," and to the disappointed wretch who gazes on them "with the eyes of sour misanthropy." The horse that was turned by his benevolent owner into a carpenter's shop, with a pair of green spectacles prefixed to his nose, and mistook the dry pine shavings for his legitimate fodder, was very much in the condition of a youth looking upon life and yielding to the natural enthusiasm of his unwarped spirit. Like the noble brute, however, the young man is undeceived as soon as he tries to sustain himself with the vanities which look so tempting and nutritious. He may, like a Wolsey, a Charles V., or a Napoleon, attain to the heights of power before the delusive glasses drop off; but even though the moment be delayed until he lies gasping in the clutch of that monarch to whom the most absolute of sovereigns and the most radical of republicans alike must yield allegiance, it is sure to come, and show him the ashes that lay hid beneath the fair, ripe-looking rind of the fruit he climbed so high to obtain. Life passes before us like a vast panorama, day by day and year by year unrolling and disclosing new scenes to charm us into self-forgetfulness. At one time, we breathe the bracing air of the moun-

tains; at another, our eyes are gladdened by the sight
of sunshiny meadows, or of fertile and far-reaching
prairies; and then the towered city, with its grove of
masts and its busy wharves, makes all mere natural
beauty seem insignificant in comparison with the
enterprise and ambition of man; until, at last, the
canvas is rolled away, the music ceases, the lights are
put out, and we are left to realize that all in which
we delighted was but an illusion and a "fleeting
show."

Nevertheless, in spite of the vanities that surround us,—in spite of the sublime world-sickness of
Solomon and the Preacher, and the fierce satire of
Juvenal, (who was as anxious to ascertain the precise
weight of Hannibal as if that illustrious *dux* had
been a prize-fighter,)—there is considerable reality
in life. The existence of so much sham and make-
believe implies the existence of the real and true. Sir
Thomas Browne tells us that "in seventy or eighty
years a man may have a deep gust of the world";
and it were indeed melancholy if any one with hair
as gray as mine should look despairingly over the
field of human existence and effort, and cry, "All is
barren."

Life, as I have before said, is whatever we choose
to make it. Its true philosophy is that divine art
which enables us to transmute its every moment into
the pure gold of heroic and changeless immortality.
Without that philosophy, it is impossible for the
world not to seem at times as it did to the desponding
Danish prince, "a sterile promontory," and a "foul
and pestilent congregation of vapours." Without it,
life is like an elaborate piece of embroidery, looked

at from the wrong side; we cannot but acknowledge the brilliancy of some of its threads, and the delicate texture of the work, but its lack of system, and of any appearance of utility, fatigues the mind that hungers after perfection, and tempts it to doubt the divine wisdom and goodness from which it originated. With it, however, we gaze with admiration and awe upon the front of the same marvellous work. Our sense is no longer puzzled by any straggling threads, or loose ends; the exquisite colours, the contrast of light and shade, and the perfect symmetry and harmony of the design, fill the heart of the beholder with wonder and delight, and draw him nearer to the source of those ineffable perfections which are but imperfectly symbolized in the marvels of the visible universe.

The philosophy which can do all this is *sincerity*. "I think sincerity is better than grace," says Mr. T. Carlyle; and the Scotch savage is right. All the amenities of life that spring from any other source than a true heart, are but gratuitous hypocrisy. The kind-hearted knight whom I have already quoted showed how highly he esteemed this virtue when he said, "Swim smoothly in the stream of nature, *and live but one man.*" This double existence, that most of us support,—that is, what we really are, and what we wish to be considered,—is the source of many of our faults, and most of our vexation and wretchedness. He is the truly happy man who forgets that "appearances must be kept up," and remembers only that "each of us is as great as he appears in the sight of his Creator, and no greater." A great French philosopher has truly said, "How many controver-

sies would be terminated, if the disputants were obliged to speak out exactly what they thought!" And
surely he might have gone farther in the same line of
thought; for how much heartburning, domestic unhappiness, dishonesty, and shameful poverty might
be prevented, if my neighbour Jinkins and his wife
were content to pass in the world for what they are,
instead of assuming a princely style of living that
only makes their want of true refinement more apparent, and if Johnson and his wife could be induced
not to imitate the vulgar follies of the Jinkinses!
Believe me, incredulous reader, there is more wisdom
in old Sir Thomas's exhortation to "live but one
man" than appears at first sight.

But to leave this great primary virtue, which policy teaches most men to practise, though they love it
not,—there are two or three principles of action
which I have found very useful in my career, and
which form a part of my philosophy of life. The
first is, never to anticipate troubles. Many years
ago, I was travelling in a part of our common country not very thickly settled, and, coming to a place
where two roads met, I applied, in my doubt as to
which one I ought to take, to an old fellow (with a
pair of shoulders like those of Hercules, and a face
on which half a century of sunshine, and storm, and
toddies had made an indelible record) who was repairing a rickety fence by the wayside. He scanned
me with a look that seemed to take in not only my
personal appearance, but the genealogy of my brave
ancestor, who might have fallen in a duel if he had
not learned how "to distinguish between the man and
the act," and then directed me to turn to the left, as

that road saved some three or four miles of the distance to the farm-house to which I was journeying. As it was spring-time, I manifested some anxiety to know whether the freshets, which had been having quite a run of business in some parts of the country, had done any damage to a bridge which I knew I must cross if I took the shorter road. He sneered at my forethought, and said he supposed that the bridge was all right, and that I had better "go ahead, and see." I was acting upon his advice, when a shout from his hoarse, nasal voice caused me to look back. "I say, young man," he bawled out to me, "never cross a bridge till you come to it!" There was wisdom in the old man's rough-spoken sentence—"solid chunks of wisdom," as Captain Ed'ard Cuttle would fain express it—and it sank deep into my memory. There are very few of us who have not a strong propensity to diminish our present strength by entertaining fears of future weakness. If we could content ourselves to "act in the living present,"—if we could keep these telescopic evils out of sight, and use all our energies in grappling with the difficulties that actually beset our path,—how much more we should achieve, and how greatly would our sum of happiness be increased!

Another most salutary principle in my philosophy is, never to allow myself to be frightened until I have examined and fairly established the necessity of such a humiliation. I adopted this principle in my childhood, being led to it in the following manner: I was visiting my grandfather, who lived in a fine old mansion-house in the country, with high wainscotings, capacious fireplaces, heavy beams in the ceilings, and wide-arching elms overshadowing the snug porch where two or three generations had made love. Sixty years and more have elapsed since that happy time, yet it seems fresher in my memory than the events of only quarter of a century back. My grandfather was a lover of books, and possessed a good deal of general information. He thought it as advisable to keep up with the history of his own times as to be skilled in that of empires long since passed away. It is not to be wondered at that he should have treasured every newspaper—especially every foreign journal—that he could lay his hands upon. It was under his auspices that I first read the dreadful story of the Reign of Terror, and acquired my anti-revolutionary principles.

I shall never forget the bright autumnal afternoon when the mail coach from Boston brought a package of books and papers to my grandfather. It was the last friendly favour, in fact the last communication, that he ever received from his old Tory friend, Mr. Barmesyde, whom I mentioned with respect in a former essay; for that genial old gentleman died in London not long after. The parcel had made a quick transit for those days, Mr. Barmesyde's letter being dated only forty-six days before it was opened by my grandsire, and we enjoyed the strong fragrance of its uncut contents together. The old gentleman seized upon a copy of Burke's splendid Essay on the French Revolution, which the package contained, and left me to revel in the newspapers, which were full of the dreadful details of that bloody Saturnalia. I got leave from my grandfather (who was so deep in Burke that he answered me at random) to sit up an hour later than usual. Terrible as all the things of which I read seemed to my young mind, there was a fascination about the details of that sanguinary orgie that completely enchanted me. My imagination was full of horrible shapes when I was obliged to leave the warm, cheerful parlour, and Robespierre, Danton, and Marat were the infernal chamberlains that attended me as I went up the broad, creaking staircase unwillingly to bed. A fresh north-west breeze was blowing outside, and the sere woodbines and honeysuckles that filled the house with fragrance, and gave it such a rural look in summer, startled me with their struggles to escape from bondage. Had it been spring, my young imagination was so excited that I should have feared that they might imitate the insurgents of whom I had been reading and begin to shoot! In the night my troubled slumbers were disturbed by a noise that seemed to me louder than the discharge of a heavy cannon. I sat up in the high, old-fashioned bed, and glared around the room, which was somewhat lighted by the beams of the setting moon. There was no mistake about my personal identity—I was neither royalist nor jacobin; there was no doubt that I was in the best "spare chamber" of my grandfather's house, and not in the Bastile, and that the dark-looking thing in the corner was a solid mahogany chest of drawers, and not a guillotine; but all these things only served to increase my terror when I noticed a dark form standing near the foot of the bed and staring at me with pale, fiery eyes. I rubbed my own eyes hard, and pinched myself severely, to make sure that I was awake. The room was as still as the great chamber in the pyramid of Cheops. I could hear the old clock tick at the foot of the stairs as plainly as if I had been shut up in its capacious case. In the midst of my perturbation it made every fibre of my frame tremble by striking *one* with a solemn clangour that I thought must have waked every sleeper in the house. The stillness that followed was deeper and more terrifying than before. I heard distinctly the breathing of the monster at the foot of the bed. I tried to whistle at the immovable shape, but I had lost the power to pucker. At last, I formed a desperate resolution. I knew that, if the being whose big, fierce eyes filled me with terror were a genuine supernatural fiend, it was all over with me, and I might as well give up at once. But, if perchance a human form were hid beneath that dreadful disguise, there was some room for hope of ultimate escape. To settle this point, therefore, became necessary to my peace of mind, and I determined that it should be done. Bending up "each corporal agent to the terrible feat," I slid quietly out of bed. The monster was as motionless as before, but I noticed that his head was covered with a white cloth, which made his head seem ghastlier than ever. Setting my teeth firmly together, and clinching my little fists to persuade myself that I was not afraid, I made the last, decisive effort. I walked across the room, and stood face to face with that formidable shape. My grandfather's best coat hung there against the wall, its velvet collar protected from the dust by a white cloth, and the two gilt buttons on its back glittering in the moonlight. This was the tremendous presence

THE PHILOSOPHY OF LIFE

that had appalled me. The weakness in the knees, the chattering of my teeth, and the profuse perspiration which followed my recognition of that harmless garment, bore witness to the severity of my fright. Before I crawled back into the warm bed, I resolved never in future to yield to fear, until I had ascertained that there was no escape from it; and I have had many occasions since to act upon that principle.

Speaking of fear, a friend of mine has a favourite maxim, "Always do what you are afraid to do;" to which (in a limited sense, so far as it relates to bodily fear) I subscribed even in my boyhood. I was returning one evening to my grandfather's house, during one of my vacation visits, and yielded to the base sentiment of timidity so far as to choose the long way thither by the open road, rather than to take the short cut, through the graveyard and a little piece of woodland, which was the ordinary path in the daytime. I pursued my way, thinking of what I had done, until I got within sight of the old mansion and its guardian elms, when shame for my own cowardice compelled me to retrace my steps a quarter of a mile or more, and take the pathway I had so foolishly dreaded. The victory then achieved has lasted to this hour. Dead people and their habitations have not affrighted me since; indeed, some grave men whom I have met have excited my mirth rather than my fears.

But overcome our fears and our propensity to borrow trouble, as we may,—in spite of all our philosophy, life is a severe task. I have heard of a worthy Connecticut parson of the old school, who

enlarged upon the goodness of that Providence
which dealt out time to a man, divided into minutes,
and hours, and days, and months, and years, instead
of giving it to him, as it were, in a lump, or in so
large a quantity that he could not conveniently use it!
Laugh as much as you please, gentle reader, at the
seeming absurdity of the venerable divine, but do not
neglect the great truth which inspired his thought.
Do not forget what a great mercy it is that we are
obliged to live but one day at a time. Do not overlook the loving kindness which softens the memory
of past sorrows, and conceals from us those which
are to come. I have no respect for that newest
heresy of our age, which pretends to read the secrets
of the unseen world, nor any sympathy with those
morbid minds that yearn to tear away the veil which
infinite wisdom and mercy hangs between us and the
future. With all our boasted learning we know little
enough; but that little is far too much for our happiness. How many of our trials and afflictions could
we have borne, if we had been able to foresee their
full extent and to anticipate their combined poig-
nancy? Truly we might say with Shakespeare,—

> "O, if this were seen,
> The happiest youth—viewing his progress through,
> What perils past, what crosses to ensue—
> Would shut the book, and sit him down and die."

He only is the true philosopher who uses life as
the usurer does his gold, and employs each shining
hour so as to insure an ever-increasing rate of interest. He does not bury his gift, nor waste it in fri-
volity. Like the old Doge of Venice, he grows old

but does not wear out: *Senescit, non segnescit.* And he truly lives twice, as an old classical poet expresses it, inasmuch as he renews his enjoyment of the past in the recollection of his good actions and of pleasures "such as leave no sting behind."

BEHIND THE SCENES

THERE is no pleasure so satisfactory as that which an old man feels in recalling the happiness of his youthful days. All the woes, and anxieties, and heart-burnings that disturbed him then have passed away, and left only sunshine in his memory. And this retrospective enjoyment increases with every repeated recital, until the scenes of his past history assume a magnificence of proportion that bewilders the narrator himself, and sets the principles of optics entirely at defiance. It is with old men looking back on their younger days very much as it is with people who have travelled in Italy. How do the latter glow with enthusiasm at the mere mention of the "land of the melting lyre and conquering spear"! How do their eyes glisten as they tell of the time when they mused among the broken columns of the Forum, or breathed the air of ancient consecration under the majestic vaults of the old basilicas, or walked along the shores of the world's most beautiful bay, and watched the black form of Vesuvius striving in vain to tarnish with its foul breath the blue canopy above it! They have forgotten their squabbles with the *vetturini,* the draughtless chimneys in their lodgings, and the dirty staircase that conducted to them; the fleas, with all the other disagreeable accompaniments of Italian life, have fled into oblivion; and Italy lives in their memories only as a land of gorgeous sunsets, and of a history that dwarfs all other human annals. And so it is with an old man looking back upon his youth: he forgets how he cried over his arithmetic lessons; how unfilial his feelings were when his governor refused him permission to set up a theatre in the cellar; how sheepishly he slunk through all the back alleys on the day when he first mounted a tail-coat and a hat; how unhappy he was when he saw his heart's idol, Mary Smith, walking home from school with his implacable foe, Brown; how his head used to ache after those *noctes cænæque deûm* with his club at the old Exchange Coffee House; and what a void was created in his heart when his crony of cronies was ordered off by a commission from the war department. There is no room in his crowded memory for such things as these. Sitting by his fireside, as I do now, he recalls his youth only as a season of bats and balls, and marbles, of sleds, and skates, and bright buttons, and clean ruffled collars, of Christmas cornucopias of hosiery, and no end of Artillery Elections and Fourths of July, with coppers enough to secure the potentiality of obtaining egg-pop to an alarming extent.

How he fires up if you mention the theatre to him! He will allow that Mr. Gilbert and Mr. Warren are most excellent in their way; but bless your simple heart, what is the stage now compared to what it was in the first part of this century? And he is about right. It is useless for us, who remember the old Federal Street playhouse, and the triumphs of Cooke and the great Kean, to try to go to the theatre now. Our new theatre is more stately and splendid than

Old Drury was, but our players do not reach my youthful standard. I miss those old familiar faces and voices that delighted me in times long past, and the stage has lost most of its charms. I can find my best theatrical entertainment here at home. I call up from among the shadows that the flickering fire-light casts upon the wall, the tall, knightly figure of Duff, the brisk, busy, scolding Mrs. Barnes, the sedate and judicious Dickson, the grotesque Finn, the stately and elegant Mrs. Powell, looking like the personification of tragedy, and bluff old Kilner, fat and pleasant to the sight, and with that hearty laugh that made all who heard it love him.

What is the excitement occasioned by the Ellsler or Miss Lind compared to that which attended the advent of the elder Kean? What crowds used to beset the box office in the ten-footer next to the theatre, from the earliest dawn until the opening! I often think, when I meet some of our gravest and grayest citizens in their daily walks, what a figure they cut now compared with the days when they were fighting their way into the box office of the old theatre! Talk of enthusiasm! What are all our political campaigns and public commemorations compared with that evening during the last war with Great Britain, when Commodore Bainbridge came into Boston Bay after his victory over the Java! That admirable actor, the late Mr. Cooper, was playing Macbeth, and interrupted his performance to announce the victory.

But, pardon me, I did not sit down here to lose myself in the reminiscences of half a century ago. Let me try to govern this truant pen, and keep it more closely to my chosen theme. Do you remember, beloved reader, your second visit to the theatre? If you do, cherish it; let it not depart from you, for in the days that are in store for you, when age and infirmity shall stand guard over you, and you are obliged to find all your pleasures by your fireside, the memory of your second play will be very precious to you. You will find, on looking back to it through a vista of sixty years or more, that all the pleasure you then enjoyed was placed on the credit side of your account, and has been increasing by a sort of moral compound interest during the long years that you have devoted to delights less innocent, perhaps, and certainly less satisfactory, or to the pursuit of objects far more fleeting and unreal than those which then fascinated your youthful mind. I say your "second play," for the first dramatic performance that the child witnesses is too astonishing to afford him its full measure of gratification. It is only after he has told his playmates all about it, and imitated the wonderful hero who rescued the beautiful lady in white satin, and dreamed of the splendour of the last great scene, when all the persons of the drama stood in a semicircle, and the king, with a crown of solid gold upon his head, addressed to the magnanimous hero the thrilling words,—

"It is enough: the princess is thine own!"—

and all the characters struck impressive attitudes, and the curtain descended upon a tableau lighted up by coloured fires of ineffable brilliancy,—it is only after all these things have sunk deep into the young mind, and he has resolved to write a play himself, and never to rest satisfied until he can bring down the house with the best of the actors he has seen, that he fully appreciates the entertainment which has been vouchsafed to him.

What a charm invests the place where we made our first acquaintance with the drama! It becomes an enchanted spot for us, and I doubt if the greatest possible familiarity in after life can ever breed contempt for it in our hearts. For my own part, I regarded the destruction of the old theatre in Federal Street, and the erection of warehouses on its hallowed site, as a positive sacrilege. And I cannot pass that spot, even at this late day, without mentally recurring to the joys I once tasted there. Perhaps some who read this may cherish similar sentiments about the old Tremont Theatre, a place for which I had as great a fondness as one can have for a theatre in which he did not see his first play. The very mention of it calls up its beautiful interior in my mind's eye,—its graceful proscenium, its chandeliers around the front of the boxes, its comfortable pit, where I enjoyed so much good acting, and all the host of worthies who graced that spacious stage. Mr. Gilbert was not so fat in those days as he is now, nor Mr. Barry so gray. What a picturesque hero was old Brough in the time when the Woods were in their golden prime, and the appearance of the Count Rodolpho on the distant bridge was the signal for a tempest of applause! Who can forget how Mr. Ostinelli's bald head used to shine, as he presided over that excellent orchestra, or how funny old Gear's serious face looked, as he peered at the house through those heavy, silver-bowed spectacles? Per-

haps for some of my younger readers the stage of
the Museum possesses similar charms, and they will
find themselves, years hence, looking back to the
happy times when Mr. Angier received their glittering quarters, and they hastened up stairs, to forget
the wanderings of Æneas and the perplexities of
arithmetic in the inimitable fun of that prince-regent
among comedians, Mr. William Warren.

But wherever we may have commenced our dramatic experience, and whatever that experience may
have been, we have all, I am sure, felt the influence
of that mysterious charm which hangs over the stage.
We have all felt that keen curiosity to penetrate to
the source of so much enjoyment. Who has not had
a desire to enter that mysterious door which conducts
the "sons of harmony" from the orchestra to the
unknown depths below the stage? It looks dark and
forbidding, but we feel instinctively that it is not so,
when we see our venerated uncle Tom Comer carrying his honest and sunshiny face through it so often.
That green curtain, which is the only veil between
us and a world of heroes and demigods,—how en-
viously do we look at its dusty folds! With what
curiosity do we inspect the shoes of varied make and
colour that figure in the little space between it and
the stage! How do we long to follow the hero who
has strutted his hour upon the stage into the invisible
recesses of P. S. and O. P., and to know what takes
the place of the full audience and the glittering row
of footlights in his eyes when he makes his exit at the
"upper entrance, left," or through the "door in flat"
which always moves so noiselessly on its hinges! I
think that the performance of the "Forty Thieves"

awakened this curiosity in my mind more than almost any other play. I longed to inspect more closely those noble steeds that came with such a jerky gait over the distant mountains, and to know what produced the fearful noise that attended the opening of the robbers' cave. I believed in the untold wealth that was said to be heaped up in those subterranean depths, but still I wished to look at the "cavern goblet," and see how it compared with those that adorned the cases of my excellent friends, Messrs. Davis and Brown. I can never forget the thrill that shot through me when Morgiana lifted the cover of the oil jar, and the terrible question, "Is it time?" issued from it, nor my admiration for the fearlessness of that self-possessed maiden when she answered with those eloquent and memorable words, "Not yet, but presently." I believed that the compound which Morgiana administered so freely to the concealed banditti was just as certain death to every mother's son of them as M. Fousel's *Pabulum Vitæ* is renewed life to the consumptives of the present day; and, years after I had supposed my recollections of the "Forty Thieves" to have become very misty and shapeless, I found myself startled in an oriental city by coming upon several oil jars of the orthodox model, and I astonished the malignant and turbaned Turk who owned them, and amused the companion of my walks about Smyrna, by lifting the lid of one of them, and quoting the words of Morgiana. My superstitions concerning that pleasant old melodrama of course passed away when I became familiar with the theatre by daylight, and was accustomed to exchange the compliments of the morning with the estimable gentleman who played Hassarac; but the illusion of its first performance has never been entirely blotted from my mind.

Some years ago it was my privilege to visit a place which is classical to every lover of the drama and its literature. Drury Lane Theatre, now that its ancient rival, Covent Garden, has passed away, and been replaced by a house exclusively devoted to the lyric muse, is the only theatre of London which is associated in every mind with that host of geniuses who have illustrated dramatic art from the times of Garrick to our own. That gifted and versatile actor, Mr. Davenport, who stands as high in the favour of the English as of the American public, conducted me through that immense establishment. We entered the door, which I had often looked at with curiosity as I passed through the long colonnade of the theatre, encountering several of those clean-shaven personages in clothes that would be much refreshed if they were allowed to take a nap, and, after traversing two or three dark corridors, found ourselves upon the stage. The scene of so many triumphs as have there been achieved is not without its attractions, even though it may look differently *en déshabille* from what it does in the glitter of gaslight. The stage which has been trod by the Kembles, the Keans, Siddons, Macready, Young, Palmer Dowton, Elliston, Munden, Liston, and Farren, is by no means an ordinary combination of planks. We know, for Campbell has told us, that

> "—— by the mighty actor brought,
> Illusion's perfect triumphs come;
> Verse ceases to be airy thought,
> And sculpture to be dumb."

Yet what a shadowy, intangible thing the reputation of a great actor would seem to be! We simply know of him that in certain characters his genius held the crowded theatre in willing thraldom, and made the hearts of hundreds of spectators throb like that of one man. Those who felt his wondrous power have passed away like himself; and all that remains of him who once filled so large a space in the public eye is an ill-written biography or a few hastily penned sentences in an encyclopædia.

I was too full of wonder at the extent of that vast stage, however, to think much of its ancient associations. Those lumbering stacks of scenery that filled a large building at the rear of the stage, and ran over into every available corner, told the story of the scenic efforts of Old Drury during nearly half a century. How many dramas, produced "without the slightest regard to expense," and "on a scale of unparalleled splendour," must have contributed to the building up of those mighty piles! The labyrinthine passages, the rough brick walls, darkened by time and the un-Penelope-like spiders of Drury Lane, were in striking contrast to the stage of that theatre as it appears from the auditorium. The green-room had been placed in mourning for the "goodlie companie" that once filled it, by the all-pervading, omnipresent smoke of London. Up stairs the sight was still more wonderful. The space above the stage was crowded full of draperies, and borders, and dusty ropes, and wheels, and pulleys. Davenport enjoyed my amazement, and led me through a darksome, foot-wide passage above the stage, through that wilderness of cordage to the machinists' gallery.

BEHIND THE SCENES

Take all the rope-walks that you have ever visited, dear reader, and add to them the running gear of several first-class ships, and you may obtain something of an idea of the sight that then met my view. I have often heard an impatient audience hiss at some trifling delay in the shifting of a scene. If they could see the complicated machinery which must be set in motion to produce the effects they desire, their impatience would be changed to wonder at the skill and care which are so constantly exerted and make so few mistakes. A glance into two or three of the dressing-rooms, and a hasty visit to the dark maze of machinery beneath the stage for working the trap-doors, completed my survey of Old Drury, and I left its ancient walls with an increased respect for them, and a feeling of self-gratulation that I was neither an actor nor a manager.

Not long after the above visit, I availed myself of an opportunity to make a similar inspection of the *Théâtre Français,* in the Palais Royal at Paris. The old establishment is not so extensive as that of Drury Lane, but its main features are the same. There was an air of government patronage about it which was apparent in its every department. The stage entrance was through a long and well-lighted corridor that might have led to a banking-house. Its green-room was a luxurious saloon, with a floor of tessellated walnut and oak, waxed and polished so highly that you could see your figure in it, and could with difficulty avoid becoming a lay figure upon it. Its frescoed ceiling and gilded cornices, its immense mirrors, and its walls covered with the portraits of several generations of players, whose genius has made the very name of that theatre venerable throughout the civilized world, were very different from most of the green-rooms that I had seen. In the ancient colleges in Italy the walls of the class-rooms are hung with portraits of the distinguished scholars, illustrious prelates, and sometimes of the canonized saints, who once studied under their time-honoured roofs. In the same spirit, the green-room of the *Théâtre Français* is adorned with busts and pictures; and the chairs that once were occupied by a Talma, a Mars, and a Rachel are held in honour in the place where their genius received its full development. The dressing-rooms of the brilliant company which sustains the high reputation of that house are in perfect keeping with its green-room. Each of the leading actors and actresses has a double room, furnished in a style of comfortable elegance. In the wardrobe and property rooms, the imperial patronage is visible in the richness of the stage furniture and the profusion of dresses made of the costliest silks and velvets. The stage, however, is very much like that of any other theatre. There were the same obscure passages, the same stupendous collection of intricate machinery, and the same mysterious odour, as of gas and musty scenery, pervaded the whole. I was permitted to view all its arcana, from the wheels that revolve in dusty silence eighty or ninety feet above the stage to the ponderous balance weights that dwell in the darkness of the second and third stories below it; and enjoyed it so keenly that I regretted to be told that I had seen all, and to find myself once more in the dazzling sunshine of the Rue de Richelieu.

BEHIND THE SCENES

We are accustomed to speak of the theatre as a repository of shams and unrealities, and to contrast it with the actualities of every-day life. I hope that you will excuse me, gentle reader, for venturing to deny the justice of all such figures of speech. They are as false as that common use of the expressions "sunrise" and "sunset," when we know that the sun does not really rise or set at all. No, it is the theatre that is the reality, and the life we see on every side the sham. The theatre is all that it pretends to be—a scenic illusion; and if we compare it to the world around us, with its loving couples, my-dearing each other before folks, and exchanging angry words over the solitary tea-tray,—its politicians, seeking nominations and votes, and then reluctantly giving up their private interests and comforts for the "public good," (as the spoils of office are facetiously termed,)—its so-called ministers of the gospel, who speak of an offer of increased salary as "an opportunity to labour in a wider sphere of usefulness,"—and its funerals, where there is such an imposing show of black crape and bombazine, but where the genuine mourning commences only after the reading of the will of the deceased,—I am sure that we shall be justified in concluding that the fictitious affair which we try to dignify with the title of "real life" is a far less respectable illusion than the mimic scene that captivates us in the hours of relaxation.

THE PHILOSOPHY OF CANT

BE not dismayed, kind reader,—I have no inten-
tion of impressing you for a tiresome cruise in
the high and dangerous latitudes of German meta-
physics; nor do I wish to set myself up as a critic of
pure reason. In spite of Noah Webster and his in-
quisitorial publishers, I still cherish a partiality for
correct orthography; and I would not be understood,
as referring in the caption of this article to the celebrated founder of the transcendental school of
philosophy. I cannot but respect Emmanuel Kant as
a remarkable intellectual man; and I hope to be pardoned for saying that his surname might properly be
anglicized, by spelling it with a C instead of a K.
Neither did I allude to the useful art of saying "No"
opportunely, which an excellent friend of mine
(whose numerous virtues are neutralized by his propensity to fabricate puns in season and out of season)
insists upon denominating the "philosophy of can't."
That faculty which is, in more senses than one, a
negative virtue, is unhappily a much harder thing to
find than the vice of which I have a few words to say.

I do not mean cant in the worse sense of the word,
as exemplified in the characters of Pecksniff, Stiggins,
Chadband, and Aminadab Sleek, nor even in those
of that large school of worshippers of propriety and
bond-servants of popular opinion, who reverse the
crowning glory of the character of Porcius Cato, and

prefer to seem, rather than to be, good. The cant I allude to is the technical phraseology of the various virtues, which some people appear to think is the same thing as virtue itself. They do not remember that a greasy bank-note is valueless save as the representative of a given quantity of bullion, and that pious and virtuous language is of no account except its full value be found in the pure gold of virtue stored away in the treasure-chambers of the heart. For such cant as this I have less respect than for downright hypocrisy; for there is something positive about the character of your genuine villain, which certainly does not repel me so strongly as the milk-and-watery characteristics of that numerous class of every-day people who (not being good enough to serve as examples, nor bad enough to be held up as warnings) are of no use whatever in their day and generation. What possible solace can he who deals in the set phrases of consolation administer to the afflicted spirit in that hour, when (even among the closest friends) "speech is silver, but silence is golden"?

There is scarcely a subject upon which men converse, in which this species of cant does not play its part; but there are some matters in which it makes itself so conspicuous that I cannot resist the temptation to pay particular attention to them. And, as the subject is rather an extensive one, I will parley no longer in its vestibule, but pull off my overcoat, and make myself at home in its front parlour. I wish to make a few observations on cant as it manifests itself in regard to morality, philanthropy, religion, liberty, and progress. My notions will excite the sneers of some of my younger readers, I doubt not, and perchance of some older ones; but, while I claim the privilege of age in speaking out my mind, I shall try to avoid the testiness which senility too often manifests towards those who do not respect its opinions. Convinced that mine are true, I can afford to emulate "Messire de Mauprat" in his patience, and wait to see my fellow-men pass their fortieth birthday, and, leaving their folly and enthusiasm behind them, come round to my position.

The cant of Morality is so common that it is mistaken by many excellent people for morality itself. To leave unnoticed the people who consider it very iniquitous to go to the theatre, but perfectly allowable to laugh at Mr. Warren on the stage of the Museum; who enjoy backgammon, but shrink from whist with holy horror; and who hold up their hands and cry out against the innocent Sunday recreations of continental Europe, yet think themselves justified in reading their Sunday newspapers and the popular magazines, or talking of the style of the new bonnets which made their first appearance at the morning service,—to say nothing about the moralists of this school, I am afraid that the prevailing notions on matters of greater import than mere amusement are not such as would stand a very severe moral test. When I see so much circumspection with regard to external propriety, joined with such an evident want of principle, it seems to me as if the Ten Commandments of the Old Law had been superseded by an eleventh: *Thou shalt not be found out.* When I see people of education in a city like Boston, dignifying lust under the title of a spiritual affinity, and characterizing divorce as obedience to the highest natural

law,—and still more, when I see how little surprise
the enunciation of such doctrines occasions,—I no
longer wonder at infidelity, for I am myself tempted
to ask whether there is any such thing as abstract
right or abstract wrong, and to question whether
morality may not be an antiquated institution, which
humanity is now sufficiently advanced to dispense
with. It is a blessed thing that we have not the
power to read one another's hearts. To pass by the
unhappiness it would cause us, what changes it would
occasion in our moral classifications! How many
men, clad in picturesque and variegated costumes,
are labouring in the public workshops of Charles-
town, or Sing Sing, or Pentonville, who, if the heart
were seen, would be found worthier by far than some
of those ornaments of society who are always at the
head of their pews, and whose names are found
alike on false invoices and subscription lists for evan-
gelizing some undiscovered continent! What a different balance would be struck between so-called
respectability in its costly silks and its comparative
immunity from actual temptation, and needy wanton-
ness displaying its rouge and Attleborough jewelry
all the more boldly because it feels that the ban of
society is upon it!

And this brings me to the cant of Philanthropy.
That excellent word has been so shamefully abused
of late years, by being applied to the empirical
schemes of adventurers and social disorganizers, that
you cannot now say a much worse thing of a man
than that he is a "philanthropist." That term ought
to designate one of the noblest representatives of the
unselfish side of human nature; but to my mind, it

describes a sallow, long-haired, whining fellow, who has taken up with the profession of loving all men in general, that he may better enjoy the satisfaction of hating all men in particular, and may the more effectually prey upon his immediate neighbours; a monomaniac, yet with sufficient "method in his madness" to make it pay a handsome profit; a knave whose telescopic vision magnifies the spiritual destitution of Tching-tou, and can see nothing wanting to complete our Christian civilization but a willingness to contribute to the "great and good work," and whose commissions for disbursing the funds are frightfully disproportionate to the amount collected and the work done. But there is a great deal of the cant of philanthropy passing current even among those who have no respect for the professional philanthropist. With all possible regard for the spirit of the age, I do not believe that modern philanthropy can ever be made to take the place of old-fashioned Christian charity. Far be it from me to underrate the benevolent efforts which are made in this community; but I cannot help seeing that while thousands are spent in alms, we lack that blessed spirit of charity which imparted such a charm to the benevolent institutions of the middle ages. They seemed to labour among the poor on the principle which Sir Thomas Browne laid down for his charities—"I give no alms to satisfy the hunger of my brother, but to fulfil and accomplish the will and command of my God; I draw not my purse for his sake that demands it, but His that enjoined it." We irreverent moderns have tried to improve upon this, and the result is seen in legal enactments against mendicancy, in palatial prisons for

criminals, and in poorhouses where the needy **are**
obliged to associate with the vicious and depraved.
The "dark ages" (as the times which witnessed the
foundation of the greatest universities, hospitals, and
asylums the world ever saw, are sometimes called)
were not dark enough for that.

Do what we may to remedy this defect in our
solicitude for the suffering classes, the legal view of
the matter will still predominate. We may imitate
the kindliness of the ancient times, but we cannot
disguise the fact that pauperism is regarded not only
as a great social evil, but as an offence against our
laws. While this is so, we shall labour in vain to
catch the tone of the days when poverty was en-
nobled by the virtues of the apostolic Francis of
Assisi and the heroic souls that relinquished wealth
and power to share his humble lot. The voice of our
philanthropy may be the voice of Jacob, but the hand
will be the hand of Esau. That true gentleman and
kind-hearted knight whom I have already quoted,
had no patience with this contempt for poverty which
was just growing into sight in his time, but is now so
common; and he administered to it a rebuke which
has lost none of its force by the lapse of more than
two hundred years: "Statists that labour to contrive
a commonwealth without poverty, take away the object of charity, not understanding only the commonwealth of a Christian, but forgetting the prophecy
of Christ."

In making any allusion to religious cant, I am sensible that I tread on very dangerous ground. Still,
in an essay on such a subject as the present, revival-
ism ought not to go unnoticed. God forbid that a

man at my time of life should pen a light word against any thing that may draw men from their worldliness to a more intimate union with their Creator. But the revival extravagances which last year made the profane laugh and the devout grieve, merit the deprecation of every person who does not wish to see religion itself brought into contempt. I do not believe in the application of the high-pressure system to the spiritual life. Some persons seem to regard a religious excitement as an evidence of a healthy spiritual state. As well might they consider a fever induced by previous irregularity to be a proof of returning bodily health. As the physician of the body would endeavour to restore the patient to his normal state, so too the true physician of the soul would labour to banish the religious fever from the mind of his patient, and to plant therein the sure principles of spiritual health—a clearly-defined dogmatic belief, and a deep conviction of the sinfulness of sin. We all need to be from time to time reminded that true religion is not a mere effervescence, not a vain blaze, but a reality which reflects something of the unchangeable glory of its divine Author. It is not a volcano, treasuring within its bosom a fierce, destructive element, sullenly smouldering and smoking for years, and making intermittent exhibitions of a power as terrible as it is sublime. No; it is rather a majestic and deep-flowing river, taking its rise amid lofty mountains whose snowy crags and peaks are pure from the defilement of our lower world, fed from heaven, bearing in its broad current beauty, and fertility, and refreshment, to regions which would else be sterile and joyless, and emptying at last into a shoreless and untroubled sea, whose bright surface mirrors eternally the splendour of the skies.

That the cant of Liberty should be popular with the American tongue is not, perhaps, to be wondered at. A young nation,—which has achieved its own independence in a contest with one of the most powerful governments in the world,—which has grown in territory, population, and wealth beyond all historical precedent,—and which has a new country for its field of action, so that its progress is unimpeded by the relics of ancient civilization or the ruins of dead empires,—could not reasonably be expected to resist all temptations to self-glorification. The American eagle is no mere barnyard fowl—content with a secure roost and what may be picked up within sight of the same. He is the most insatiable of birds. His fierce eye and bending beak look covetous, and his whole aspect is one of angry anxiety lest his prey should be snatched from him, or his dominion should be called in question. In this regard he differs greatly from his French relative, who squats with such a conscious air of superiority on the tops of the regimental standard-poles of the imperial army, and surveys the forest of bayonets in which he makes his nest as if he felt that his power was undisputed. And we Americans are not less uneasy and wild than the bird we have chosen for our national emblem, and appear to think that the essential part of liberty consists in keeping up an endless talk about it. Our cant of freedom needs to be reminded of Tom Hood's observation concerning religious cant:—

"'Tis not so plain as the old hill of Howth,
A man has got his bellyful of meat,
Because he talks with victuals in his mouth!"

With all our howling about liberty, we Americans are abject slaves to a theory of government which we feel bound to defend under all circumstances, and to propagate even in countries which are entirely unfitted for it. This constitutional theory is a fine thing to talk about; few topics afford so wide a range to the imaginative powers of a young orator. It is not therefore to be wondered at, that the subject should be so often forced upon us, and that so many startling contrasts should be drawn between our governmental experiment and the thousand-years-old monarchies of Europe. These comparisons (which some people who make republicanism such an article of faith, that they must find it hard to repeat the clause of the Lord's prayer, "Thy *kingdom* come," —are so fond of drawing) remind me of the question that was discussed in the Milesian debating society —"Which was the greatest man, St. Patrick or the Fourth of July?" and the conclusions drawn from them are very like the result of that momentous debate, which was decided in the affirmative.

For my own part, I have got past the age when eloquence and poetry are of much account in matters of such vital importance as government. When I buy a pair of overshoes, my first object is to get something that is water-proof. So, too, in the matter of government, I only wish to know whether the purposes for which government is instituted—the protection of the life, property, and personal liberty of its subjects—are answered; and, if they are, I am ready to swear allegiance to it, not caring a splinter of a ballot-box whether it be founded on hereditary succession or a roll of parchment, or whether its

THE PHILOSOPHY OF CANT

executive authority be vested in a president, a king,
or an emperor. That is the best government which
is best administered; it makes little difference what
you call it, or on what theory it is built. I love my
country dearly, and yield to no one in my loyalty to
her government and laws; but (pardon me for being
so matter-of-fact, and seemingly unpatriotic) I would
willingly part with some of this boasted liberty of
ours, to secure a little more wisdom in making laws,
and a good deal more strength in executing them. I
count the privilege of talking politics and of choosing
between the various political adventurers who aspire
to be my rulers, as a very insignificant affair com.
pared with a sense of security against popular vio.
lence and the dishonesty of dealers in the necessaries
of life. And I cannot help thinking, that for the
inhabitants of a country where there is little rev.
erence for authority or willing obedience to law,
where the better class of the citizens refuse to take
any part in politics, and where the legislative power
is enthroned, not in the Senate, nor in the House of
Representatives, but in the Lobby,—for the inhabitants of such a country to boast of their liberty
aloud, is the most absurd of all the cants in this canting world.

Little as I respect the cant of liberty, I care even
less for the cant of Progress. I never had much patience with this worship of the natural sciences, which
is rapidly getting to be almost the only religion
among certain cultivated people in this quarter. I
remember in my boyhood startling by my scientific
apathy a precocious companion who used to bother
his brains about the solar system, and one useless

[375]

ology and another, in the precious hours which ought
to have been devoted to Robinson Crusoe and the
Arabian Nights' Entertainments. He had been
labouring hard to explain to me the law of gravita-
tion, and concluded with the bold statement that,
were it not for that law, an apple, with which he had
been illustrating his theory, instead of falling to the
earth, might roll off the unprotected side of this sub-
lunary sphere into the abyss of space,—or something
to that effect. He could not conceal his contempt for
my want of scientific ardour, when I asked him
whether he should really care if it did roll off, so long
as there was a plenty left! I did wrong to joke him,
for he was a good fellow, in spite of his weakness.
It is many years since he figured himself out of this
unsatisfactory world, into a state of existence where
vision is clearer even than mathematical demonstra-
tion, and where x does not "equal the unknown quantity."

Pardon this digression: in complaining of the
vaunted progress of this rapid age, I am making little
progress myself. It appears to me that the people
who laud this age so highly either do not know what
true progress is, or suffer themselves to mistake the
means for the end. Your cotton mills, and steam engines, and clipper ships, and electric telegraphs, do
not constitute progress; they are means by which it
may be attained. If gunpowder, immediately after
its invention, had been devoted to the indiscriminate
destruction of mankind, could such an invention have
justly been termed progress? If the press were used
only to perpetuate the blasphemies and indecencies
of Mazzini and Eugene Sue, who would esteem

Gutenberg and Fust as benefactors, or promoters of true progress? And if the increased facilities for travel, and the other inventions on which this age prides itself, only tend to make men's minds narrower by absorbing them in material interests, and their souls more mean by giving them the idol of prosperity to worship, then is this nineteenth century a century of progress indeed, but in the wrong direction. And if our mode of education only augments the ratio of crime among the lower class, and makes superficial pretenders of the higher orders of society, it is not a matter which will justify our setting ourselves quite so high above past ages and the rest of the world.

I cannot see what need nor what excuse there is for all this bragging. A great many strong men lived before Agamemnon,—and after him. We indeed do some things that would astonish our forefathers; but how are we superior to them on that account? We enslave the lightnings of heaven to be our messengers, and compel the sun to take our portraits; but if our electric wires are prostituted to the chicanery of trade or politics, and the faces which the sun portrays are expressive of nothing nobler than mercantile shrewdness and the price of cotton, the less we boast of our achievements, the better. Thucydides never had his works puffed in a newspaper, Virgil and Horace never poetized or lectured for a lyceum; Charlemagne never saw a locomotive, nor did St. Thomas Aquinas ever use a friction match. Yet this unexampled age possesses, I apprehend, few historians who would not shrink from being compared with the famous Greek annalist, few poets worthy to wear the crowns of the friends of the great Augustus, few rulers more sagacious and firm than the first Emperor of the West, and few scholars who would not consider it a privilege to be taught by the Angelic Doctor.

True progress is something superior to your puffing engines and clicking telegraphs, and independent of them. It is the advancement of humanity in the knowledge of its frailty and dependence; the elevation of the mind above its own limited acquirements, to the infinite source of knowledge; the cleansing of the heart of its selfishness and uncleanness; in fact, it is any thing whatever that tends to assimilate man more closely to the divine Exemplar of perfect manhood.

THE END.